# CLASSIC CASCADE CLIMBS

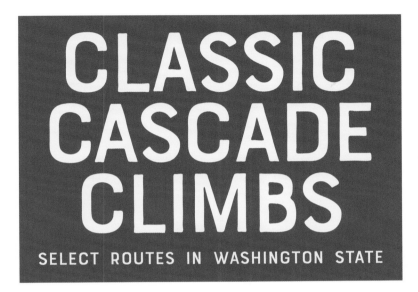

# CLASSIC CASCADE CLIMBS

## SELECT ROUTES IN WASHINGTON STATE

JIM NELSON, TOM SJOLSETH & DAVID WHITELAW

MOUNTAINEERS
BOOKS

**MOUNTAINEERS BOOKS** is dedicated to the exploration, preservation, and enjoyment of outdoor and wilderness areas.

1001 SW Klickitat Way, Suite 201, Seattle, WA 98134
800-553-4453, mountaineersbooks. org

Mountaineers Books and its colophon are registered trademarks of The Mountaineers organization.
Printed in China
Distributed in the United Kingdom by Cordee, www.cordee.co.uk

First edition, 2021

Copyeditor: Kris Fulsaas
Design and layout: Kate Basart/Union Pageworks
Route overlays: John McMullen
Topos: David Whitelaw and John McMullen
Cartographer: Lohnes+Wright
Cover photograph: *Climber on Forbidden Peak* (Photo by Scott Kranz)
Back cover photograph: *Jessica Campbell on the crux pitch of* Der Sportsman, *Prusik Peak.* (Photo by Max Hasson)
Frontispiece: *Evelina Dearborn on Mount Stuart's Northeast Face, October 1983* (Photo by Jim Nelson)

Library of Congress Control Number: 2021933786

Mountaineers Books titles may be purchased for corporate, educational, or other promotional sales, and our authors are available for a wide range of events. For information on special discounts or booking an author, contact our customer service at 800-553-4453 or mbooks@mountaineersbooks.org.

Printed on FSC®-certified materials

ISBN (paperback): 978-1-68051-046-1
ISBN (ebook): 978-1-68051-047-8

*An independent nonprofit publisher since 1960*

# CONTENTS

# OVERVIEW MAP

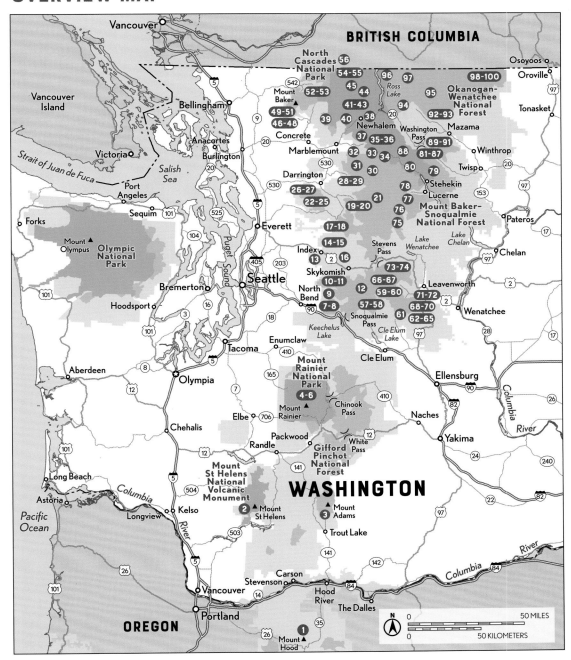

*Gordy Skoog atop Mount Formidable making the first winter ascent, 1981 (Photo by Lowell Skoog)*

# INTRODUCTION

Washington State! A green Pacific paradise of grand scope and opportunity. Time and geology have created a region of unparalleled beauty and continuous variety. It is a climber's paradise, to be certain, and nearly every corner of the state offers some kind of prize, large or small, famous or forgotten. There are deep and endless canyons of granite, many miles of basalt pillars and cracks, incredible alpine rock climbs, and always the awesome snow domes of the volcanoes.

From the ice-clad summit of Mount Rainier to the hot granite of Tumwater Canyon, there is legendary climbing here of every type, for every season, and at every grade. Whether you are just visiting or lucky enough to call this place home, looking for camaraderie or solitude, seeking

*Bob Cotter and Bill Pilling approaching Mount Stuart's Northeast Face (Photo by Jim Nelson)*

exploration or classic climbs, we hope our suggestions will provide just what you want.

We've all heard the smack-talk about the rain, and inevitably some trips will change in character as a result. The truth is, however, still fairly simple: the summers are simply incredible. Between the equinoxes, from the middle of June to the beginning of September, there is often negligible precip, and most of the climbs described in this volume will be in great shape. Lowland rock climbing in eastern Washington, sheltered from Pacific storms by the great shower curtain of the Cascades, is often possible from March to November. And plenty of climbing is done in the winter, too.

Washington has been called home by a long and distinguished list of inspirational climbers, from Lage Wernstedt and Hermann Ulrichs to John Roper and Colin Haley. For those with the inclination and imagination, there remain many lifetimes of new and unclimbed routes to be dreamed and realized. Some will merely pass through Seattle on the

*Peaks of the Northern Pickets from the southwest, with Phantom Peak in the center; left from Phantom are Ghost Peak, Crooked Thumb, and the Challengers. Mount Redoubt is behind Challenger; the distant peak left of center is Mount Spickard.* (Photo by John Scurlock)

road between Yosemite and Squamish; for others, those great locations will seem wonderful training grounds for the real business of state: Washington State.

## VOLCANO HISTORY

Indigenous peoples have inhabited the Pacific Northwest for thousands of years and developed their own myths and legends about the Cascades. In these legends, St. Helens, with its pre-1980 graceful appearance, was regarded as a beautiful maiden over whom Hood and Adams feuded. Native tribes also had their own names for many of the peaks: Tahoma, the Lushootseed name for Mount Rainier; Koma Kulshan or simply Kulshan for Mount Baker; Louwala-Clough or Loowit, meaning "smoking mountain," for Mount St. Helens.

In 1792 British navigator George Vancouver explored Puget Sound and gave English names to the high mountains he saw. Mount Baker was named for Vancouver's third lieutenant, Joseph Baker; Mount Rainier was named after Admiral Peter Rainier. Vancouver named Mount Hood after Lord Samuel Hood, an admiral of the Royal Navy. Mount St. Helens was named for Alleyne FitzHerbert, first Baron St. Helens, a British diplomat.

In 1805 the Lewis and Clark Expedition passed through the Cascades on the Columbia River, which for many years was the only practical route through that part of the range. Looking at Mount Adams, they thought it was Mount St. Helens. When they later saw Mount St. Helens, they thought it was Mount Rainier. The Lewis and Clark Expedition, and the many settlers who followed, met the last obstacle on their journey at the Cascades Rapids in the Columbia River Gorge. Before long, the whitecapped mountains that loomed above the rapids were called the "mountains by the cascades," and later simply the Cascades. The earliest use of the name Cascade Range is found in the writings of botanist David Douglas.

## THE CASCADES

The amazing scope of the Cascades makes it difficult to characterize the range in any all-encompassing way. Its changing geology, swirling weather, and overall size all provide a variety of choices as well as a variety of conditions.

In general, the Cascades rise from relatively low footings in the south, and the southern interests in this book are with the volcanoes—Mounts Hood, Adams, St. Helens, and Rainier. In the central region of Washington State, between Snoqualmie Pass and the Boulder River, the range takes on a more jagged uplift of nonvolcanic and largely nongranitic peaks like The Tooth, Mount Garfield, and Mount Index. This central region also has several well-known granitic intrusions like the Stuart Range and the Darrington group as well as others. Finally, in the 80 miles or so of the northernmost part of the state, fabled summits like Liberty Bell, Forbidden Peak, Bear Mountain, and Slesse Mountain make for a dramatic climax to the range and are a profound lure for climbers. It is still the most wild and rugged of the regions described in these pages.

The original version of this book described some 500 glaciers and nearly 100 square miles of ice in this scenic chunk of the Cascades. Twenty-five years later, these glaciers are certainly diminished. The glacier underneath the south face of Forbidden Peak appeared to be at least 50-60 feet thick in 1980 and is today perhaps 6-8 feet thick in August. Things *have* changed.

The Cascades *are* still a wild range, however. The rugged nature of the Cascades, especially those areas to the north, is exactly what has kept these regions challenging. Steep ground, overgrown vegetation, wet slabs, and notorious bushwhacking have all been experienced by at least some climbers in the Cascades! A good deal of the torment *can* be lessened with experience, and learning one's craft in the Cascades has contributed to so many great climbers who have called Washington home.

*Dylan Johnson on Mount Slesse, March 2015* (Photo by Colin Haley)

Most destinations in the Cascades require permits and other bureaucratic considerations, and of course many of the climbs in this book are among the more popular. By now, few people using this book will even remember the no-permit days when the Enchantment Lakes were free to anyone with the stamina to hike up there. In the face of proximity to Seattle, there ultimately were too many people with the conditioning for it, and we now have a permit-by-lottery system for that area. But even so, on a great many of these adventures, you'll meet so few people that it will be fun to chat with those you do encounter.

With the necessity of making reservations months in advance, the spontaneous approach to going up when the weather was good has now been reduced to chance. For some, this kind of annoyance has been countered with fitness. Probably everything in the Enchantments, for instance, has been climbed car to car in a day or soloed.

For as far as we can see, there will always be places in the Cascades that harbor beautiful secrets. Certainly, the Picket Range to the north with its unsavory and athletic approaches will remain a condensation of all that's gnarly in Washington mountaineering, but there are still more secrets than can ever be known.

And these places are not so hard to reach, either; just hike up to where everyone else turns right, put this book away, and hang a left!

*Fred Beckey and Kit Lewis on Illusion Peak in the Chilliwack's, July 1986* (Photo by Jim Nelson)

# HOW TO USE THIS GUIDE

This book is an attempt to show where to climb, not how to climb. We have divided the range into westside and eastside, and for each side of the Cascades the climbs are listed from south to north. See the overview map for each climb's general location.

## WASHINGTON STATE'S HIGHEST MOUNTAINS

Until Fred Beckey's *Cascade Alpine Guide* series was published in 1973, knowledge of peaks and climbing routes was limited and often passed on by word of mouth between groups of climbers. Older maps were grossly incomplete, lacked detail, and were often inaccurate. It wasn't possible to identify all of the most prominent peaks in the range until 1975 when the USGS 7.5-minute quadrangle library for the range was completed. Less than a year later, the 100 highest peaks in Washington State had been identified and become the target of a certain group of ambitious climbers calling themselves "the Bulgers."

The Bulgers, a name devised as a result of a twist on the name of a certain poem, were a group of climbers interested in conquering the Top 100. The six members of the original group included John Lixvar (Lizard), Russ Kroeker (Koala), Mike Bialos (Buffalo), Bette Felton (Zookeeper), John Plimpton (Long John), and Bruce Gibbs (Giraffe). Independently, these Bulgers ticked off the Top 100 peaks. In 1980 Russ Kroeker became the first person to climb them all after summiting Sinister Peak. The idea of the Top 100 spread among climbing circles and has now become quite popular. At the time of publishing, seventy-seven people have climbed all 100.

In addition to the 100 peaks the Bulgers included on their list, climbers pursuing the Bulger List recognize another seven peaks that should have been included in Washington's true 100 highest because of their elevation and prominence. The other seven peaks—Castle Peak, Luna Peak, Mount Ballard, Lincoln Peak, Colfax Peak, Sherman Peak, and Liberty Cap—were included in a separate list, compiled by Jeff Howbert and John Roper between 1987 and 2001, called the T100 x P400, or Top 100 by 400 feet of prominence (see below). The seven peaks replaced on the original Bulger List to establish the T100 x P400 were Blackcap Mountain, Little Annapurna, Mount Rahm, Horseshoe Peak, Dark Peak, Sahale Peak, and Seven Fingered Jack. At the time of this writing, nineteen people have climbed the T100 x P400.

## PROMINENCE

Prominence is the vertical distance a given summit rises above the lowest col on the highest ridge connecting it to a higher summit. Or, explained another way, it is the elevation difference between the summit of a peak and the lowest contour that contains the given peak and no higher peaks. Imagine the ocean rising to the exact point where a certain peak is the highest point on its very own island. At that point, the prominence is the elevation of the peak above the risen ocean.

## WHAT'S INCLUDED FOR EACH CLIMB

Each mountain or peak includes not only its elevation but also its prominence—how much the mountain rises from the lowest point on the connecting ridge to its highest connected neighbor mountain. If the mountain is included on the Top 100 list, we include its ranking in brackets, immediately following its prominence. We provide a general overview of each mountain—its position, climbing history, notable features, and other tidbits. For some mountains we feature one climb; for others, two or more.

Under the Land Manager heading, we provide the name of the managing agency and basic permit information: National parks sometimes require entrance fees. Climbing permits—some free, some fee-based—are required on a few mountains. Most climbs begin from trailheads that require a Northwest Forest Pass or interagency recreation pass for parking. Requirements for backcountry or wilderness permits, such as those issued in national parks or quota areas like the Enchantments, vary: some are free, others require a small fee; some are seasonal, others are required year-round. Generally, most wilderness permits are free—self-issued at the trailhead—for day and overnight trips, but for up-to-date information, contact the land manager (listed in Resources at the back of this book).

All the climbs list an overall grade, and some include a Yosemite decimal rating, water-ice rating, mixed-climb rating, aid rating, and/or PG rating; see the next section for details. The climb overviews include a time range, which might be a few hours to several days. Some climb overviews include recommended gear and/or season, as well as other considerations from water availability to bugs to . . . mountain goats!

For each climb we provide an approach (with a grade rating), which includes driving directions to a trailhead, hiking directions, and off-trail directions to the base of the climb. The route description of most climbs is accompanied by a route overlay photo and occasionally a topo; each climb finishes with a description of the descent.

Following most of the climbs, we list a selected history of notable ascents on the mountain by year, including the approximate difficulty grade and climbers' names. Abbreviations include FA (first ascent), FWA (first winter ascent), FFA (first free ascent), and FKT (fastest known time). **NOTE:** We have not included absolutely all climbs in some cases, particularly on the volcanoes, where we focus on the major glaciers and ridges, and on peaks like Dragontail where so many routes and variations are difficult to chart and make sense of.

## RATINGS

Route ratings can be useful in determining the difficulty of a climb, but keep in mind that they aren't absolutes; there are variables and the ratings can be somewhat subjective. They are undeniably helpful, however, so we include grade, class, and water-ice ratings for the routes described.

### CLIMB GRADE

We give a grade, ranging from I to VI, for each climb to give an approximate idea of a climb's difficulty at a glance. The grade rating is for the technical part of the climb and descent and does not include the approach. The overall grade is intended only as a quick approximate overview or starting point for trip planning. Grade estimates are for climbers with average experience and average fitness. Many experienced climbers regularly climb Grade IV and V climbs in only a couple of hours; our grade ratings are intended for the average recreational climber.

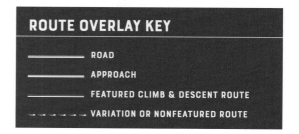

ROUTE OVERLAY KEY

———————— ROAD
———————— APPROACH
———————— FEATURED CLIMB & DESCENT ROUTE
- - - - - - VARIATION OR NONFEATURED ROUTE

## TOPO KEY

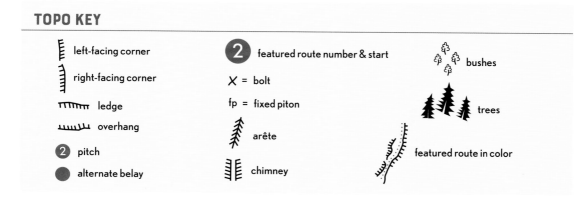

left-facing corner

right-facing corner

ledge

overhang

2  pitch

alternate belay

2  featured route number & start

X = bolt

fp = fixed piton

arête

chimney

bushes

trees

featured route in color

One thing to understand is that grade ratings are subject to a number of variables. Seasonal conditions, especially for snow and glacier climbs, can easily change a Grade II glacier in spring to a Grade III or more in fall. Think of the grade as an assessment of overall length or time, commitment or difficulty of retreat, and technical difficulty. Here's an overview:

**GRADE I & II:** Climbs made in a short day, with minimum seriousness or commitment

**GRADE III:** Climbs requiring less than a full day

**GRADE IV:** Climbs requiring a long day or more

**GRADE V:** Climbs that may require one night on the climb

**GRADE VI:** Climbs that require more than one night on the climb

*Bryan Burdo pushing the standards on Dolomite Tower, August 1990 (Photo by Pete Doorish)*

## ROCK RATINGS

For technical difficulty on rock, we use the Yosemite Decimal System's class ratings of 1–6 (with an occasional PG—parental guidance—rating for the climb's seriousness).

**CLASS 1 & 2:** Requires walking and steep hiking

**CLASS 3:** Requires use of hands, mostly for balance; often referred to as scrambling; easy climbing but may include moderate exposure; often includes loose rock, requiring careful assessment and routefinding

**CLASS 4:** Easy climbing but often with more exposure or consequence of mistake than class 3; approaching class 5 in difficulty, but with no shortage of footholds

**CLASS 5:** Broken into the Yosemite Decimal System from 5.0 to 5.15, but open-ended when the climb is harder; the class 5 rating (5.7, for example) applies specifically to the hardest move or sequence and could be limited to only 5 feet of climbing. What is a 5.7 exactly? A climb rated 5.7 is harder than a 5.6 and easier than a 5.8. Basically it's a comparative rating system; a climb rated 5.7 should be about the same difficulty as other climbs rated 5.7.

**CLASS 6:** Also known as aid climbing, or using gear for hand- or footholds; indicated with A0–A5

It's important to understand that the technical rating is a small piece of the information regarding a climb's overall difficulty or grade. For example, a climb rated Grade III, 5.10 could be a six-pitch rock climb of mostly mid-5th class and one well-protected move of 5.10, while another climb rated Grade III, 5.8 might have five pitches of sustained 5.8 and be less well protected. Most would say that the climb rated 5.10 is the easier climb, even though it has the harder technical rating.

## SNOW AND ICE RATINGS

While the Yosemite Decimal System is used for rating difficulties on rock, an equivalent system for snow does not exist. We often use "moderate" or "steep" to describe snow slopes in climb descriptions. We consider slopes approaching 30 degrees to be steep because the consequences of a slip on them can be considerable.

For ice, we reluctantly give ratings for Water Ice 1–6 (abbreviated WI 1–WI 6); we usually use a rating given by the first-ascent party. We also use a Mixed 1-13 rating on occasion (abbreviated M1–M13). This rating is for rock or mixed rock and ice climbing where crampons are worn. It's important to understand that ice ratings can easily change from day to day as much as a full grade or two—or more—as the conditions of these routes can change rapidly.

## APPROACH GRADE
While six grades are the established norm for climbing grades, we feel that four grades work well for rating approaches. Our approach grade ratings are intended to give a quick indication of an approach's difficulty, as a starting point for trip planning.

## DON'T FORGET THE BASICS!
Many climbs can be done in a day or less, but others require several days due to lengthy approaches or longer climbing routes. Whether you're out for a day or overnight, always follow responsible backcountry practices:
- Leave natural features undisturbed.
- Secure food from animals.
- Thoroughly treat or boil drinking water obtained from natural sources.
- Use backcountry toilets when available; bury waste at least 200 feet from all water sources—don't bury toilet paper: pack it out.
- Consider leaving pets at home.
- Locate campsites to minimize impacts.
- Build fires only where safe and permitted—consider bringing a stove instead.
- Do not litter your route with flags or cairns.

## A NOTE ABOUT SAFETY

Safety is an important concern in all outdoor activities. No guidebook can alert you to every hazard or anticipate the limitations of every reader. Therefore, the descriptions of roads, trails, routes, and natural features in this book are not representations that a particular place or excursion will be safe for your party. When you follow any of the routes described in this book, you assume responsibility for your own safety. Under normal conditions, such excursions require the usual attention to traffic, road and trail conditions, weather, terrain, the capabilities of your party, and other factors. Keeping informed on current conditions and exercising common sense are the keys to a safe, enjoyable outing.

—Mountaineers Books

In addition to climbing gear, always bring the Ten Essentials.
1. Navigation: map, compass, GPS, etc.
2. Headlamp
3. Sun protection: sunscreen, glacier glasses, etc.
4. First-aid kit
5. Knife
6. Fire: matches, firestarter, etc.
7. Shelter: bivy bag, space blanket, tent, etc.
8. Extra food
9. Extra water
10. Extra clothes

## ADDITIONAL RESOURCES
Good resources can be very helpful with trip planning; see the Resources section at the back of this book for recommendations. This is also where we list information for the land managers for the climbs.

*The Southern Pickets from the east: (left to right) Little Mac Spire, East McMillan Spire, Strandberg Pyramid, Mount Degenhardt, Mount Terror, The Blob, Twin Needles, Ottohorn, and (in front of Mount Baker) Frenzel Spitz* (Photo by Steph Abegg)

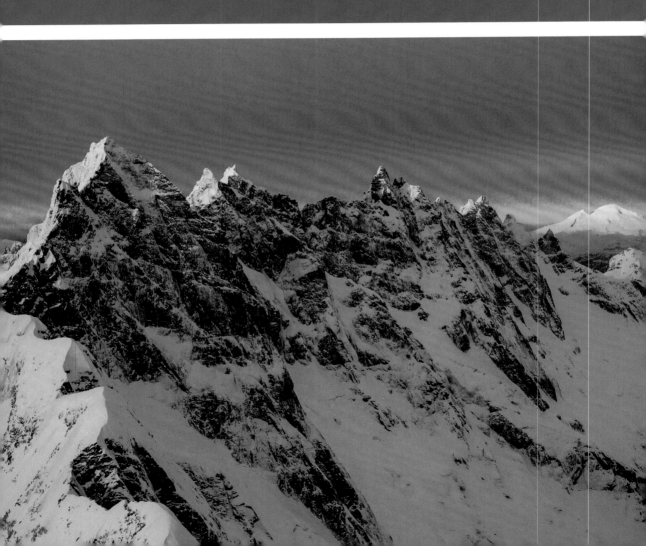

# WESTSIDE CASCADES

# SOUTHERN CASCADES

## MOUNT HOOD (OREGON)   11,243'

**PROMINENCE: 7706'**

### PALMER GLACIER

Hood's exciting daggerlike profile, ease of access, and variety of routes have for decades made it an interesting mountain for climbers of all abilities. The mountain is very popular, the standard route is superclassic, and, in good conditions, some of the technical routes on the mountain are among the finest of their type in the Cascades.

Some might dismiss Hood outright as a typical Northwest snow slog. With good luck, perfect snow, and ideal timing, the standard route may appear to be almost casual, although the final slopes are certainly "do-not-fall" terrain in even the best conditions. From Timberline Lodge, the ski lift reaches 8500 feet, operates throughout the summer, and typically makes a high camp unnecessary. Unfortunately, the perception that the climb is a walk-up tempts many who are unprepared. Hazards not to be underestimated include sudden harsh weather, crowds, altitude, ice, and rockfall. Sadly, fatalities on Hood are not uncommon.

On the west side, the Reid Glacier Headwall is also a great moderate route. In winter or spring, the striking North Face gully routes above the Eliot Glacier and, on the east face, the intricate mixed routes above the Newton Clark Glacier can become stellar climbs. On the historic side, Fred Beckey's fabled Yocum Ridge, originally done in 1959, remains a spectacular climb.

### LAND MANAGER

Mount Hood Wilderness, Mount Hood National Forest, Zigzag or Hood River Ranger District. Wilderness permit required year-round on the south-side climbing route, available at Wy'East Timberline Day Lodge; Sno-Park permit required November 1–April 30.

*Mount Hood's alluring north face rises above Hood River valley orchards.* **(Photo by Ed Cooper)**

*Mount Hood from the south: Palmer Glacier: (A) Old Chute; (B) Palmer Glacier; (C) Pearly Gates (Photo by John Scurlock)*

## NOTE
Rescues for persons without cell phones or mountain locator units (MLUs) may be subject to fines.

## 1. PALMER GLACIER: GRADE III

**TIME:** 1–2 days. Optimal conditions are when the upper mountain is snow covered. Once the snow melts enough to expose rocks, the objective dangers become considerable. In addition, freezing temperatures are also recommended. On average the best conditions are January through about April or May. Expect exposure to icefall or worse on warm days.

## APPROACH
From Interstate 5 at Vancouver, drive south across the Columbia River and take US Highway 26 east to the town of Government Camp, Oregon. Turn left (north) onto Timberline Road and follow it to Timberline Lodge; park in the lower lot (5920 feet). The climbers register is near the entrance to the day lodge.

## ROUTE
From the lodge, the climbing route follows the right (east) edge of the ski area, avoiding the ski runs. Pass the Silcox Hut, then the Palmer Ski Lift (8540 feet). Continue past Crater Rock to where the White River Glacier meets the Coalman Glacier, forming a gentle snow ridge known as the Hogsback (10,550 feet). This glacial arête has a bergschrund that widens through the season as the glacier pulls away from the slopes above. Climb over or traverse around the 'schrund and climb steepening slopes toward the Pearly Gates, a gully leading through cliff bands to the summit ridge, just west of the top.

*Climbing parties on Mount Hood's Hogsback* (Photo by Pete Erickson)

**OPTIONS:** There are other routes through the summit headwall, but the Pearly Gates holds snow well and often has better snow. From the Hogsback and below the bergschrund, there are two other established route options to the west of the Pearly Gates. The Old Chute route climbs the headwall above the Coalman Glacier; the West Crater Rim route traverses the Coalman Glacier Headwall, finishing via the west ridge.

## DESCENT

Descend the climbing route. It is essential to understand the descent in poor visibility. Avoid a fall-line descent trending southwesterly (toward Zigzag Canyon)—it misses the top of the ski lifts and the safe route to Timberline Lodge. Once below Crater Rock, follow magnetic south; this vector involves considerable traversing and leads close to the top of the lifts and the Silcox Hut. From there, follow the lifts down.

## SELECTED HISTORY

**1857** Mount Hood, FA.W. Chittenden, J. Deardorff, W. Buckley, L. Powell, H. Pittock.

# MOUNT ST. HELENS/LOOWIT 8365'

## PROMINENCE: 4605' [84]

### MONITOR RIDGE

Prior to 1980, St. Helens's distinctive and symmetrical Fuji-style shape was a familiar icon of the southern Cascades. After the blast, little remained of its famous profile, and 1300 feet of its summit cone had vanished, as they say, into thin air. Ash rained across eastern Washington, and debris flows over Washington closed routes to the mountain. Access was finally restored in 1987, and St. Helens became an instant classic as a spring kickoff to the climbing season.

When snow covered, the southern slopes are an appealing playground for snow riders looking for adventures beyond ski area boundary tapes. Winter can be harsh, but also empty and beautiful. As the spring days lengthen, the southern slopes are known for producing acres of forgiving and consolidated corn snow.

### LAND MANAGERS

Mount St. Helens National Volcanic Monument, Gifford Pinchot National Forest, climbing permit required year-round: April 1–October 31, limited permits must be purchased in advance online (see Resources); November 1–March 31, free climbing permits self-issued at Marble Mountain Sno-Park. Parking fee, Northwest Forest Pass, or interagency recreation pass required for parking at Climbers Bivouac Trailhead; December 1–March 31, Sno-Park permit required for parking at Marble Mountain Sno-Park.

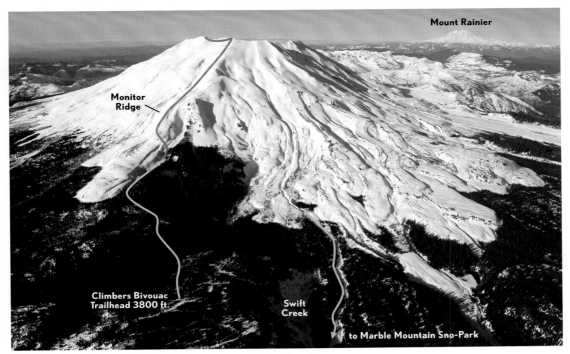

*Mount St. Helens from the south: Monitor Ridge* **(Photo by Alasdair Turner)**

## 2. MONITOR RIDGE: GRADE II

**TIME:** 6–10 hours. Accidents happen on this route when people slide or glissade and are unable to avoid hazards. Know your craft if you are glissading! Other hazards include sudden harsh weather, altitude, snow travel, and navigation challenges. At the crater rim, there is often a snow cornice which may be unstable and perched above a thousand-foot void. Take great care! There are no active glaciers on this route; however, snowfields can be very icy and may have large cracks. Check the forecast and watch the weather, as conditions can change rapidly. Be prepared for whiteouts and other weather extremes.

### APPROACH, GRADE I

There are two starting points: Climbers Bivouac Trailhead (3800 feet), and Marble Mountain Sno-Park (2700 feet) when access to the higher trailhead is snowed in.

**CLIMBERS BIVOUAC TRAILHEAD:** From Interstate 5 at Woodland, take exit 21 east on State Route 503 to the town of Cougar. At 6.4 miles beyond Cougar, just after the Swift Reservoir viewpoint, turn left on Forest Road 83. Follow FR 83 for 3 miles, then bear left onto FR 81 for another mile to FR 830. Turn right at FR 830 and continue about 0.4 mile to the Climbers Bivouac Trailhead at 3800 feet; there is car camping here, but no water.

From Climbers Bivouac, take the Ptarmigan Trail No. 216A for the first 2 miles of the well-marked path through forest, reaching the Monitor Ridge Climbers Trail No. 216H just before tree line at 4680 feet.

**MARBLE MOUNTAIN SNO-PARK:** Follow the directions above, but at the fork for FR 81, continue on FR 83 for 3 miles to the Sno-Park (2700 feet).

Follow the Swift Creek drainage north, reaching timberline at about 6600 feet. Be aware of the avalanche risk in both winter and spring.

### ROUTE

Once the winter snow cover is gone, the Monitor Ridge Climbers Trail No. 216H ascends through blocky boulders where the trail is indicated with blue markers on poles. Beyond the rocky section, plenty of loose scree and sand follows on or near the Monitor Ridge moraine. A final loose slope leads quite abruptly to the rim of the volcanic crater. Use caution anywhere near the crater rim year-round.

When the route is snow covered, let the conditions guide the ascent route. Snow can vary from soft enough to require flotation on snowshoes or skis to frozen hard, requiring crampons. During the spring transition period from winter snow to summer snow, it is possible to have both hard and soft snow on the same day. With snow cover, a cornice overhangs the crater rim.

### DESCENT

Descend the climbing route.

# MOUNT ADAMS/KLICKITAT 12,276'

## PROMINENCE: 8116' [3]

### SOUTH SPUR

While the idea for a "presidential range" of mountains was peddled in the 1830s in several locations, the great mass of Mount Adams is one of a few instances where the names stuck. From even close range, the mountain looks a bit like its bigger brother to the north and apparently nearly equals Rainier in area above tree line. A lava flow from near the South Butte is perhaps the most recent eruption on the mountain and may be less than 2000 years old.

It is a large and complicated monument—like other volcanoes, a stacked cake of harder layers interspersed with soft pumice, ash, and crumbling breccia. The loose foundations of our Northwest snow matter little on this route, however, and climbers and snow riders now slog up a path where a century ago mule teams laden with summit sulfur labored on behalf of the Glacier Mining Company.

The South Spur route is a long uphill hike by late summer and, along with St. Helens, the only Washington volcano that does not require glacier travel. The south ridge does hold snow late into some summers, but has no glacier. The route is often great for skis and snowboards until about late June or early July. Despite the pedestrian nature of the path, hazards still not to be underestimated include sudden changes in weather, altitude, snow travel, and, most importantly, whiteout conditions. Crampons may be helpful in some conditions.

While the southern glaciers are in full retreat, the mountain currently hosts a dozen glaciers totaling nearly nine square miles of ice cover. The largest of these are the Adams, Klickitat, and Lyman Glaciers, all originating from the summit ice cap. Other than the southern routes, the mountain sees very few visitors.

Adams also has a beautiful backcountry, like Rainier, but without the crowds. The glaciers on the northern and eastern aspects offer classic glacier climbs in a wilderness setting. Circumnavigations can be made with about 80 percent being on established trails and connecting with a nice high route for the rest. The lands south, west, and north of the summit are within the Mount Adams Wilderness, and everything east of the summit belongs to the Yakama Nation.

**LAND MANAGER**

Mount Adams Wilderness, Gifford Pinchot National Forest, Mount Adams Ranger District. Cascades Volcano Pass (fee) required above 7000 feet May 1–September 30; free self-registered wilderness permit required October 1–April 30.

## 3. SOUTH SPUR: GRADE II

**TIME:** 1–2 days. Look for the South Climb Trailhead to open around early July. The Lunch Counter at 9300 feet is a popular camp area for two-day ascents. More sheltered and less popular camp areas are also available in the Morrison Creek drainage at around 7400 feet.

*Mount Adams looking south to Mount Hood, with the Columbia River far below; Mount Jefferson, and Three Fingered Jack are in the distance.* **(Photo by John Scurlock)**

Mount Rainier

Pikers Peak 11,657 ft.

Lunch Counter 9300 ft.

Avalanche Glacier

Crescent Glacier

Mazama Glacier

South Climb Trailhead 4700 ft.

*Mount Adams from the south: South Spur* (Photo by John Scurlock)

## APPROACH, GRADE II

From the town of Trout Lake on State Route 141, turn onto a road signed "Mount Adams Recreation Area." Continue north, following signs to Morrison Creek Campground via Forest Road 80 and FR 8040; the 3-mile section of FR 500 beyond Morrison Creek Campground is extremely rough and narrow—drive carefully! Continue on FR 500 to its end just beyond Cold Springs Campground and the South Climb Trailhead at 4700 feet.

## ROUTE

Hike the South Climb Trail No. 183, crossing the Round the Mountain Trail No. 9 at 6280 feet and Morrison Creek at 6800 feet. At about 7400 feet, the trail reaches the moraine and follows it west and below the tiny Crescent Glacier. Snowfields and moraine continue beyond the Crescent Glacier to the Lunch Counter, a distinctive shoulder plateau at about 9300 feet. With a 4600-foot elevation gain and about 4.5 miles from the trailhead, the Lunch Counter is the traditional high camp for two-day ascents. Above the Lunch Counter, the route steepens and ascends snowfields past the false summit of Pikers Peak, at 11,657 feet, then across the summit plateau and up.

## DESCENT

Descend the climbing route.

## SELECTED HISTORY

**1854 SEPTEMBER** North Ridge. III. A. G. Aiken, Edward Allen, Andrew Burge.

**1863 SUMMER** South Spur. II. Henry Coe, Sarah Fisher, Julia Johnson, Mr. Phelps.

**1921 AUGUST** Rusk Glacier Castle. III. Claude Rusk party of seven.

**1924** Northwest Ridge. III. Lindsley Ross, John Scott, Fred Stadter.

**1938 JUNE** Klickitat Glacier. Joe Leuthold, Russ McJury, Wendall Stout.

**1945 JULY** Adams Glacier. III. Fred Beckey, Dave Lind, Robert Mulhall.

**1948 SEPTEMBER** Lyman Glacier. III. Robert Craig, Cornelius "K" Molenaar.

**1957 SEPTEMBER** White Salmon Glacier. II+. Gene Angus, Roger Moreau.

**1961 JULY** Wilson Glacier. III. Fred Beckey, Herb Staley.

**1962 JULY** South Klickitat Glacier. III. Dave Mahre, Lex Maxwell, Ralph Uber.

# LITTLE TAHOMA  11,138'

## PROMINENCE: 858' [4]

### WHITMAN GLACIER

The LT, a jagged remnant of rock, perches like a worshipper on the flanks of its giant idol. Little Tahoma is the remnant of a much larger Mount Rainier that has grown up, blown up, and grown up again, leaving this peak as a broken shard from another time. This is the fifth-highest peak in a state full of mountains, and it is still dwarfed by the mass of the Big R. Although upstaged by Rainier, it is a classic-shaped peak, steep on all sides with a tiny summit. The route is a snow and glacier climb with some difficulties, culminating in unforgettable views of Rainier's Ingraham and Emmons Glaciers.

### LAND MANAGER

Mount Rainier National Park, headquartered in Ashford; entrance fee or park pass required. Annual Climbing Cost Recovery Fee required in advance online before applying for required climbing permit. Wilderness permit required for overnight trips; park website has current specifics (see Resources). Permits for east side of mountain handled through White River Wilderness Information Center; for south side, through Paradise Ranger Station.

## 4. WHITMAN GLACIER: GRADE II+

**TIME:** 1–3 days. The mountain can be approached from Paradise or from the White River side. Starting from Paradise is the preferred winter and spring route; the White River approach works well once the access road opens in late spring.

*Claire Bonham-Carter on the classic ski approach from Paradise to Little Tahoma; Mount Adams, and peaks of the Tatoosh Range are to the south. (Photo by Pete Erickson)*

*Little Tahoma from the southeast: Whitman Glacier (Photo by John Scurlock)*

## APPROACH, GRADE III

**VIA WHITE RIVER:** From Enumclaw, drive southeast on State Route 410 for about 40 miles and then turn right (west) onto White River Canyon Road toward Sunrise. Reach the White River entrance to the park in 1 mile. Another 3 miles leads to a small parking area near the Fryingpan Creek bridge at 3800 feet. If this is full, be prepared to walk or hitchhike from an alternate parking area.

The forested trail quickly joins the Wonderland Trail and follows the Fryingpan Creek valley, in about 4 miles reaching the open meadows of Summerland at 6000 feet. Continue above Summerland on the Wonderland Trail for approximately 0.3 mile and leave the trail at 6100 feet.

Head uphill to the southwest and skirt cliffs on the right (northwest) before climbing south to Meany Crest at about 7200 feet. A bit farther, at the edge of the Fryingpan Glacier, near Point 7573 there are spacious campsites. Ascend the Fryingpan Glacier, trending west below the rocks of Whitman Crest at about 8700 feet. A gap at 9050 feet leads over Whitman Crest and onto the Whitman Glacier.

## SELECTED HISTORY

**1894 AUGUST**  East Shoulder. II+. J. B. Flett, Henry H. Garrison.

**1959 JUNE**  North Face. IV, 4th and 5th class. Dave Mahre, Gene Prater.

**1959 AUGUST**  Northeast Face. III, 4th class. Dave Mahre, Lex Maxwell, Bob McCall.

**1980 JANUARY**  North Face, FWA. George Dunn, Eric Simonson.

**1981 JANUARY**  West Ridge. V, 5.7. Matt Christensen, Paul Cook.

**2012 MAY**  South Face. III. Loren Campbell, Mike Gauthier.

**VIA PARADISE:** From SR 7 at Elbe, turn east onto SR 706 and drive to the Nisqually entrance into the park; continue on Paradise Road to the ranger station and parking lot at Paradise (5400 feet).

Follow the Skyline Trail 1.5 miles to Panorama Point (6900 feet), then the Pebble Creek Trail (or snow) toward Camp Muir.

From 8600 feet on the Muir Snowfield, below Moon Rocks, traverse northeast below Anvil Rock onto the upper Paradise Glacier. Once you have rounded below Anvil Rock, head northeast and traverse the Cowlitz Glacier toward Cathedral Rocks, avoiding the crevasse fields below 8400 feet. Cross Cathedral Rocks, a rock cleaver that divides the Cowlitz from the Ingraham Glacier, at a gap near 8450 feet. Once on the Ingraham, cross to the east side of the glacier as crevasses allow toward a prominent notch near 8800 feet. Chossy slabs work to the notch and the Whitman Glacier. Continue up the Whitman Glacier toward Little Tahoma's summit, joining the route from White River at about 9000 feet.

## ROUTE

Ascend the Whitman Glacier where the slope angle increases as you climb, reaching the top of the glacier at approximately 10,300 feet. The final 800 feet of the route, depending on the snow cover, ascends 2nd- and 3rd-class rock that is notoriously loose. Though the climbing is nontechnical, use caution due to loose rocks. Climber-caused rockfall may be a significant issue on the final portion of the route.

## DESCENT

Descend the climbing route.

# MOUNT RAINIER/TAHOMA  14,410'

## PROMINENCE: 13,210' [1]

### EMMONS-WINTHROP GLACIER; LIBERTY RIDGE

You know you want to! Rainier, spectacularly visible from metropolitan areas, stands as an obvious challenge for locals whether they are climbers or not. Sunrise from high on the mountain is sublime, an experience not to be missed. The mountain is truly huge, standing so far above its neighbors that it is ranked Number 21 in the world for topographic prominence. While actual prominence is even higher, for climbers it means routes with more than 9000 feet of elevation gain.

With that much altitude, and located so close to tidewater, it is the most glaciated peak in the Lower 48. The upper mountain is fully exposed to storms from the Pacific Ocean, and immense glaciers have carved huge cirques and amphitheaters with long, jagged ridges between them. There are a great many classic climbs all the way around

*Mount Rainier's broad summit area showing the three summits (left to right): Point Success, Columbia Crest, and Liberty Cap. (Photo by John Scurlock)*

Mount Rainier; some are in fact world-class and none are casual. With altitude, severe weather, and large glaciers near roads and civilization, the mountain has been an ideal training ground for bigger things. A great many successful Himalayan climbers have trained and learned their craft here on Mount Rainier.

For those attempting Rainier on their own, recognizing and understanding hazards are necessary steps for being able to manage risk. Skills associated with snow and glacier travel, altitude, weather extremes, and group dynamics are good areas in which to have had real experience before attempting Rainier on your own. Mike Gauthier, longtime climbing ranger and author of *Mount Rainier: A Climbing Guide*, has observed that "the mountain can serve up lessons of hardship for those who underestimate it or, more often, those who overestimate themselves."

A great deal has been written about glacier travel, altitude sickness, and everything else that can happen on a mountaineering adventure like Rainier. While it's not currently in fashion, taking an extra day or two, and an extra quart or two of water, can turn nausea and headache into a big smile. Do you really want to go back to work that badly?

### LAND MANAGER

Mount Rainier National Park, headquartered in Ashford; entrance fee or park pass required. Annual Climbing Cost Recovery Fee required in advance online before applying for required climbing permit. Wilderness permit required for overnight trips; park website has current specifics (see Resources). Permits for east side of mountain handled through White River Wilderness Information Center; for south side, through Paradise Ranger Station.

### NOTE

Careful preparation and flexibility can make the difference between a great climb and tragedy. Severe winter-like storms on the mountain are not uncommon during the summer. Avalanches can be a threat year-round, not just in winter. Statistically, June has seen the most fatalities from icefall and avalanche. Do not underestimate the altitude even if you have experience on these routes. Cell service on the mountain is spotty at best.

*Mount Rainier from the northeast: Emmons-Winthrop Glacier* (Photo by John Scurlock)

*Circumventing the bergschrund crevasse on the Emmons-Winthrop Glacier; Rainier's northwest summit, Liberty Cap, is seen in the distance. (Photo by Mike Warren)*

## 5. EMMONS-WINTHROP GLACIER:
### GRADE III

**TIME:** 3-5 days round-trip; 8-12 hours round-trip from Camp Schurman. The Emmons-Winthrop route is one of the great glacier routes of North America, with glacier travel and snow and ice slopes to 40 degrees. Reaching the summit requires a vertical elevation gain of more than 10,000 feet over more than 8 miles. Proper physical conditioning and time spent acclimatizing can offset the effects of fatigue that lead to mistakes and injuries.

Crowds on a route this popular also create hazards. Rope teams climbing above and below each other and at bottleneck areas require care and thoughtful etiquette. Give uphill traffic the right-of-way. They are doing the hard work, so let them pass. The uphill traffic must work harder if the boot pack is destroyed by those joyfully stomping down from the top.

The description below is for the standard Emmons-Winthrop Glacier route via Camp Schurman. For those wanting a more adventurous approach, accessing the Winthrop Glacier via St. Elmo Pass (7400 feet) is a nice alternative to the Inter Glacier approach.

### APPROACH, GRADE III
From Enumclaw, drive State Route 410 southeast about 40 miles and turn right (west) onto White River Canyon Road toward Sunrise. Reach the White River entrance to the park in 1 mile. Continue 5 miles to White River Campground and the Glacier Basin Trailhead (4350 feet).

Follow the Glacier Basin Trail 3.1 miles to Glacier Basin and campsites at 5900 feet. A workable itinerary for sea-level-based climbers might include first camping at Glacier Basin, and then at Emmons Flats or Camp Schurman on day two, before making the summit attempt on the third day. Alternately, day one could end at Camp Schurman, with day two being an acclimatization day, and the summit on day three.

From Glacier Basin backcountry camp, follow a climbers path and moraine to the snout of the Inter Glacier at 6800 feet. The glacier is small but has some crevasses. It is also known for rockfall during warm temperatures. Near the top of the glacier, skirt left (east) toward a rocky area where Camp Curtis is situated at 9000 feet. This provides a good angle to assess the route and take a photo to help navigate crevasses.

From Camp Curtis, a short descent leads to the Emmons Glacier (8900 feet) and the slog up to Camp Schurman at 9500 feet. There are many camp spots at Schurman and barrels for depositing human waste.

To get above the crowds, an alternative is Emmons Flats at 9800 feet. August and September may present difficulties accessing the Emmons from Camp Curtis. An alternate route ascends to the top of Steamboat Prow, then descends loose gullies. Use caution in this area.

## ROUTE

From high camp at either Camp Schurman or Emmons Flats, climb southwesterly up the Emmons Glacier as crevasses allow. The first half of the route—the so-called Corridor—is often a smooth, wide path ascending at approximately 30 degrees. Upon exiting the Corridor somewhere around 11,200 feet, the route typically traverses rightward (north) on steepening slopes. At this point, the Winthrop and Emmons Glaciers merge. The route to the summit varies greatly depending on the year and season. A long traverse northwest on the Winthrop Glacier is not unusual. Between 13,500 feet and 13,700 feet, a bergschrund usually forms that is a bottleneck on busy days. The long traverse around the end of the 'schrund should be considered on crowded days, especially on the descent.

**WINTHROP GLACIER VARIATION:** A more adventurous and less-traveled route starts from Camp Schurman and traverses more to the right (west-northwest) from high camp. Depending on conditions, the Winthrop offers an interesting and less populous alternative to the Emmons. It may be more practical to descend the Emmons route to Steamboat Prow.

## DESCENT

Descend the climbing route.

# 6. LIBERTY RIDGE: GRADE IV

**TIME:** 3-5 days round-trip. One-day single-push ascents can be a good strategy for experienced and well-acclimated climbers, when snow conditions allow. Liberty Ridge is one of the world's great climbs, unmistakable and begging to be climbed. With more than a vertical mile of technical terrain—50-degree snow or ice—the stunning north ridge of Mount Rainier stands comfortably at the bar with many of the planet's most beautiful climbs. The ridge is a catwalk of relative security amid the unspeakable chaos of the mountain's north face. It is only from up close that you begin to sense the bass notes of real danger. Watch carefully, read everything; the ridge provides protection from most but not all exposure to avalanches.

Unless climbers have spent time acclimatizing in advance, they may be tempted to camp at Thumb Rock (10,800 feet), once considered a protected campsite; Thumb Rock is now considered to be threatened as a result of recent accidents, including a fatality in May 2019. This will undoubtedly affect strategy for Liberty Ridge climbers. Other than Thumb Rock, there really are no flat areas for even the smallest tent between the glacier at 8800 feet and the top at 14,000 feet.

A good weather report is more important for this climb than most; the relentless 50-degree angle makes retreat difficult, and with most storms approaching from the southwest—the other side of the mountain—there can be little warning. Chilling for several nights at Camp Schurman would be the best scenario, allowing for a faster ascent, ideally without high camps.

The route is protected from collapsing seracs initially but is quite exposed to rockfall, especially on the lower third. Above about 12,400 feet, the route is minimally exposed to serac fall, but realistically, factors like fatigue, fitness, altitude, and especially weather are more likely to cause problems.

*Using skis on the approach and on the descent of the Emmons Glacier allowed Colin Haley, Eric Carter, and Nick Elson to complete a roundtrip climb of Liberty Ridge in just over nine hours from the trailhead.* **(Photo by Colin Haley)**

Ice avalanches on the route are rare but are the suspected cause of several serious accidents, including the loss of six climbers in a June 2014 tragedy.

While the first ascent was made in late September, early summer has become more popular. Early season provides more snow cover, less ice climbing, and, hopefully, usually less exposure to rockfall. Spring weather can be severe, and avalanche threats are real in May and June. While Paradise may have summer conditions, the 50-degree slopes on the mountain's north side probably won't. Climbers in the Cascades are statistically just as likely to get avalanched in May as in any other month.

## APPROACH, GRADE III

The climb can be approached from two directions. From the east via White River has several advantages: you start a bit higher, and returning to the starting point is much shorter after descending the Emmons-Winthrop Glacier.

*Mount Rainier from the north: Liberty Ridge* (Photo by John Scurlock)

From the north via Carbon River is often used for winter and early-spring ascents.

**WHITE RIVER-GLACIER BASIN:** From Enumclaw, follow State Route 410 southeast about 40 miles and turn right (west) onto White River Canyon Road toward Sunrise. Reach the White River entrance to the park in 1 mile and follow the approach to the Glacier Basin Trailhead (4350 feet) and Glacier Basin (5900 feet) given for Emmons-Winthrop Glacier (Climb 5). A workable itinerary for sea-level climbers is to start late on the first day and bivy at Glacier Basin, then ascend to a high camp on lower Curtis Ridge on day two, with the summit and descend on day three.

From Glacier Basin, follow a climbers path leading toward the Inter Glacier, at about 6500 feet. Take a climbers path to the right (northwest) to St. Elmo Pass at 7400 feet, and from the west side of the pass make a long traverse across the Winthrop Glacier at about 7200 feet. The traverse continues across talus and scree on the broad lower slopes of Curtis Ridge. Drop onto the Carbon Glacier near 7200 feet and aim for the base of the route at 8600 feet.

**CARBON RIVER-IPSUT CREEK:** From Enumclaw, follow SR 410 southwest to Buckley, then SR 165 south about 23 miles to the park's Carbon River entrance and drive to the road end at 1900 feet.

Walk the road a couple miles to Ipsut Creek Campground at 2300 feet. Find the trailhead at the upper end of the former parking lot and follow the Wonderland Trail east about 3 miles, crossing the Carbon River on a suspension bridge. Just beyond the bridge, take the uphill (right) fork to a small meadow known as Moraine Park at 6100 feet. Just above the meadow, hike southeast on a moraine and reach the Carbon Glacier somewhere between 7000 and 7500 feet. Slog the glacier and aim for the west side of Liberty Ridge at about 8600.

## ROUTE

From either approach, most parties climb the right side of Liberty Ridge (snow or scree) to the small campsite at Thumb Rock (10,800 feet). These slopes are prone to rockfall, especially during the period when the snowmelt exposes the "rock." Snow conditions above Thumb Rock are unpredictable, can change overnight, and vary year to year. The route is often snow climbing for much of the early summer, with more likelihood of ice as the season progresses. The angle averages about 50 degrees.

From Thumb Rock, a steep section (often rock) is often skirted on the left, regaining the ridge crest some 400 feet above. With better conditions, this section can also be climbed directly or turned on the right. Once back on the crest, the route's steepness continues, intimidating as you pass the Black Pyramid at 12,400 feet. Above 13,000 feet, the angle eases a bit and the route joins the Liberty Cap Glacier. Find a route across the bergschrund (may require ice climbing), followed by a traverse of Liberty Cap, Rainier's northwest summit at 14,112 feet. From Liberty Cap, head east, and then south across the broad summit plateau and finally up to Columbia Crest.

## DESCENT

The descent is usually made via the Emmons-Winthrop Glacier route.

## SELECTED HISTORY

**1857 JULY** Kautz Glacier to 13,800+ feet. III. August Kautz party of four.

**1870 AUGUST** Gibraltar Ledges. III. Hazard Stevens, Philemon Van Trump.

**1870 OCTOBER** Via Gibraltar Ledges. Geologists Samuel Emmons, Allen Wilson.

**1884 AUGUST** Emmons Winthrop -Glacier route III. Warner Fobes, George James, Richard Wells.

**1890 AUGUST** FA by a woman. Evelyn Fay Fuller.

**1891 AUGUST** Tahoma Glacier. III. Warren Riley and dog, Alfred Drewry, Philemon Van Trump.

**1905 JULY** Success Cleaver. III. F. Kizer, three Mazamas, two Sierra Club members.

**1920 JULY** Fuhrer Finger. II+. Peyton Farrer, Hans Fuhrer, Heinie Fuhrer, Joe Hazard, Thomas Hermans.

**1922 FEBRUARY** Via Gibraltar Ledges, FWA. Jacques Bergues, Jacques Landry, Jean Landry, Charles Perryman.

**1935 SEPTEMBER** Ptarmigan Ridge. IV. Wolf Bauer, Jack Hossack.

**1935 SEPTEMBER** Liberty Ridge IV. Jim Burrow, Arnie Campbell, Ome Daiber.

**1937 JULY** Sunset Amphitheater. III. Fred Thieme, Wendell Trosper.

**1938 AUGUST** Sunset Ridge. III. Lyman Boyer, Arnie Campbell, Don Woods.

**1948 JULY** Nisqually Glacier. III. Robert Craig, Dee Molenaar.

**1957 JUNE** Edmunds Headwall. IV. Fred Beckey, Don Gordon, Tom Hornbein, Herb Staley, John Rupley.

**1957 JULY** Curtis Ridge. IV, 5.5 A1. Gene Prater, Marcel Schuster.

**1960 JULY** Russel Cliff. III. Don Jones, Jim Kurtz, Dave Mahre, Gene Prater.

**1961 JUNE** Willis Wall. IV. Charles Bell.

**1963 JULY** South Tahoma Headwall. III+. Fred Beckey, Steve Marts.

**1965 JULY** Sunset Amphitheater Headwall. III+. Dave Mahre, Don McPherson, Gene Prater, Fred Stanley, Jim Wickwire.

**1966 JULY** Central Mowich Face. IV. Dee Molenaar, Dick Pargeter, Gene Prater, Jim Wickwire.

**1972 MARCH** Ptarmigan Ridge, FWA. Al Errington party.

**1975 FEBRUARY** Willis Wall, FWA. Dusan Jagersky, Reilly Moss.

**1976 JANUARY** Liberty Ridge, FWA. Party unknown.

# SNOQUALMIE PASS HIGHWAY/I-90

## THE TOOTH                         5604'

**PROMINENCE: 244'**

### SOUTH FACE; TOOTH FAIRY

This is perhaps the most-visited summit in the Snoqualmie Pass region, and some might hazard that it's among the most popular climbs in the state. Indeed, there seems to be a large group of Tooth fans who make the slog up there on a regular basis. The 5-mile, 2000-foot-elevation-gain approach is, of course, casual compared to the Pickets but nonetheless athletic for what it is.

Set above the scenic Source Lake in the Alpental valley, the volcanic (Oligocene) Tooth's low elevations and southern exposures result in two climbs that are often dry and usually in good condition. The south face, which was first climbed more than ninety years ago, features four moderate short pitches interspersed with ledges. The far more recently established *Tooth Fairy*, around on the southwest face, is a modern sport climb done in six short pitches to the summit.

The proximity of Seattle precludes any expectations of a wilderness experience here. For decades, one of this state's climbing institutions has included the Tooth on its list of necessary climbs.

### LAND MANAGER

Alpine Lakes Wilderness, Mount Baker–Snoqualmie National Forest, Snoqualmie Ranger District. Northwest Forest Pass or interagency recreation pass required for parking. Free self-registered wilderness permit required for day and overnight trips.

*The Tooth from the northeast: south face* (Photo by John Scurlock)

## 7. SOUTH FACE: GRADE II, 5.4

**TIME:** 6–10 hours. **GEAR:** small rack to 2½ inches; crampons helpful in early season. On a weekend, the South Face route will almost always have someone else on it, usually both climbing up and rappelling off. Allow generous extra time for these situations and bring patience and a headlamp.

### APPROACH, GRADE II

Drive Interstate 90 to Snoqualmie Pass and take exit 52; turn left to cross under the freeway and follow signs to the Alpental parking lot and Snow Lake Trailhead at 3200 feet. Please do not use ski area parking lots on weekends or holidays, especially at Alpental; if you are not a patron of the ski area, park in the lower lot, the first parking lot on the left as you travel up the Alpental road; it's located just below the Alpental footbridge. Consider carpooling whenever possible and be sensitive and respectful to ski area guests, the ski area, and their parking policies and signs.

Follow the Snow Lake Trail No. 1013 about 2 miles to a junction where the old trail is labeled "Source Lake Trail." Continue straight on the old path where the new Snow Lake Trail makes a sharp bend to the right. Continue up the valley on the old trail less than a mile to the talus field that fills the end of the cirque above tiny Source Lake. This is the headwaters of the Snoqualmie River.

Descend a couple hundred feet and cross the talus field until under cliffs. Several tracks work up and left through short sections of forest and boulder fields until reaching the basin underneath the east face of The Tooth. Once in the basin at 4400 feet, move left and find the boot track in the grass on the left edge of the gravel. Scramble boulders up to the gravelly pass immediately south of Pineapple Pinnacle. Slip through the pass and then stomp around the west side of the pinnacle until a short scramble leads to the start of the route at Pineapple Pass.

### ROUTE

**PITCH 1:** From the notch, climb cracks and large, steep but solid blocks about 100 feet to a belay ledge at the base of another short, steep wall. **PITCH 2:** Climb a steep wall (5.3) with balance climbing about 60 feet to a big ledge with trees. The first two pitches can be combined if the route is not already crowded. **PITCH 3:** The third and least technical pitch works a rope length of ledges and short steps to the base of the final wall. **PITCH 4:** Shuffle up and along a left-traversing ramp called the Catwalk (exposed low 5th class), pass a vintage ring piton, and carry on until reaching easier ground and the summit. **VARIATION 5.6:** Climb the last short bit of steep wall directly to the summit area.

### DESCENT

Descend the route via rappels from trees to climber's right on the route. Multiple single-rope rappels are easier to manage than long raps here due to trees, blocky snags, and other climbers.

## 8. TOOTH FAIRY: GRADE II, 5.9+

**TIME:** 8–12 hours round-trip from car. **GEAR:** 13 sport and alpine draws, single 60m rope. Crampons will get you up the snowfield (and onto the route!) ahead of others.

### APPROACH

Follow the approach for the South Face, but at the point where the South Face approach scrambles up to Pineapple

*Lauren Allen sends pitch 5 of the* **Tooth Fairy.** *(Photo by Jacob Lopilato)*

Pass, continue skirting The Tooth's southeast face, heading down and around to the north. In about 250 feet, locate the route on a steep arête directly beneath the summit overhangs. Anchors should be visible on the initial pitches.

## ROUTE

**PITCH 1:** On the right side of the arête, scramble 25 feet up a ledgy ramp and step left onto the main face. Cross another ramp, and a short 5.8 section reaches the chains. **PITCH 2:** Work up a bit and clip the first bolt with a full-length runner. Step immediately right (5.9) and around the corner onto the big steep face. Exciting 5.8 continues to the arête crest and an exposed belay on the edge. **PITCH 3:** Move up and left a bit (5.4) and then up again on lower-angle rock. Find the belay on a good ledge 15 feet left of the arête. **PITCH 4:** This fun pitch starts just right of the belay and then works up a short slab to a steep, pretty face. A couple 5.8 moves finish the face and lead to a great ledge. **PITCH 5:** Climb up and left from the anchor and make an athletic sequence through the notch and up onto the little slab. Work right on the slab and get into the steep slot (5.9) leading up. Continue up a corner onto a rampy ledge just beneath the steep stuff. About 15 feet of steepish 5.9+ works up to the lip. The chains are 6 feet above. **PITCH 6:** The summit can be reached in one pitch with a 60m rope. A short 5.6 section above the anchor blocks the view of the rest of the pitch. Pass a rappel

## SELECTED HISTORY

**1916 JUNE** North Ridge. II, 5.0. Charles Hazlehurst, C. G. Morrison.

**1928 SEPTEMBER** South Face. II, 5.5. C. L. Anderson, Herman Wunderling.

**1928 SEPTEMBER** South Face, solo. Hans-Otto Giese.

**1938 JULY** West Face. II, 5th class. Ray Clough, Charles Kirschner.

**1942 OCTOBER** Southwest Face. II+, 5.7. Fred Beckey, Helmy Beckey, Louis Graham.

**1952 MARCH** South Face, FWA. Vic Josendal, Dick McGowan, Pete Schoening.

**1959 SEPTEMBER** East Face. II+, 5.7. Roger Jackson, Michael Kennedy.

**1984 DECEMBER** East Face, FWA. Scott Fisher, Jim Nelson.

**2018 JULY** Southwest Face, *Tooth Fairy*. II, 5.9. Jim Nelson, David Whitelaw.

station at midpitch and note that loose rock on the easy terrain near the summit directly threatens the base of the route.

## DESCENT

Rappelling the route with no one else around works just fine; two of the stances, however, are indeed minimal and no place for groups. Further, the last 50 feet to the top are

*The Tooth from the south: (A) Tooth Fairy, (B) South Face (Photo by John Scurlock)*

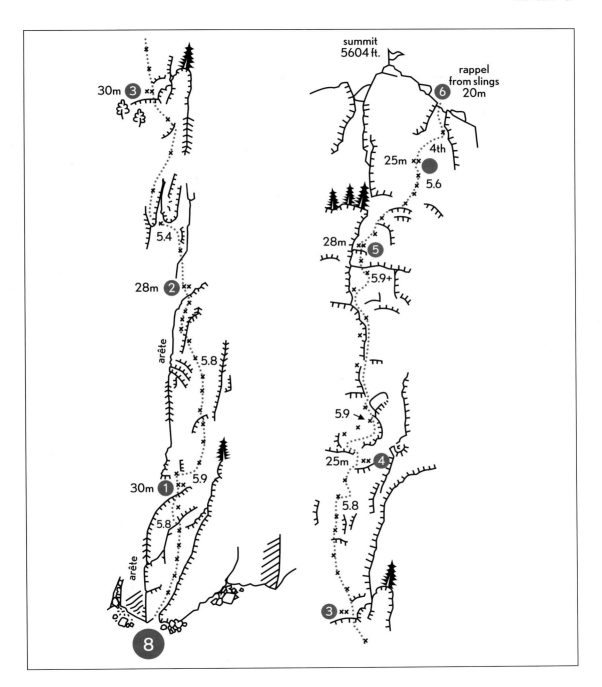

low-angle and easy, but loose rock will probably move as the rap rope is pulled. Others may start to climb while you are on the summit and not realize you are above them.

Consider descending via another route if others are climbing below. The obvious choice is to descend the south face, although it may have a circus of its own in progress. So get in line for that or descend the north ridge, which is easy but will likely require a few bits of gear and two short rappels.

# SNOQUALMIE MOUNTAIN   6278'

## PROMINENCE: 998'

### NEW YORK GULLY
Except for a few local skiers, the north side of Snoqualmie Mountain was mostly unexplored terrain in 1985 when a couple of transplanted New England ice climbers established this classic mixed route. Jim Ruch, who made the first ascent with Bob Cotter, enjoyed the route so much he was eager to climb it again. Returning with Carl Diedrich, Ruch commented that the mixed climbing was some of the best he had done. The third ascent wasn't made until February 2001 by Mark Bunker and Colin Haley.

The existence of this climb adds more depth to a growing subgenre of Cascade climbing. A number of mini nordwands have now come into fashion—among them, spectacular lines on Colonial Peak, Mount Index, White-horse Mountain, Colfax Peak, and many others. These routes are generally not appealing in summer but have found a following in winter, the only time one can find classic mixed climbing in the Cascades. For what seems like just a few moments each year, when conditions are just right, these faces can offer mixed climbing on rock, snow, and ice. For some, climbing on snow- and ice-covered rock defines alpine climbing.

As the winter opportunities on Snoqualmie Mountain basalt have become more popular, additional routes and variations have been put up on Snoqualmie's north-west face. Starting near the toe of the central buttress, the nine-pitch *Pineapple Express* was climbed in 2005 and its variation *Blue Moon* a few years later.

Favorable snow conditions and avalanche awareness should be considered a prerequisite for this approach, climb, and descent. The southwest slopes of Snoqualmie Mountain (including the Phantom Slide) are target zones for avalanche explosives delivered via artillery or helicopter. Avalanche-control activities and the closure of those slopes are always communicated in advance. A map and sign in the main Alpental parking lot contain additional information.

Getting out in the winter and learning to judge constantly changing conditions can be a great accomplishment. Occasionally the choss is covered in a stable blanket of consolidated snow and ice on some aspects. Bring a little gear, a couple pins, and a lot of nerve!

### LAND MANAGER
Alpine Lakes Wilderness, Mount Baker-Snoqualmie National Forest, Snoqualmie Ranger District. Northwest Forest Pass or interagency recreation pass required for parking. Free self-registered wilderness permit required for day and overnight trips.

*Colin Haley enjoys an early repeat of Snoqualmie Mountain's* New York Gully. *(Photo by Mark Bunker)*

# 9. NEW YORK GULLY: GRADE III⁺, 5.8 WI 3 M5 A1 OR M5⁺

**TIME:** 12-15 hours. **GEAR:** mostly rock pro to 3 inches, including pitons; possibly ice screws in rare conditions. Below-average temperatures are greatly appreciated, the colder the better. However, warm "pineapple express" storms can also have a positive effect on the snowpack. Freezing temperatures following a short warming are often a good recipe for winter climbing. The weather determines the character of the climbing, which will change dramatically as the cycles of freeze and thaw work their alchemy.

## APPROACH, GRADE III

Drive Interstate 90 to Snoqualmie Pass and take exit 52; turn left to cross under the freeway and follow signs to the Alpental ski area upper parking lot at 3200 feet. Please do not use ski area parking lots on weekends or holidays, especially at Alpental; if you are not a patron of the ski area, park in the lower lot, the first parking lot on the left as you travel up the Alpental road; it's located just below the main (center) lot with the Alpental footbridge. Consider carpooling whenever possible and be sensitive and respectful to ski area guests, the ski area, and their parking policies and signs.

Walk up the road just past the main lot until below the Phantom Slide area. This major slide path is the reason there are no big trees. A short way above the road and just west of cliffs, navigate through two short cliff bands in the woods to get started. Often there is a boot path through this area. Ascend the Phantom Slide to around 4600 feet, where a traverse west leads to just below the west ridge crossing at 5250 feet.

*Snoqualmie Mountain from the northeast,* New York Gully: *(A)* Pineapple Express, *(B)* Blue Moon, *(C)* New York Gully *direct start,* *(D)* New York Gully, *(E)* Turf Testament, *(F)* Snostril (Photo by John Scurlock)

## SELECTED HISTORY

**1898** South Ridge, FA. I. Albert Sylvester USGS survey party.

**1928 FEBRUARY** FWA. Hermann Ulrichs, Jeffrey Cameron.

**1968 SEPTEMBER** Northwest Face. II+. Dan Davis.

**1985 MARCH** Northwest Face, *New York Gully*. III+, 5.8 WI 3 M5 A1 or M5+. Bob Cotter, Jim Ruch.

**2005 FEBRUARY** Northwest Face, *Pineapple Express*. IV, 5.8 WI 3+ M6. Dan Cauthorn, Roger Strong.

**2009 FEBRUARY** Northwest Face, *Blue Moon*. IV, 5.8 WI 4 M6. Craig Gyselinck, Wayne Wallace.

**2009 FEBRUARY** Northwest Face, *New York Gully*, direct start. III+. Mark Bunker, Wayne Wallace.

**2018 MARCH** Northwest Face, *Turf Testament*. III, 5.8 WI 4 M6. Mark Bunker, Rolf Larson.

**2021 JANUARY** Northwest Face, *Snostril* and *Temres*. III, WI 4 M5. Tom Bierne, Doug Hutchinson, Christian Junkar.

## ROUTE

From the west ridge at 5250 feet, descend a short way into Thunder Basin below the mountain's northwest face. The climb begins on the right side of the face with several hundred feet of easy snow climbing in the Snot Couloir. **PITCHES 1–2:** The route begins with two long pitches toward a tree snag near the base of a long right-slanting box gully. **PITCH 3:** Climb the box gully past a difficult chock stone to a belay on the left wall where there is a little snow to stand on. This pitch may still have a fixed pin or two from the first ascent and at more than 213 feet (65m) is the crux of the route. **PITCH 4:** Start on the right-hand wall and continue straight up to the end of the gully, then move across a short slab to the base of the off-width corner. **PITCH 5:** The beginning of this pitch is steep, and an aid move may be helpful; climb a move or two up the off-width before clipping a Cotter/Ruch knifeblade on the left wall, then continue another 30 feet to a belay at a tree. **PITCH 6:** Head right about 250 feet on 4th-class mixed terrain, up to a saddle to the right of the subsummit. From here, make a quick rap into a snow gully that leads up to the west ridge and the summit a bit beyond.

## DESCENT

Descend the mountain's southwestern slopes back to the Alpental valley.

# MOUNT GARFIELD     5519'

**PROMINENCE: 839'**

### WEST PEAK, INFINITE BLISS; MAIN PEAK, SOUTH RIB

Garfield is a multipeak massif of modest height and even more modest reputation. The south face of the main peak had been an identifiable challenge for decades, but none of the main potential was explored until fairly recently. Its unremarkable summit elevation cleverly hides the fact that it has huge sweeps of stone that would more commonly be expected on the high peaks than here on the edge of the range.

Fred Beckey prophetically called Garfield a "hazardous enigma," tagged to a photo of the then-unclimbed south face of the main peak. The whole place attracted only minimal interest until the West Peak became the center of still another backwoods bolting battle.

In addition to the impressive highly recrystallized mix of mostly dacite, minor andesite, and rhyolite in breccia on the main and middle peaks, there are at least a half dozen other dizzy spires and summits of significance. Garfield towers above the scenic Snoqualmie River valley, a major recreation area only an hour from Seattle.

### LAND MANAGER

Alpine Lakes Wilderness, Mount Baker-Snoqualmie National Forest, Snoqualmie Ranger District. Northwest Forest Pass or interagency recreation pass required for parking. Free self-registered wilderness permit required for day and overnight trips.

## 10. WEST PEAK (4896'), INFINITE BLISS: GRADE V, 5.10+

**TIME:** 1 day. **GEAR:** 17 draws (34 if simul-climbing). The big shining slabs on the west peaks are obvious and there were several early routes. Still, nothing was on anyone's tick list until this modern line up the middle of the slabs was established by Leland Windham and Steve Martin in 2003. With nearly a half mile of climbing on a mountainside in the Cascades, the route really can't be called a sport route. This is a superfun 23-pitch bolted climb up a huge face that's easy to get to. There are several easy sections with big runouts, and some confusion has resulted. However, any move harder than 5.6 is well protected, and the crux pitches are fully bolted sport pitches with incredible position.

The descent is thankfully back down the route. Still, being umpteen pitches off the ground anywhere requires some experience. Fiddling around for only a few extra minutes per pitch can mean rappelling in the dark.

## APPROACH, GRADE I

Drive Interstate 90 toward North Bend and take exit 34 to 468th Street; follow it to the junction with SE Middle Fork Road, which becomes Forest Road 56. Drive 12.3 miles to the Middle Fork–Taylor River Road junction just after the Taylor River bridge (about 1200 feet) and park at a five-car spot 1 mile beyond the bridge.

The unmarked but well-worn trail is about 100 yards farther up the road. Hike 30–45 minutes steeply uphill to the base of the route and look for bolts.

## ROUTE

**PITCHES 1–6:** The climb begins with six low-5th-class pitches on clean slab to the right of a watercourse to a ledge. **PITCH 7:** Begin with 50 feet of 3rd class and finish on a large ledge. This whole section is fully exposed to rockfall from parties above, including pitches 15–17 where there is loose rock. **PITCH 8:** Begin about 20 feet to the right from pitch 7 before climbing into the "stone ditch" and up. After pitch 8, the bolts become more frequent as the climbing steepens. **PITCH 9:** Follow a dike before moving left to a ledge; 5.9 with 10 bolts. **PITCH 10:** Reach a ledge; move the belay 50 feet left to start the next pitch. **PITCH 11:** 5.10

*Leland Windham points to his route,* Infinite Bliss, *on Mount Garfield.* (Photo by Monty VanderBilt)

*Mount Garfield from the southwest: West Peak,* Infinite Bliss (Photo by John Scurlock)

with 9 bolts. **PITCH 12:** 5.7 with 6 bolts. **PITCH 13:** Angle to the right to a notch in the skyline; 5.2 with 1 bolt. **PITCH 14:** Climb left toward a corner, then back to the right toward the belay; 5.8 with 8 bolts.

**PITCH 15:** Climb leftward past a bolt, left around a bush, then straight up; 5.2 with 2 bolts. **PITCH 16:** Carefully follow the 3rd-class ramp up and right to the stunted cedar at about 200 feet—the 3-bolt belay anchor is another 80 feet of 4th class directly above the cedar. **NOTE:** there are other small evergreens on this pitch, but only one cedar. **PITCH 17:** Angle slightly leftward for 170 feet to the belay directly below a rock scar; 4th class without bolts. **PITCH 18:** End on a ledge; 5.8 with 8 bolts. You have worked hard to get this far; the final pitches are pure bliss.

**PITCH 19:** 5.10+ with 17 bolts. **PITCH 20:** A short pitch with 2 bolts. **PITCH 21:** Cross a gully and climb a long

5.10- corner with 15 bolts. **PITCH 22:** Climb the dike, followed by a traverse right to a small ledge; 5.8 with 11 bolts. **PITCH 23:** 5.10 with 11 bolts. The climb finishes on Infinite Peak, a subsummit east of the main West Peak.

### DESCENT
Two 60m ropes work well for the rappels, with the longest rappels being about 180 feet (55 meters).

## 11. MAIN PEAK, SOUTH RIB: GRADE V, 5.10

**TIME:** 1-2 days. **GEAR:** rack to 3 inches, including some thin blade pitons. With only one known ascent of this route, there is not much available information. Pete Doorish, who climbed three routes on this chert and metachert side of

Garfield, suggested people would enjoy this climb. There is a rough topo in the *Cascade Alpine Guide* by Fred Beckey. A scouting climb of the 1940 route is not a bad idea before attempting the more technical routes on the mountain.

## APPROACH

Follow the approach for the preceding climb. Continue on Middle Fork Road about 2 miles farther to a parking lot at 1100 feet next to a wide gravel wash 2.6 miles from the Taylor River bridge.

The climb was originally approached via the central south-face gully and included a 5.10 section when snow is not in the gully. Subsequent parties have approached using the path for the 1940 route on the southwest face, following a mix of dry streambed and forest. At the top of slabs at about 3100 feet, leave the 1940 route, making a descent into the Great Canyon gully, then traverse across a large ledge system east to the south face's central gully.

## ROUTE

**PITCHES 1-3:** From the central gully below the south face, begin with mid-5th-class climbing to a prominent point on the rib. **PITCHES 4-5:** Face climbing with adequate protection ascends through a headwall. **PITCH 6:** Easier climbing reaches the top of a pillar with trees. **PITCHES 7-8:** Above the pillar, climb the rib directly (mid-5th class) to a ledge below a steeper wall. **PITCH 9:** Climb the right side of the steep wall (5.10). **PITCHES 10-15:** Ascend by easier climbing. **PITCH 16:** Ascend a dihedral (5.6) near the center of the face.

## DESCENT

From the summit, scramble down rock and heather slopes of the northwest face, then continue west to the Leaning Spire–Main Peak

South Rib. *Mount Garfield from the south, south rib: (A) 1940 route, (B) South Rib, (C) Southeast Face, (D) East Ridge* (Photo by John Scurlock)

## SELECTED HISTORY

### MAIN PEAK

**1940 AUGUST** Southwest Route. III+. Jim Crooks, Judson Nelson.

**1941 NOVEMBER** West Summit, *Leaning Spire*. III, 5.2. Fred Beckey, Louis Graham, Walt Varney.

**1990 JUNE** East Rib. IV, 5.7. Alex Cudkowicz, Pete Doorish.

**1991 SEPTEMBER** South Rib. V, 5.10. Russ DeVaney, Pete Doorish.

**1991 SEPTEMBER** Southeast Face. V, 5.11. Pete Doorish.

### WEST PEAK (4896')

**1940 AUGUST** West Ridge. III. Tom Campbell, Stan Garson.

**1963 FEBRUARY** South Face. III+, 5.5. Gerry Roach, Dick Springgate, John Wells.

**2003 AUGUST** South Face, *Infinite Bliss*. V, 5.10. Leland Windham, Steve Martin.

### EAST PEAK (5480')

**1951 APRIL** II. Party unknown.

Col at 5050 feet. From the col, descend the second gully to the first gully, reaching the junction of the two gullies at a Y. Below the Y, the route is devious and difficult to describe.

Stay above and west of the Great Canyon gully. Parties generally make anywhere from three to six single-rope rappels over the entire descent.

# MOUNT DANIEL                    7960'

## PROMINENCE: 3480'

### SOUTHEAST RIDGE

Formed from dacite, andesite, and rhyolite, Daniel makes an ideal introduction to snow mountaineering. It is a landmark peak with a whopping 3500 feet of prominence. It is also a gentle peak with five summits and the largest glaciers between Chinook and Stevens Passes. Located in the heart of the Cascades and approached on good trails, Daniel makes a great choice for fall and later-season climbs.

The highest point for Daniel is the west summit. The USGS map implies the east peak is the summit at 7859 feet. Topo maps show the middle and west peaks to be about equal in height, but field observations show the west summit to be higher by a bit. A visit to the northwest peak includes crossing both the Daniel and Lynch Glaciers.

*Mount Daniel from the south: southeast ridge* (Photo by John Scurlock)

## SELECTED HISTORY

**1925 AUGUST**  FA. A Mountaineers party recorded an ascent, although Daniel was likely climbed previously by surveyors.

With the glaciers in retreat, several new alpine lakes have formed. Pea Soup Lake below the Lynch Glacier has grown, and where the color was once milky with glacier flour, its color is now aquamarine. The glacial retreat here has been substantial. As with elsewhere in the range, several of these local glaciers are expected to vanish in the very near future. Explore the glaciers or avoid them; there is room to roam. Late summer is best for exploring the changes.

### LAND MANAGER

Alpine Lakes Wilderness, Okanogan-Wenatchee National Forest, Cle Elum Ranger District. Northwest Forest Pass or interagency recreation pass required for parking. Free self-registered wilderness permit required for day and overnight trips.

## 12. SOUTHEAST RIDGE: GRADE II

**TIME:** 1–2 days. The long, gravelly southeast ridge is a straightforward nontechnical route followed by high traverse to the highest peak. Without glacier travel, the southeast ridge also serves as the logical descent route when climbing the Lynch Glacier.

### APPROACH, GRADE II+

Drive Interstate 90 east from Snoqualmie Pass and take exit 80, driving north 3 miles to the town of Roslyn. From Roslyn take Salmon la Sac Road (State Route 903) 16 miles, through the town of Ronald and on to Salmon la Sac. Just before reaching the Cle Elum River, turn right onto Cle Elum Valley Road (Forest Road 4330) toward Fish Lake.

*Mount Daniel from the north; the approach to the lower Lynch Glacier is shown* (**Photo by Lowell Skoog**)

*Mount Daniel from the northeast* (Photo by John Scurlock)

Continue 12 more miles to a fork near the end of the road. Take the left fork for an additional several hundred feet and find the Cathedral Rock Trailhead on the left at about 3350 feet.

The Cathedral Rock Trail No. 1345 slogs a series of switchbacks through old-growth forest, passing the Trail Creek Trail No. 1322 at 2 miles (stay right) and later Squaw Lake at 4841 feet. The trail meanders through meadows and alongside ponds before reaching the Pacific Crest Trail No. 2000 at 4 miles. Take the PCT west uphill a short way to Cathedral Pass at 5600 feet. From the pass, traverse below the southwest side of Cathedral Peak, giving away a few hundred feet of elevation before reaching Peggys Pond at just shy of 5600 feet, 5 miles from the trailhead.

## ROUTE

The most direct route begins just north of the pond. From Peggys Pond, head up and west toward Point 7020 feet on Daniel's southeast ridge. Continue on the ridge but traverse below Point 6762 feet to gain a little pass at 7550 feet below Daniel's east summit. Keep traversing below the east summit and persevere over toward the middle and main summits. Once the snow is gone, the traverse below the East Peak is steep scree and dirt. The final ascent to the twin higher summits is straightforward. The upper Lynch Glacier is easily accessible from the summit area for explorations farther west.

## DESCENT

Descend the climbing route.

# STEVENS PASS HIGHWAY/US 2

## MOUNT INDEX           5991'

**PROMINENCE: 2991'**

### INDEX TRAVERSE

The Mount Index peaks look so steep, rugged, and intriguing that they seem surely to rival the Dru or Whitney as climbs. The mountain's east and north faces are on full display from the Stevens Pass Highway, while the equally imposing western faces are mostly hidden from easy view. Of the three peaks, only the South (Main) Peak has a moderate scramble route to the summit. Climbing the North or Middle Peak involves committing to multipitch technical routes—short lists of the Cascades' most difficult mountains typically include both. The three peaks of Index (not even 6000 feet high) may have the largest collection of difficult climbs in the Cascades.

*Wayne Wallace with Index North Peak behind, and the Skykomish River valley far below* (Photo by Tom Sjolseth)

## SELECTED HISTORY

### MAIN (SOUTH) PEAK

**1911 OCTOBER**  First recorded ascent, Anderson Creek. II. Evidence of previous ascent at summit.

**1963**  FWA. Cecil Bailey, Stan Jensen, Jim Pritchard.

**1964 SEPTEMBER**  South Norwegian Buttress. V, 5.7 A4. Alex Bertulis, Eric Bjornstad.

**1984 JANUARY**  East Gully. IV+. Fred Dunham, Bill Sumner.

**1987 AUGUST**  South Norwegian Buttress only. III, 5.10. Bryan Burdo, Greg White.

**1988 JULY**  South Norwegian Buttress, 1964 route, FFA. V, 5.9. Bryan Burdo, Steve Risse.

### MIDDLE PEAK (5493')

**1950 AUGUST**  North–south traverse. V, 5.7. Fred Beckey, Pete Schoening.

**1960 JUNE**  West Face. V. Fred Beckey, Don Gordon.

**1960 JULY**  South–north traverse, solo. Ed Cooper.

**1961 AUGUST**  East Face. V, 5.7 A3. Eric Bjornstad, Ed Cooper.

**1977 JANUARY**  North–south traverse, FWA. Larry Cooper, Mike Marshall, Don Page, Byron Robertson.

**1978 DECEMBER**  North Face. V, WI 3. Doug Klewin, Dan McNerthney.

**1985 JULY**  North Norwegian Buttress. VI, 5.9 A3. Pete Doorish, Dale Farnham, Charlie Hampson.

**2003 JULY**  North Norwegian Buttress, right of 1985 route. VI, 5.10 A4. Todd Karner, Roger Strong, William Tharpe, Blair Williams.

**2020 JULY**  North Norwegian Buttress, left of 1985 route. VI, 5.9 A3. Sam Boyce, Lani Chapko, Kyle Willis.

### NORTH PEAK (5360')

**1929**  North Face. III+, 5.6. Lionel Chute, Victor Kaartinen.

**1951 JULY**  East Face. IV, 5.7. Fred Beckey, Richard Berge, Jim Henry, Pete Schoening.

**1954 JULY**  West Face. IV+. Don Gordon, Pete Schoening.

**1963 JANUARY**  FWA. V. Pat Callis, Dan Davis.

**1971 AUGUST**  Southeast Buttress. IV+, 5.7 A2. Garrett Gardner, Bill Lingley.

**1989 FEBRUARY**  West Face, *Eve Dearborn*. V, WI 3. Mark Bebie, Jim Nelson.

**2006 FEBRUARY**  West Face, *Murphy's Law*. V, WI 3. Ade Miller, Stuart Taylor.

To this day, little is known about most routes. The seldom-visited Middle Peak was first climbed 1950, then not again until 1960. On the second ascent of the Middle Peak, with Don Gordon, Fred Beckey commented in the 1961 *Mountaineer Annual*: "Don had made a previous attempt and his discrete choice of the proper entree into a key gully kept us from becoming lost in a near-vertical jungle of brush and trees set at an almost unbelievable forest angle. It is an area that will probably never be subjected to the logger or the recreational climber. Any error of course on the lower 1000 feet will likely result in the climber abandoning the ascent."

Many of these routes are seldom climbed because of their serious nature, but largely that is due to the less-attractive characteristics one finds on many low-elevation peaks in the Cascades. The very hard, brittle metagabbro, minor gneissic amphibolite, and gabbro flasser gneiss rock, combined with an excess of vegetation, have conspired to make for difficult and unappealing climbing. Even so, the allure is strong and the potential for winter climbing should not be overlooked. A winter ascent of the North Peak over three days in 1963 got things started and the route is now considered a classic. More-serious routes, like the north face of the Middle Peak climbed in December 1978, await repeat ascents, and a couple of major winter lines remain uncharted as of 2020.

**LAND MANAGER**
Mount Baker-Snoqualmie National Forest, Skykomish Ranger District. Northwest Forest Pass or interagency recreation pass required for parking. Free self-registered wilderness permit required for day and overnight trips.

## 13. INDEX TRAVERSE, NORTH TO SOUTH: GRADE V, 5.7

**TIME:** 1–2 days. This is a long climb, and ascents without a bivy are not common. An under-24-hour traverse was made in February 2007 by Mark Bunker and Colin Haley. Don't let the low technical rating of 5.7 give the wrong impression; this is a serious and committing climb. Wayne Wallace commented after his 2005 ascent with Tom Sjolseth, "Once again I find myself in utter awe of the efforts of the generations of climbers from the past. Just because a

route was done long ago doesn't mean it wasn't a hard-core route. The Index Traverse solidified that opinion for Tom and I. The climb ranks among the great traverses in the country for sure!"

### APPROACH, GRADE II
Drive the Stevens Pass Highway (US Highway 2) to mile marker 35.2, just west of the turnoff to the town of Index. Turn south onto Mount Index Road. Drive 0.3 mile and bear right. Continue several hundred feet to a parking area on the left at 600 feet.

Walk the Lake Serene Trail No. 1068 as it follows an old logging road for 1.6 miles to the newly built trail. The trail crosses below Bridal Veil Falls before continuing up many switchbacks for 2 miles to Lake Serene. Follow the trail around the north side of the lake, and find a route along the talus aiming for the north peak.

*Mount Index from the northeast, summer conditions: (A) South Norwegian Buttress, (B) North Norwegian Buttress, (C) Index Traverse* (Photo by John Scurlock)

## ROUTE

The climbing begins with two or three pitches on the brushy northeast spur ending below a steep wall. Pass the wall to the east into a low-angle gully, followed by a sharp turn west where a ledge leads north above the steep wall. Ledges continue west into the trees. Climbing through trees leads up to the north bowl.

Climb snow or slabby rock, followed by steeper climbing exiting the bowl, then follow ledges to the right to the beginning of the upper north rib. The north bowl and exit to the upper rib are 3rd–4th class, more difficult when wet. Protection is minimal and careful routefinding imperative. An alternate route traverses low and eastward across the north bowl, gaining the north rib at a lower point and adding several pitches of enjoyable rock climbing.

The character of the climb changes for the better upon reaching the upper rib, where two or three very enjoyable pitches lead to heather benches high above Lake Serene. Scramble 10-15 minutes up and over false summits to the North Peak summit at 5360 feet.

From the summit descend a couple hundred feet of 3rd class to a west-facing gully. Traverse the southwest side of the first gendarme below the north summit, followed by a steep rappel. More down-climbing and another one to three rappels reach the North-Middle notch. Climbing directly from the notch is steep and poorly protected (5.9). A recommended option is to the east where lower-angled climbing is located. Mid-5th-class climbing leads to the north-ridge crest; follow the ridge toward a false summit. The false summit can be bypassed on the east; otherwise a

*Mount Index from the northeast, winter conditions (A) East Gully (Main Peak), 1984, (B) North Face (Middle Peak), 1978, (C) North Face (North Peak), 1929* **(Photo by John Scurlock)**

short rappel is followed by 3rd-class climbing to the Middle Peak summit (5493 feet).

Complex routefinding down to the Middle-Main notch involves some guesswork and, with luck, very little rappelling. From the Middle-Main notch, a short, steep wall (5.6) climbs up and right, followed by a chimney-gully. Mostly easier climbing, mixed with exposed heather (crampons helpful), continues to the Main (South) Peak's summit.

## DESCENT

The descent from the Main Peak summit traverses the west side of two subsidiary summits, followed by slabs and heather meadows. Just above the pass with tarns, turn east into a broad gully at about 5300 feet. The gully narrows and steepens, becoming 3rd class and including a rappel. Descend until able to skirt cliffs north at about 4000 feet. Traverse to the ridge above Lake Serene and follow it down to the northeast. This ridge becomes very steep and narrow for several hundred feet before reaching a pass at 3100 feet. A brushy descent west leads to the southeast end of Lake Serene.

# INDEX TOWN WALL

### DAVIS-HOLLAND AND LOVIN' ARMS

Index Town Wall is probably the closest granite to Seattle—perhaps even the closest to the car. It's about an hour and half from Seattle, and the very closest climbs are just minutes from the car. There are two big tiers of beautiful, Yosemite-like steep granite: the Upper and Lower Town Walls, which have drawn climbers to the quiet little town of Index since the '60s.

The nearly vertical upper walls approach 500 feet in places, with the first climbers here putting up a number of respectable aid routes, often requiring more than a day of climbing. Later generations began to free-climb all the amazing and beautiful cracks, and Index today remains a true center for Northwest rock climbing.

### LAND MANAGER

Forks of the Sky State Park, a unit of Wallace Falls State Park. Lower Town Wall currently owned by Washington Climbers Coalition; check their website (see Resources) for seasonal closures during falcon nesting.

# 14. DAVIS-HOLLAND AND LOVIN' ARMS: GRADE III, 5.10C

**TIME:** 1 day. **GEAR:** set of nuts, doubles of cams from fingers to 3 inches; optional 5-inch cam protects undercling above belay to start pitch 3. Choosing only one or two routes from this historic location is like choosing only one or two jelly beans from a lifetime-sized bag. There are many really great climbs at Index, and we chose this on Upper Town Wall not only for its popularity but for its ambiance and position.

The climb follows the first three pitches of a route climbed in 1964 by Dan Davis and John Holland. These pitches were free-climbed in the 1970s, with most parties rappelling after pitch 3 to avoid the vegetated upper pitches of the original climb. In 1980 Don Brooks pushed a line straight above the pitch 3 belay, creating the *Lovin' Arms* extension, which goes at 5.11b by the original route or 5.10c by a later variation that most climbers now follow. The climb is known for its sustained difficulty and variety of climbing. From pitch 2's left-leaning thin-hands corner to the overhanging quartz edges of the route's final 40 feet—enjoy!

*Jessica Campbell on the final pitch of* **Davis-Holland** *to* **Lovin' Arms** *(Photo by Max Hasson)*

*Ginnie Jo Blue on the fifth pitch of* Davis-Holland *to* Lovin' Arms (Photo by Max Hasson)

*Index climbing areas and town from the southeast:* Davis-Holland *and* Lovin' Arms *(Photo by John Scurlock)*

## APPROACH

Drive the Stevens Pass Highway (US Highway 2) to the well-marked turnoff to the left (north) for the town of Index. Follow the curving little road less than 1 mile until a big metal bridge leads left, across the river and into Index. Continue west through town to Avenue A and find the Lower Town Wall parking area at 480 feet, just across the street from the river. Allow 30-40 minutes for the walk from the car.

Find a path near the railroad tracks that leads back east along the tracks. Past the Lower Town Wall, an obvious path leads north up into the forest and switchbacks past other small rocks and big timber before coming out under the Upper Town Wall. Walk a bit left (west) along the base on a well-used path to arrive at the route, an obvious left-leaning corner and crack.

## ROUTE

**PITCH 1:** Climb the obvious right-leaning flake–finger crack (5.9) to a ledge. Work right and left and up again on small steps to find the bolted anchors in the right-facing corner. **PITCH 2:** Climb the amazing finger and hand crack in the corner (5.10a) and reach another bolted anchor. **PITCH 3:** Work up and to the right from the belay, climbing around the roof and then back left into a right-facing corner. Work up the corner (5.10c) and pass the crux on very thin holds to

reach another anchor with bolts and a ledge. From here, the original *Davis-Holland* route heads left, but continue now on *Lovin' Arms*.

**PITCH 4:** Continue straight up with thin face holds and techy moves to reach a good hand-sized crack (5.10a). Take the crack up to an obvious chimney and belay at bolts on its upper left. **PITCH 5:** This pitch presents a few options. The original route went to the right from the anchors with a single bolt for aid (5.10c A0 or 5.11c) to reach cracks. A popular variant (5.10a) continues up the chimney for 20 feet or so and then exits to the right on a sort of crack or ramp traverse (5.9) to a small corner. Climb the crack in the corner (5.10a) until bigger holds appear. Continue up and right until a cruxy mantle finishes the pitch on a ledge with anchors. **PITCH 6:** This rather sporty pitch climbs up from the belay, then works up the quartzy face and passes a bolt to reach decent cracks. Numerous but difficult holds on steep terrain (5.9) lead directly up to the anchors.

## DESCENT

Numerous descent options depend on the length of your rope(s). It is certainly straightforward to rap the route with two 60m ropes. Historically, people have walked off to the left and made some short raps in an obvious gully.

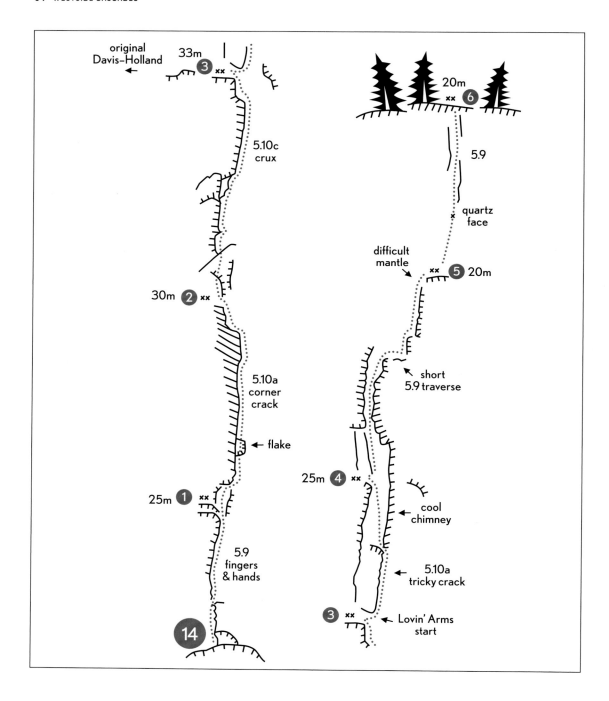

original
Davis–Holland
←

33m
**3** xx

5.10c
crux

30m **2** xx

5.10a
corner
crack

← flake

25m **1** xx

5.9
fingers
& hands

**14**

20m **6**

5.9

quartz
face
×

difficult
mantle → xx **5** 20m

short
5.9 traverse ←

25m **4** xx

cool
chimney ←

5.10a
tricky crack ←

**3** xx

Lovin' Arms
start ←

# BARING MOUNTAIN                6125'

## PROMINENCE: 2445'

### NORTH FACE, COOPER-GORDON; DOLOMITE TOWER, SOMA-VANISHING POINT

Baring is easily visible from many points in Seattle. The upper third of its dramatic north face is an obvious vertical wall seen in profile from 35 miles away. US Highway 2 passes ultraclose to the south, and still, few people ever venture in for a look. Certainly, the legends from the '60s have served to insulate this big wall from everything except the popular conception of a gigantic, out-of-focus horror show looming above Barclay Lake.

Baring supports one of the grandest rock walls in the Cascades. What would it take to climb such an imposing rock face? Year after year, the most successful climbers of the period were turned back. The rock was compact, and

piton cracks were few. The migmatic gneiss rock is much different from granite, and hand drilling took forever. While much of the climbing was free, the difficulty of placing reliable protection suggested aid.

Baring's gigantic north face is framed on the right by the spectacular and semiautonomous subpeak known as Dolomite Tower. Its sheer walls and pointy-appearing summit are arguably as compelling an objective as the main peak.

Indeed, since the first ascent, several generations of climbers drove by on US 2 before people like Pete Doorish, Bryan Burdo, and others began to recognize the potential for truly great modern rock climbs on these underconsidered walls. In a nutshell, what happened was that both Doorish and Burdo established several lines on both Baring itself and Dolomite Tower and then returned multiple times to upgrade their efforts. The result is an area with several difficult, steep modern routes that deserves more attention.

*Mount Baring from the north; Dolomite Tower is in the foreground, with the main peak behind.* (Photo by John Scurlock)

## LAND MANAGER

Wild Sky Wilderness, Mount Baker-Snoqualmie National Forest, Skykomish Ranger District. Northwest Forest Pass or interagency recreation pass required for parking. Free self-registered wilderness permit required for day and overnight trips.

# 15. NORTH FACE, COOPER-GORDON: GRADE IV, 5.10

**TIME:** 1 day. **GEAR:** medium rack to 3 inches. Much of the psych-out associated with Baring Mountain stems from difficulties and dramas that took place during attempts to make the first ascent of this route. Pete Schoening and Richard Berge made the first two attempts on this face in 1951, which ended at the left end of a difficult traverse on the third step. Berge fell to his death in 1952 while retreating in the dark with Fred Beckey and Tom Miller.

For a time, the climb was known as the *Pioneers Route* due to the numerous attempts by many of the top climbers of the day, including Fred Beckey, Berge, Ed Cooper, Don Gordon, and others. Numerous people, including Fred, worked out the route over a couple of seasons until Ed and Don finally completed the route, Fred having had to return to work. So much for calling Fred a dirtbag! The second ascent was not made until 1983.

## APPROACH, GRADE II

Drive the Stevens Pass Highway (US Highway 2) to the nearly nonexistent community of Baring; at milepost 41,

turn left (north) to cross railroad tracks. Continue on the Barclay Creek Road (Forest Road 6024) and follow signs as it turns to gravel; in about 5 miles reach the Barclay Lake Trailhead at 2300 feet. The approach hike is a Cascades

*Baring Mountain from the northeast: (A) East Face, 1992, (B) North Face, 1960, (C) North Face, 1984, (D) Soma, 1990, (E) Vanishing Point, 1999 (Photo by John Scurlock)*

1

5.7

9

5.4

8

5.3

5.10 roof

7

3rd

several rope lengths

5.4

Rockfall Point

6

5.4

5

5.6

5.3

4

steeper rock

5.7

slab

5.4

3

short 5.6

5.5

2

gully

4th

4th

1

4th

1984 Doorish route

15

3rd class to top

shoulder

3rd

24

5.12-

13

5.11- belay cave

23

5.7

5.7 around corner

original finish

tree ledges

12

11

5.8/5.9

21

5.7 ramp

10

20

5.11+

5.8/5.9

chimney

x 5.10c

x

9

19

18

5.8

5.10- steep

8

5.5

3rd

7

17

4th

5.5

6

16

flake

5.6

sloping ramp

15

5.8+

5

14

5.4

5.6    fp

13

5.4

Dolomite Camp

4

5.7

3rd

12

3

4th class

5.7

11

4th

2

5.0

10

5.3

5.7

1

9

5.6 traverse

8

classic! It gains elevation quickly and can take up to three or four hours; checking it out in advance may save some frustration on dark alpine mornings.

Take the Barclay Creek Trail No. 1055 about 1.5 miles, to the northwest end of the lake (2422 feet). Leave the trail and cross the outlet stream. Make an ascending traverse on a climbers path aiming to the northeast.

## ROUTE

The climb starts well to the left of Dolomite Tower. Hike or climb around the bottom of the huge forested buttress that forms the bottom 1000 feet of the route. Scramble up a big gully to the northeast of the main buttress until eventually passing beneath a big overhang at the start of the 1984 Doorish route located just right of a big gully-corner. The *Cooper-Gordon* route begins a bit left of the gully, although several variations have gone up the gully and then moved left to get on the main line. Essentially four or five pitches climb 3rd-, 4th- and low-5th-class terrain to reach a minor buttress top known as Rockfall Point. From Rockfall Point, climb a bit of 5.4, followed by two or three pitches of 3rd- and 4th-class ground to reach a forested ledge area. This is where the numbered pitches shown on the topo begin.

**PITCH 1:** Climb a cool 5.7 face up and right for about 50 feet and belay at a bush. **PITCH 2:** Hand-traverse out to the right (5.7) on good rock with excellent position. Work right a bit more and then up to a belay. **PITCHES 3-4:** Two pitches of 4th and 3rd class work up forested rock to reach a large area known as Dolomite Camp. **PITCH 5:** This is a great 130-foot pitch of face climbing (5.6) directly above Dolomite Camp that passes a fixed pin and reaches an obvious belay bush. **PITCH 6:** Another great 165-foot pitch angles up and left on a sloping crack. Find a fixed pin in the crack and then work straight up (5.6) to easy ground and the belay. **PITCHES 7-8:** These pitches go mostly straight up 4th-class terrain, gradually subsiding to 3rd class and ultimately reaching an obvious ledge at another minor buttress top.

**PITCH 9:** This spectacular pitch, known as the "Traverse of the Pioneers," starts a bit right of center on the ledge and then traverses out to the left (exposed, some 5.10-) underneath a series of roofs. Continue until finding a fixed pin and the roofs can be turned on the left and up to a belay with a bolt. **PITCH 10:** This 80-foot pitch moves up, passing a

bolt and a fixed pin; look for a place where a natural thread protects a 5.10c face move up to a small left-facing corner. Climb up to a pin and move left (5.8-5.9). Work up to a belay at a good ledge. **PITCH 11:** Move left over a boulder feature (5.8) and then climb a great 5.9 crack up to a big ledge with trees at the top of another big step in the north wall. **PITCH 12:** Work up and left on a 3rd-class tree ledge to reach a little saddle or minor col feature. From here move up and right another 15-20 feet into a sort of belay cave or alcove that marks the start of the fourth and final step of the mountain. **NOTE:** From the small col feature, the original route continued left on 3rd-class terrain to reach the shoulder and then the summit. Make a half-pitch traverse (5.7) out to the right and belay on a prow. **PITCH 13:** Continue up the prow (5.7) and then somewhat to the right to find an obvious ledge system. **PITCH 14:** 3rd-class terrain leads to the summit in 150 feet or so.

## DESCENT

Wander down the southwest slope several hundred feet, leading to a high bowl that holds some snow until about the middle of summer. Find the Baring Mountain climbers trail at the lower west end of the bowl at 4800 feet. The trail follows the northwest-trending forested ridge for about 1 mile. At the second 4000-foot saddle on the ridge, the trail drops steeply to the northeast, losing 1700 feet and reaching the trailhead in about 0.5 mile.

# 16. DOLOMITE TOWER, SOMA-VANISHING POINT: GRADE V, 5.12

**TIME:** 1-2 days. **GEAR:** nuts and cams to 2½ inches, about 15 quickdraws, 60m ropes. The central prow of the tower's northeast face was originally climbed solo by Pete Doorish, who placed hand-drilled bolts. A few years later, Doorish returned with help to work on the route as a free climb, *Soma*. Replacing the ¼-inch bolts, upgrading belay anchors, and locating minor variations resulted in an amazing climb on this spectacular wall. The climbing is a mix of crack and face climbing and about 60 percent traditional pro. Inspired by the free-climbing potential, Bryan Burdo worked through the '90s to combine sections of *Soma* with uncharted terrain, creating *Vanishing Point*.

*Pete Doorish on* Soma *(Photo by Bryan Burdo)*

*Bryan Burdo on* Soma, Dolomite Tower *(Photo by Pete Doorish)*

## APPROACH, GRADE III

This is a technical approach, with much scrambling combined with occasional 5th-class climbing; allow three or four hours. Follow the approach for the preceding climb, and leave the trail about 0.5 mile before Barclay Lake, where the trail crosses Barclay Creek.

Head upstream a short way until able to cross Barclay Creek on logs. Continue upstream several hundred feet, then leave the stream to reach a large talus field with large boulders. Follow the drainage beyond the talus field to a prominent gully, climbing in and out of the gully as necessary. Where the gully becomes a 5th-class chimney, a ledge system leads to the right to a steep forested rib. The route up the rib navigates around cliffs and slabs where many fixed ropes have been left through the years. At the top of the forested rib, climb left (east) into the gully where 400 feet of mostly scrambling leads to a long 5.8 bolted slab pitch trending leftward. Above this pitch, follow a broad ledge left about 300 feet to a groove-gully-chimney system. Halfway up this gully, bolts protect the wall to the right, ending at a two-bolt belay. Continue up and left

across a slab with a bolt at the start. Up and left from the bolt leads to a large bench directly below the route.

## ROUTE

**PITCH 1:** Climb the bolted line left of the arête (5.10+) for less than 100 feet. **PITCH 2:** Climb about 100 feet on either *Vanishing Point*'s bolted line to the left (5.10+) or *Soma*'s 5.10 hand crack to the right. **PITCH 3:** Climb past a bolted stance (5.11), then up to the right past stacked blocks, moving to a corner to the right of the arête. Belay on a sloping ledge with a bolt on the left wall. **PITCH 4:** Continue up the corner crack (5.11) to a belay ledge out left and below a roof. **PITCH 5:** This long, mostly bolted pitch is on or near the arête (5.11+) with an alternate belay a short way past the roof. **PITCH 6:** Follow bolt-protected climbing on the arête (5.12). **PITCH 7:** Continue up the arête for a few bolts (5.11) before moving left to a shallow dihedral. The pitch finishes with some runout 5.8, ending at a two-bolt belay on a small ledge. **PITCH 8:** Begin with a very steep bolted face (5.12), followed by a bolted arête to a hanging belay under the large roof.

**PITCH 9:** The original route (*Soma*) climbs cracks and the face to the right of the arête and right of the roof; for *Vanishing Point*'s roof pitch (5.12!), climb through the right side of the roof, then left with bolt-protected climbing on the face above to a bolted belay. **PITCH 10:** *Vanishing Point*; climb steeply (5.10+), then to the right toward an arête. **PITCH 11:** *Vanishing Point*; climb bolts and gear near the arête (5.10) to a belay on slab. **PITCH 12:** Climb the slab, then a crack (5.9), to the bolted roof.

## SELECTED HISTORY

**1897 JULY** Baring Mountain. II. John Charlton, Albert Sylvester USGS survey party.
**1960 JULY** Northeast Rib, *Pioneers Route*. IV, 5.8 A2 or 5.10. Ed Cooper, Don Gordon.
**1983** *Pioneers Route*, FFA. IV, 5.10. Pete Doorish, John Silletto.
**1984 FEBRUARY** *Pioneers Route*, FWA. Pete Doorish, Dale Farnham.
**1984 JULY** North Face, left side. V, 5.10 5.12-. Alex Cudkowicz, Bryan Burdo, Pete Doorish, Dale Farnham.
**1988 SEPTEMBER** North Face, center route. V, 5.11. Alex Cudkowicz, Pete Doorish.
**1990 AUGUST** North Face, right side. V, 5.10+. Pete Doorish, Paul Woodrum.
**1992 OCTOBER** East Face. IV, 5.11-. Pete Doorish, Laura Woods.

## DOLOMITE TOWER

**1986 SEPTEMBER** North Prow. V, 5.9 A3. Pete Doorish.
**1990 JUNE** East Face. III+, 5.8. Pete Doorish, Franci Ries.
**1990 AUGUST** North Prow, *Soma*. V, 5.12-. Bryan Burdo, Pete Doorish.
**1992 JUNE** Northwest Face, right side. V, 5.11. Pete Doorish.
**1992 AUGUST** Northwest Face, left side. V, 5.12 A0. Laurel Black, Bryan Burdo, Pete Doorish.
**1992 AUGUST** Northwest Face, *Northwest Passage* (center route). V, 5.12-. Pete Doorish, Paul Woodrum.
**1993 JULY** Northeast Rib. V, 5.11+. Laurel Black, Pete Doorish.
**1994 SEPTEMBER** West Face, left route. II+, 5.8. Pete Doorish, Franci Ries.
**1994 SEPTEMBER** West Face, right route. II+, 5.9. Pete Doorish, Franci Ries.
**1999** *Vanishing Point*. V, 5.12. Bryan Burdo, Scott Stanton.

## DESCENT

Descend to the southwest, finding the Baring Mountain climbers trail at the lower west end of the high bowl at 4800 feet. The trail follows the northwest-trending forested ridge for about 1 mile. At the second 4000-foot saddle on the ridge, the trail drops steeply to the northeast, losing 1700 feet and reaching the trailhead in about 0.5 mile.

*Dolomite Tower: (A) Northeast Rib 1993, (B) North Prow/Soma, 1986/1990, (C) Vanishing Point 1999, (D) Northwest Passage, 1992 (Photo by John Scurlock)*

# DARRINGTON & SUIATTLE AREA

Darrington is largely part of the Boulder River Wilderness located about two hours north and east of Seattle. From the tiny logging town of Darrington, the Mountain Loop Highway heads east and south to Barlow Pass, then west into Granite Falls, and all along this highway there are trailheads with access to peaks both near and far. For some climbs, the closer approach is through Granite Falls. But Darrington itself sits directly beneath Whitehorse Mountain near the junction of two cascading valleys that each contain beautiful and compelling granite features.

Historically, the climbing has taken place in the Clear Creek valley on features like Exfoliation Dome, Green Giant Buttress, and Three O'Clock Rock. In recent decades, climbers have shifted their focus to developing routes on Squire Creek, routes that are among the longest in the Northwest.

D-Town is a slab-climbing mecca, and almost nothing here even approaches vertical except the east face of Exfoliation Dome, also known as Witch Doctor Wall. There are incredible textured friction slabs, insane knobs on steeper walls, and even a few flakes and splitter cracks! Rumors of big runouts on rusty gear are decades out of date almost everywhere in Darrington, and these routes display modern gear and sensibilities.

*Carl Skoog enjoys the granite slab on Vesper Peak's north face.* (Photo by Lowell Skoog)

# VESPER PEAK                        6214'

**PROMINENCE: 1574'**

## TRUE GRIT; RAGGED EDGE

Vesper Peak is located west of the main Cascades crest and somewhat in line with the Darrington group. Indeed, it is granitic slab climbing on a remote and lovely peak. The slabby aspect of Vesper's north side has been talked about forever, but the north-face routes from the past were not inviting programs. Sadly, north-facing features in the Cascades tend to remain wet and are usually messy compared to rock with southern exposure. Vesper is no different, and these routes took a good bit of cleaning to bring into line. Give the face a day or two to dry out following wet weather.

That said, the higher elevations and regular climber traffic should keep these fun new routes clean and enjoyable. The hike up to this venue is steep, and while most climbers usually finish these routes in a day, there are also numerous high bivouac sites for those who prefer a fine wilderness evening to another day back at the office.

## LAND MANAGER

Mount Baker-Snoqualmie National Forest, Verlot Public Service Center or Darrington Ranger District. Northwest Forest Pass or interagency recreation pass required for parking. Free self-registered wilderness permit required for day and overnight trips.

# 17. TRUE GRIT: GRADE III, 5.8

**TIME:** 1 day. **GEAR:** single rack of cams to 2½ inches, including small cams; ice axe and perhaps light crampons can be useful until about midseason. The best season is July through September. Of the three north-face routes, this is the middle and slightly more direct. It is a good moderate route with sound rock and a stress-free walk-off descent.

## APPROACH, GRADE II

From the town of Granite Falls east of Everett, drive east on the Mountain Loop Highway (State Route 530). In about 28 miles, reach the posted intersection with Sunrise Mine Road (Forest Road 4065). Stay on the mine road another 2 miles to the Sunrise Mine Trailhead at 2350 feet. The hike is about 4 miles, with 3500 feet of gain.

Hike the Sunrise Mine Trail No. 707, crossing the South Fork Stillaguamish River at less than 1 mile. From the river, the trail climbs steeply to the high valley between Sperry Peak and Morning Star Peak, then climbs out of the valley, switchbacking steeply up a narrow rocky chute to Headlee Pass at 4750 feet. From the pass, the trail continues west into the basin between Vesper and Sperry Peaks. In the basin, pass a small lake and its outlet flow, then make for the pass between Sperry and Vesper.

At the 5800-foot level, a small col allows access to an alpine bench with steep heather that extends west across the north face of Vesper: this bench is the key to reaching

*Vesper Peak from the north* (Photo by John Scurlock)

these routes. Both routes begin near the right end of this bench system underneath the main summit.

## ROUTE

**PITCH 1:** Climb about 200 feet (60m), starting on low-5th-class slabs and passing a broken ramp on the left (5.4) to a bolted belay below a chimney. **PITCH 2:** Climb a groove to the narrow chimney, then finish the 100-foot (30m) pitch with a bolted slab (5.7) to a comfortable ledge. **PITCH 3:** Bolted 5.7 slab climbing leads to a thin left-facing corner, and more slab work continues above to finish the 100-foot (30m) pitch. Find the bolted belay at a small ledge that marks the start of the next pitch's crack system. **PITCH 4:** Climb the lovely finger and hand crack (5.8) past some cruxy moves and a couple of pro-bolts to reach the bolted belay stance in 130 feet (40m). **PITCH 5:** Climb about 50 feet of grotty slab (5.8) to reach the summit ridge in another 30 feet (25m total).

## DESCENT

Walk off a short distance to the southeast and then back down into the basin you hiked up into.

# 18. RAGGED EDGE:
## GRADE III, 5.7

**TIME:** 1 day. **GEAR:** single rack of cams to 3½ inches, doubles from ½ to 1 inch. The best season is July through September. Of the three lines on the north face, this is the right-hand one. While moderate, the climbing is very sustained at the

5.7 grade. Originally *Ragged Edge* started where *True Grit* does now and worked up and right thus avoiding the exposed scramble. It is likely that the route climbs part of the 1969 route for pitches 1 and 4.

*Vesper Peak from the north: (A)* True Grit, *(B)* Ragged Edge *(Photo by John Scurlock)*

## SELECTED HISTORY

**1918 OR EARLIER** East slope. I, 2nd class. Prospectors or USGS party.

**1968 JULY** North Face, east side. II+, 5.8. Bruce Garett, Jim Langdon.

**1969 AUGUST** North Face, center route. III, 5.8. B. J. Heath, Mike Heath, Tom Oas, Bill Sumner.

**1970 JUNE** North Face, right side. II+, 5.8. John Bonneville, Julie Brugger, Earl Hamilton, Mark Weigelt.

**1970 SEPTEMBER** North Face, right side. III, 5.6. Marc Harnois, Don Williamson.

**2013 AUGUST** North Face, *Ragged Edge*. II+, 5.7. Darin Berdinka, Gene Pires.

**2015 SEPTEMBER** North Face, *True Grit*. II+, 5.8. Darin Berdinka.

**2017 SEPTEMBER** North Face, *Fish and Whistle*. II+, 5.10-. Darin Berdinka.

### APPROACH

Follow the approach for *True Grit* (Climb 17). From the start of *True Grit*, exposed heather scrambling leads down and around the buttress toe to reach the start of *Ragged Edge*. Originally this route started where *True Grit* does now and worked up and right, thus avoiding the exposed scramble.

### ROUTE

**PITCH 1:** Climb a short layback flake (5.6) and then take an easy groove to easier slabs. From the highest grassy ledge, traverse sharply right about 35 feet and arrange a gear belay underneath a white dike on the slab. **PITCH 2:** Fire up the dike (5.7), passing three bolts, then traverse way right again. Work an easy short gully and find the bolted anchor on the crest. **PITCH 3:** Interesting sequences out right and back left again lead to a shallow arête (5.7) protected by fixed pins. **PITCH 4:** Move to the right of the arête and work up a section of somewhat loose steeper blocks. Use care climbing back and forth and finish at the bolted anchor. **PITCH 5:** Climb an exposed 5.7 slab past two bolts; at the second clip, make an exciting traverse right about 50 feet to the fixed anchor. **PITCH 6:** A pleasant 5.5 summit arête completes the route, passing a couple more fixed pins.

### DESCENT

Walk off a short distance to the southeast and then back down into the basin you hiked up into.

# SLOAN PEAK 7835'

**PROMINENCE: 3875'**

### SLOAN GLACIER, CORKSCREW; SOUTHEAST FACE, LOWER SHELF

Visible from many summits throughout the Cascades, Sloan is a very prominent peak rising above all others west of the Cascade crest. Strikingly steep on all sides, surprisingly it has a mostly third-class trail to the top.

While approaching from opposite sides of the mountain, the *Corkscrew* and southeast face routes join for the final 400 feet. The *Corkscrew* route traverses very high across the south face on a goat trail at 7400 feet, while the other approach climbs 600 feet of the southeast face before joining the *Corkscrew* goat trail at 7400 feet. Both routes have early-season challenges: a river crossing for the *Corkscrew* and snow sliding off slabs for the southeast face. These are two good but moderate routes on a very prominent peak.

The orthogneiss rock is largely solid, and the mountain has opportunities for technical climbs. Some of the cleanest rock is found on the southeast and southwest faces. Winter ascents have been few, but access is reasonable and there is much scope for winter activity.

Many of the surrounding peaks were first climbed by local pioneers, at a time when the region was mostly unexplored by the mountaineering community. One of these pioneers, Harry Bedal, grew up with Sloan Peak literally out his front door. Remnants of his trapper's cabin can still be seen high in Bedal Basin along the southwest approach to the mountain.

### LAND MANAGER

Henry M. Jackson Wilderness, Mount Baker–Snoqualmie National Forest, Verlot Public Service Center or Darrington Ranger District. Northwest Forest Pass or interagency recreation pass required for parking. Free self-registered wilderness permit required for day and overnight trips.

# 19. SLOAN GLACIER, CORKSCREW: GRADE II⁺, 4TH CLASS

**TIME:** 1-2 days. This is the eastern approach from the North Fork Sauk River, with 2800 feet of gain to campsites at 4700 feet and numerous stream crossings followed by nebulous, unmaintained trails. The condition of the Sloan Glacier varies greatly, and by late season it can present a real challenge. A high traverse under the east face is one late-season strategy, and it is not hard to picture a day when the glacier will slide away each summer.

## APPROACH, GRADE II⁺

From Interstate 5 near Arlington, take exit 208 and drive east on State Route 530 for 32 miles to the town of Darrington. From Darrington, drive south on the Mountain Loop Highway (Forest Road 20) for 19.7 miles. Turn left (east) on North Fork Sauk Road (FR 49) and continue 4.5 miles to the Sloan Peak Trailhead at about 1900 feet. From Granite Falls, drive the Mountain Loop Highway (FR 20) east for 37 miles and turn right (east) on North Fork Sauk Road (FR 49), then follow the preceding directions to the trailhead.

*Navigating the glacier on Sloan Peak's* **Corkscrew route** (Photo by Pete Erickson)

*Sloan Peak from the east: Sloan Glacier,* Corkscrew *route* (Photo by John Scurlock)

Hike the Sloan Peak Trail No. 648 as it follows an old road approaching the North Fork Sauk River. There is no bridge across the river, and the possibility of crossing depends on season and year. After crossing the river, find the trail in forest and enter the Henry M. Jackson Wilderness at about 1 mile. The steep trail crosses Cougar Creek below a waterfall at the 2-mile mark (3100 feet), and crossing may be difficult during snowmelt. Later the trail crosses avalanche paths, which occasionally obliterate the trail. Beyond the slide area, ascend into meadows with campsites near 4700 feet.

Additional bivy sites are found at 5000 feet, 5200 feet, and 5800 feet. A boot path climbs toward the glacier, which is accessed by crossing the intervening ridge near a rock outcrop (5850 feet) or above, but not below.

## ROUTE

Reaching the glacier at about 5800 feet or higher, find a route to the top of the glacier's far southern end at 7400 feet. Later in the summer as the glacier breaks up, finding a safe route is not guaranteed. From the top of the glacier, find the *Corkscrew* goat trail traversing west across the upper south face. The trail begins with a short descent, then traverses all the way to the southwest ridge and around a small pinnacle to the west face. The upper west face follows a gully (3rd class) most of the way to the top.

## DESCENT

Descend the climbing route.

## 20. SOUTHEAST FACE, LOWER SHELF: GRADE III, 5.0

**TIME:** 1-2 days. This is the western approach from the Bedal Creek basin, with 3800 feet of gain on an unmaintained, steep trail to bivy sites at 6550 feet, and off-trail travel including some brush; the total gain to the summit is 5100 feet. While the Sloan Glacier route has late-season challenges, this route has early-season issues. Until snow patches on slabs melt off for the season, they pose risks to climbers. Once dry, the slabs leading onto the lower shelf lead quickly up to the *Corkscrew* goat trail.

## APPROACH, GRADE III

From Interstate 5 near Arlington, take exit 208 and drive east on State Route 530 for 32 miles to the town of Darrington. From Darrington, take the Mountain Loop Highway (Forest Road 20) for 17.5 miles to FR 4096 on the left, about 1 mile south of FR 49. Turn onto FR 4096 and continue for about 2 miles to the road's end at about 2800 feet. If starting from Granite Falls, drive the Mountain Loop Highway (FR 20) east for 37 miles and turn right (east) on FR 4096 and continue for about 2 miles to the road's end at about 2800 feet.

Hike the Bedal Creek Trail No. 705 as it begins within a stand of old-growth forest, entering the Henry M. Jackson Wilderness shortly, followed by a small creek crossing at 0.7 mile. The trail sees little maintenance, so expect overgrowth, which obscures the trail in places. At about 2 miles, the trail fades where a large slide path intersects Bedal Creek. Continue near the streambed and rock cairns, trending mostly along the right side. A few hundred yards uphill, aim for a forest on the north bank, where the trail continues to Bedal Basin near the site of Harry Bedal's historical trapping cabin at 4700 feet.

Aim for a ridge crossing above the south end of the basin at about 5800 feet and continue east. Pass below Sloan's beautiful and steep southwest face; a bit farther, cross the southwest ridge (more accurately a south ridge). At this crossing near Point 6619 feet, there are great bivy sites (6600 feet) with views of the south face.

*Sloan Peak from the south: southeast face, lower shelf* (Photo by John Scurlock)

## ROUTE

From the southwest (south) ridge crossing near Point 6619 feet, traverse east into the southeast basin, which has a very small seasonal glacier. Head to the far east end of cliffs guarding the lower shelf. Climb polished slabs (low 5th class) leading to easier terrain (3rd class). Near the end of the lower shelf, a short section of low 5th class followed by easier climbing joins the *Corkscrew* goat trail (see the preceding route). Follow it west, around the southwest ridge, to the upper west face.

**OPTION:** Another route on Sloan's south face is the 1948 southwest face, which follows a line directly above the 6600-foot bivy sites, with a half dozen pitches of low-5th-class rock.

## DESCENT

Descend the climbing route, which often includes a couple of rappels.

## SELECTED HISTORY

**1921 JULY** Sloan Glacier, *Corkscrew*. II+, 4th class. Harry Bedal, Nels Skaar.

**1948 JULY** Southwest Face. II, 5.0. Fred Beckey, Jack Schwabland.

**1958 SEPTEMBER** West Face. III, 5.4. Fred Beckey, Ron Niccoli.

**1963 FEBRUARY** FWA. Fred Beckey, Mike Borghoff, Tony Hovey.

**1965 JULY** Southeast Face. II, 5.7. Fred Beckey, Jerry Fuller.

**2007 SEPTEMBER** Southeast Ridge. II, 5.10. Lane Brown, Wayne Wallace.

**2009 AUGUST** Southwest Face, *Fire on the Mountain*. III, 5.10+. Blake Herrington, Rad Roberts.

**2011 DECEMBER** Northwest Face, *Full Moon Fever*. IV. Braden Downey, Will Hinckley, Kevin Hogan.

**2020 FEBRUARY** West Face, *Superalpine*. IV, WI 3–4. Kyle McCrohan, Porter McMichael.

*Sloan Peak and Glacier Peak from the southwest* (Photo by John Scurlock)

# GLACIER PEAK/DAKOBED  10,520'

## PROMINENCE: 7480' [6]

### SOUTH RIDGE, COOL GLACIER

While only 70 miles from Seattle, Glacier's summit remains hidden deep in the wilderness and surrounded by other large peaks. Known to Americans Indians as Dakobed, the mountain is a relatively small stratovolcano. Back when continental ice sheets retreated from the region, Glacier Peak began to erupt regularly, sending mud and debris raging as far as Puget Sound.

With no short approaches, Glacier is perhaps Washington's only true wilderness volcano. The southern route presented here is a straightforward snow and glacier climb, very scenic and remote. This grand course avoids glacier travel for the most part, a result of shrinking glaciers, and provides close-up views of Kololo Peak's impressive glaciers.

Midsummer is usually wonderful, but spring and even winter ascents are becoming more frequent. Once beyond the forest approach, the route is ideal for ski travel, and the opportunity for glacier mountaineering is extensive. The mountain's northern and eastern slopes support one of the larger concentrations of active glaciers in the Lower 48. These glaciers experienced a brief resurgence between about 1950 and 1980 but are currently retreating at increasing rates.

### LAND MANAGER

Glacier Peak Wilderness, Mount Baker-Snoqualmie National Forest, Verlot Public Service Center or Darrington Ranger District. Northwest Forest Pass or interagency recreation pass required for parking. Free self-registered wilderness permit required for day and overnight trips.

## 21. SOUTH RIDGE, COOL GLACIER: GRADE II

**TIME:** 1–3 days. There are no plans to repair either White Chuck River Road or the White Chuck River Trail following 2003 floods, so the longer (22-mile) southern approach,

*Glacier Peak from the east: south ridge, Cool Glacier* **(Photo by John Scurlock)**

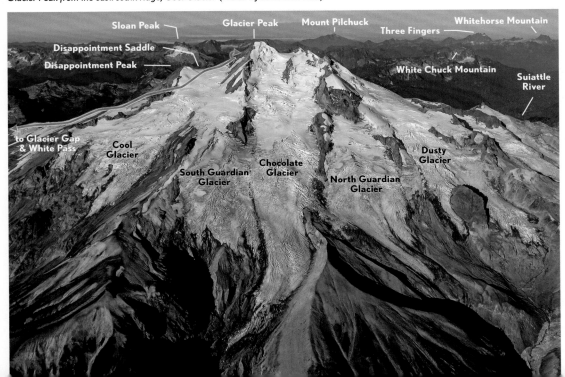

Glacier Peak from the south: south ridge, Cool Glacier (Photo by John Scurlock)

with 9400 feet of elevation gain, has become the favored route for those with limited time. Mountain hazards not to be ignored include sudden changes in weather, altitude, and glacier travel. Climbers need the ability to navigate without visibility. The ascent can be done as a leisurely backpacking trip but is also well suited to a fast and light style. **BONUS CLIMB:** Kololo Peak (8200 feet) is a short detour to the southeast from Glacier Gap.

## APPROACH, GRADE IV

From Granite Falls, drive the Mountain Loop Highway (Forest Road 20) east 37 miles to North Fork Sauk Road

(FR 49) and turn right (east) onto it. Continue 6.6 miles to the North Fork Sauk Trailhead at 1850 feet. From Interstate 5 near Arlington, take exit 208 and drive east on State Route 530 for 32 miles to Darrington, then drive another 19.7 miles south on the Mountain Loop Highway (FR 20) to FR 49 and turn left (east), continuing 6.6 miles to the trailhead.

Follow the North Fork Sauk Trail No. 649 for 5 miles to 3000 feet, where it begins a steep climb and in about 4 miles joins the Pacific Crest Trail No. 2000 just west of White Pass (6000 feet). This section with 3000 feet of elevation gain faces south, so plan accordingly during hot weather. Campsites are available near White Pass.

From White Pass, leave the trail and traverse east, then cross to the north side of the ridge somewhere near Point 6770 feet. Recommended crossing spots are a bit west of Point 6770 feet, at 6500 feet, or a bit northeast at 6620 feet. There are many potential campsites on the west side of the ridge, where much of the White Chuck Glacier has vanished.

## ROUTE

Traverse the White Chuck Glacier, aiming for a small pass—Glacier Gap—just east of Point 7739 feet. This gap at 7500 feet gives access to the western edge of the Suiattle

Glacier and, just beyond that, the start of the south ridge. Although the ridge can be taken directly up Disappointment Peak, bypassing to the east via the Suiattle and Cool Glaciers is recommended after snow has melted off the ridge's loose pumice. Beyond Disappointment Saddle at 9640 feet, a pumice ridge leads to a broad gully, then up to the summit.

## DESCENT
Descend the climbing route.

# EXFOLIATION DOME            4300'

## PROMINENCE: 200'

## BLUEBERRY ROUTE; DARK RHYTHM
Exfoliation Dome is aptly named. It has seen periodic rockfalls, just like any other large granite feature. They seem to occur somewhere on the peak every fifteen or twenty years, and it takes about that long for the white scars to turn gray again.

*Micah Lambeth follows pitch 5 of the Blueberry Route on Exfoliation Dome* (Photo by Zack Krupp)

Located just outside of the Boulder River Wilderness, Exfo was the first Darrington feature to be climbed.

The monolith is somewhat unusual in that it sports different names for the different aspects to which it faces. The broad and slabby west face is known as Blueberry Hill, and there are several popular routes on its flanks.

The largely hidden east face, also known as Witch Doctor Wall, was the scene of Fred Beckey's first adventure. Fred keyed in to the steep big face on the Witch Doctor side and established his mixed free and aid route there in 1969. Witch Doctor Wall was climbed via several other wall-type routes back in the day.

Finally, to the left (east) of the Witch Doctor face is another steep wall, directly beneath the actual summit, known as the Solar Wall. It features a couple of Zion-style modern wall routes and a surprising new free climb on excellent rock.

Exfo is not the most straightforward rock from which to descend. Almost all the routes are rappelled with two ropes on mostly bolted anchors, but irritations are encountered on most of the choices. If you aren't familiar with this peak, it's probably best to descend the climbing route.

**LAND MANAGER**

Mount Baker-Snoqualmie National Forest, Darrington Ranger District. Northwest Forest Pass or interagency recreation pass required.

## 22. BLUEBERRY ROUTE:
### GRADE III, 5.8 +

**TIME:** 1 day. **GEAR:** medium rack to 4 or even 5 inches. This has been the standard route on the peak for many years. Unlike most crag-style rock climbs, this one reaches an actual summit, and the views are phenomenal. The

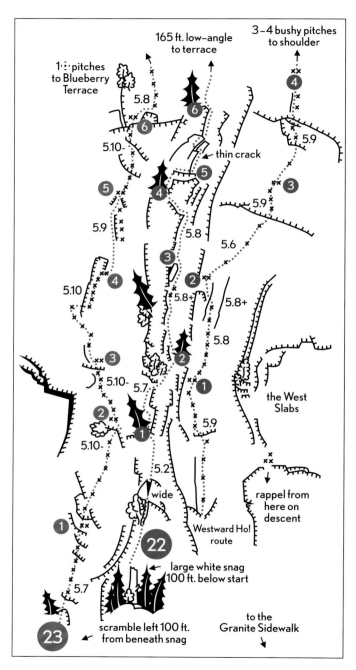

entire buttress forms a huge right-facing corner that appears frighteningly shattered when viewed from the slabs off to the right. Some claim it is getting looser, and it probably is. Whether it's any more dangerous than in previous years is difficult to say.

The climb follows broken slabs and cracks along the right-hand margin of the west face for the first six pitches, then reaches the broad ledge known as Blueberry Terrace several hundred feet below the top.

While the climb is not truly difficult, completing the route to the summit, making the descent, and then hiking down the slabs makes for a full day. Be especially wary not to get caught up on the dome if the weather changes. Descending the Granite Sidewalk in the rain would not make for an enjoyable walk-off!

## APPROACH, GRADE II

From Interstate 5 near Arlington, take exit 208 and drive east on State Route 530 for 32 miles to the town of Darrington. Enter town and in about 0.5 mile turn right onto the Mountain Loop Highway (Forest Road 20). Head south and in 2.8 miles turn right onto Clear Creek Road (FR 2060). In another 8.5 miles on this logging road, reach an obvious fork. To the right (straight) is Three O'Clock Rock, but take the left fork over a big metal bridge onto Blueberry Road (FR 2065). In the next 0.5 mile pass a couple of good camping spots. The dome has two huge granite slides-washes that descend from the wall to the road. The second of these is known as the Granite Sidewalk, the approach to all the west-face routes. Drive as close to the second granite wash as possible, about 1 mile from the bridge, and park.

Pick your way across shattered blocks, broken tree parts, and other avalanche debris until you reach the first slabs in about 10 minutes. The hike requires some decision-making and includes two short tree-climbs to link the slabs. From below the first big grotto, a tree scramble on the left works into easy bushes and then passes above the drop until a second tree-climb reaches the slabs above and left of the grotto. After this, the ascent becomes more casual as it hikes low-angled slabs directly to the start of the route near a large white snag.

*Exfoliation Dome from the north: (A)* Dark Rhythm, *(B)* Blueberry Route *(Photo by John Scurlock)*

## ROUTE

**PITCH 1:** Find an obvious wide crack in the slabs, move up (5.2), and locate the belay at the bottom of a left-facing corner with a substantial tree. **PITCH 2:** Climb the corner crack to the base of an overlap and undercling left to get around it. Continue (5.7) to a belay at a ledge with trees. **PITCH 3:** Climb right-facing flakes and cracks along the buttress edge, pass two bolts, then continue past the large "splinter" flake above (5.8+). Set up a gear anchor just past the flake. **PITCH 4:** Continue up and right, below the main buttress crest, until a couple cruxy moves (5.8) move up and left onto the crest. Belay from a tree anchor. **PITCH 5:** Make a short climb up flakes and blocks for about 75 feet and belay beneath the obvious clean finger crack. **PITCH 6:** Climb the thin crack, step left to reach the wide crack, and work up to a belay on a pedestal. **PITCH 7:** Climb slightly right as the angle kicks back, and aim for an obvious large tree. From the tree, it's a short distance to Blueberry Terrace. **PITCH 8:** Walk to the extreme left end of the terrace and make a belay at one of the last solid trees, then lead out left and up flakes and short slabs (5.7) about 75 feet or until a solid gear belay can be found. **PITCH 9:** Wander a bit and find several options, all with somewhat runout 5.8 bits in the first half of the pitch, then easier climbing and gear belays follow. **PITCH 10:** Continue up generally easy ground until the angle relaxes and you can walk to the summit ridge. Scramble up and right through blocks and trees to reach the top.

## DESCENT

Getting off Exfoliation Dome is not particularly dangerous; there are a number of ways to go, but all of them have less-than-ideal sections and all require two ropes; a single 70m rope will not be comfortable! From the summit, a bolted rappel anchor heads down to the southwest and

*Exfoliation Dome from the west: (A)* Dark Rhythm, *(B)* Blueberry Route *(Photo by John Scurlock)*

## SELECTED HISTORY

**1969** Witch Doctor Wall. IV, 5.8 A3. Fred Beckey and friends.

**1972** *Blueberry Route.* III, 5.9. Bill Sumner, Clark Gerhardt.

**1973** *Thunder Road*, solo. IV, 5.9 A3. Don Brooks.

**1973** West Slabs. III, 5.8. Manuel Gonzalez, Tom Oas.

**1974** *Checkered Demon.* IV, 5.7 A3. Dave Davis, Cal Folsom.

**1975** North Ridge. II, 5.10+ or 5.7 A1. Greg Ball, Bill Fryberger.

**1978** *23rd Psalm.* IV, 5.8 A3. Chris Greyell, David Whitelaw.

**1979** *Sunday Cruise.* III, 5.9. Duane Constantino, Chris Greyell, Dave Tower.

**2001** *Westward Ho!* II, 5.9. David Whitelaw, Mark Hanna, Chris Greyell.

**2002** *Dark Rhythm.* III, 5.10. David Whitelaw, Chris Greyell, Mark Hanna.

**2003** *Solaris.* IV, 5.10- A2. Chris Greyell, Mark Hanna, David Whitelaw.

**2003** *Voodoo Wall.* IV, 5.10 A2. Dave Burdick, Mike Swanicke.

**2007** *Rainman.* III, 5.10+. Chris Greyell, Stephen Packard, David Whitelaw.

**2008** *Jacob's Ladder.* III, 5.10 A0. Matt Perkins and friends.

**2012** *Snake Charmer.* III, 5.11-. Dave Burdick and friends.

**2012** *Ancient Melodies.* III, 5.10 A0. Mark Hanna, Danny Coltrane, Stephen Packard, J. R. Storms.

**2018** *Snagglepuss.* III, 5.8. Curt Veldhuisen, Mark Hanna, Micah Klesick.

the upper shoulder of the West Slabs. Not entirely obvious bolted anchors head down to the top of the *Westward Ho!* route, which begins very near the start of the buttress. Rapping back down *Dark Rhythm* has been known to snag ropes, so the buttress descent may be a better choice. From Blueberry Terrace, it is possible to rappel directly south off the terrace. It takes two rappels to reach the bolts at the top of *Westward Ho!*

## 23. DARK RHYTHM: GRADE III, 5.10

**TIME:** 1 day. **GEAR:** Small rack to 2 inches, including wired nuts plus 15 quickdraws. This is an exciting route that climbs

directly up the West Buttress to the left of the *Blueberry Route*. The route cleans up very quickly and provides several exciting pitches way up high on the rock.

### APPROACH, GRADE II

Follow the approach for *Blueberry Route* (Climb 22). About 75 feet below the start of the *Blueberry Route*, look for an obvious large silver-white broken snag that signals the point where it is easiest to cross the rib (actually the lower continuation of the buttress) may be most easily crossed to reach *Dark Rhythm* and routes beyond. From the snag, it's possible to scramble left about 100 feet to find the start beneath numerous mossy-looking overlaps.

### ROUTE

**PITCH 1:** Climb to the first bolt about 25 feet (PG) above a small overlap with a short crack offering protection. Follow the line of bolts up and right (5.7) to find the chains at a diagonal ledge beneath a block. **PITCH 2:** Climb up, then right, and get up onto a block. From the top of the block, bolts lead up and right across steeper slabs (5.10-). Cross a small overlap and move up to the chains. **PITCH 3:** Climb the white dike above the anchors to the left (5.10-) and find some exciting climbing over the lap above. **PITCH 4:** Climb up out of a short crack and onto the slab above; continue to the base of the "Flange." Layback and friction up the edge (5.10) to reach the chains. **PITCH 5:** Climb the short (5.7) crack above the anchors to the top of the flake and reach an obvious "seam." Friction up this (5.9) and follow natural gear to the belay. **PITCH 6:** Bolts lead up to a small step-over move, then climb up and left (5.10-) to easier moves and the belay. **PITCH 7:** Climb onto the block beside the anchor and continue with a line of bolts up the slab (5.8). Easier climbing reaches chains. **PITCH 8:** Several bolts point up and left to a chain anchor just before the trees on Blueberry Terrace. From here, follow the *Blueberry Route* to the summit.

### DESCENT

Use the same descent as the preceding climb. The presence of rope-eating flakes make attempting to rappel this route inadvisable.

# SQUIRE CREEK WALL

4958'

## PROMINENCE: 278'

### SLAB DADDY; THE HOLY GREYELL

Without question the culmination of the Darrington experience, Squire Creek Wall is a complicated 2000-plus-foot sweep of glacier-carved granite almost a mile wide. Climbers flirted with the gigantic slabby feature for some decades, but it was the last of the Darrington monoliths on which modern routes were developed. Big-wall slab routes!

Squire Creek itself tumbles out of the scenic Waterfall Basin, fed by avalanches from the ramparts of Three Fingers; from time to time the creek can be serious but it is usually less than knee deep or even lower in autumn. The basin is home to many great climbs, including the remarkable Roan Wall, which features perhaps one of the most perfect big slabs found anywhere. Just a short distance from Roan Wall, on the long ridge between Three Fingers and Whitehorse Mountain, is the spectacular Salish Peak with Chris Greyell's classic *Flight of the Falcon* route. It's undeniably a bit of a stomp to get up there, but the ambiance is pure wilderness and great rock, alone and wild.

An old logging road parallels both Squire Creek and the wall for a few miles, and while the road is decommissioned for cars, many people approach these climbs with a mountain bike. At the northern near end of the wall are the *Oso Rodeo* and *Slab Daddy* routes, the latter is among the longest routes to be found in this guidebook and, as it turns out, one of the easiest routes in the area to reach. Farther upvalley, is the Illusion Wall—the distinctive triangular buttress that forms the south corner of Squire Creek Wall—where you'll find *The Holy Greyell* route.

### LAND MANAGER

Boulder River Wilderness, Mount Baker-Snoqualmie National Forest, Darrington Ranger District. Northwest Forest Pass or interagency recreation pass required for parking. Free self-registered wilderness permit required for day and overnight trips.

# 24. SLAB DADDY: GRADE V, 5.10+

**TIME:** 1 long day. **GEAR:** small cam for pitch 5 anchor; small gear protects first sequences of pitch 11. This is Darrington's big kahuna, with 22 pitches of mostly 5.8 and harder slab climbing. Many still enjoy a bivouac either on the way up or the way down. The scenic Balcony Bivy at the top of pitch 11 saw much use during the establishment of this climb, but the Reservoir Bivy at the top of pitch 6 very often has running water. A single slippery move on pitch 20 (5.11-) is simple to pull through.

## APPROACH, GRADE II+

From Interstate 5 near Arlington, take exit 208 and drive east on State Route 530 for 32 miles to Darrington. Enter town and in about 0.5 mile turn right onto the Mountain Loop Highway (Forest Road 20). In another 0.5 mile, turn right at the Red Top Saloon onto Darrington Avenue. Follow the avenue until it exits town, passing a sign for a fish

*Brother Chris Greyell enjoys a day out on* Slab Daddy. *(Photo by David Whitelaw)*

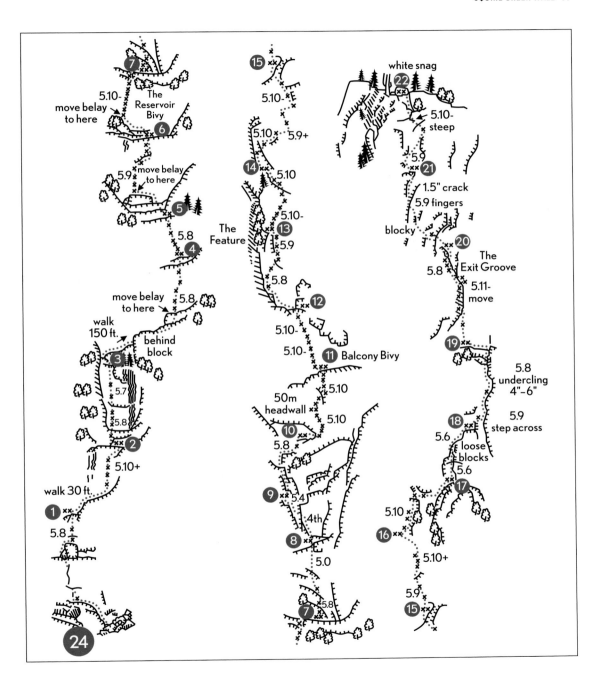

*Squire Creek Wall from the southeast: (A) The Holy Greyell, (B) Slab Daddy, (C) Oso Rodeo (Photo by John Scurlock)*

hatchery on the right. In another 0.5 mile turn left at the T intersection onto Squire Creek Road. Pass some scattered homes and follow a few switchbacks as the road leads up alongside Squire Creek. A couple of scary narrow spots in the road lead to a large and ample parking and turnaround area (1100 feet) at about 3 miles from the T intersection. Those scary narrow spots in the road may become too narrow for car traffic in the future. Many people bivy in and around their vehicles at the parking area.

Walk the old road about 0.25 mile before it reaches the landslide area. Follow the obvious track across the gravelly floor of the slide and then climb a short dirt bank (good trail) to regain the old roadbed. Bike the road past several significant washouts, and in about 1 mile, or maybe 300 feet past the second washout, follow a now-obvious path that leads off the road to the right and down into the forest toward the creek. In about 200 feet, negotiate a steep bank down to the rocky creek bottom. Move upstream about 100 feet to wade across the creek with little trouble. Cross a short flat area of fern forest, ascend a small rise, then make a hard left for the shelter of the big trees. An obvious boot path switchbacks through the forest until it's possible to make a sharp right across some slide alder and into the gully immediately below *Slab Daddy*.

## ROUTE

**PITCH 1:** From 30 feet above the lowest rock, move out left to find the first clip. Climb past a short, thin crack and a bit of 5.8 friction to the anchor. **PITCH 2:** Scramble up and right, then pass four bolts (crux 5.10+) to easier ground and the belay. **PITCH 3:** Step across the pond and make a short mantle up. Climb the knobby (5.7) slab. From the top, scramble a few feet uphill and then to the right 150 feet to reach the start of the fourth pitch. **PITCH 4:** Dark rock leads up and left (5.8) past five bolts to the anchors. **PITCH 5:** Again, climb up and left past five bolts (5.8) to the chains on a large ledge. Climb a short 12-foot wall and belay on top of the big block. Use the first bolt and a small cam for the anchor. **PITCH 6:** Climb directly up, then move right, under an overlap. From the right end of the overlap, climb the wall using crystal-filled huecos and find the belay beneath the Reservoir Bivy. From the pool, scramble up and left to start the next pitch.

**PITCH 7:** Interesting 5.10- climbing works past five or six bolts before moving to the right near the top of the pitch. The chains are 15 feet to the right. **PITCH 8:** Climb a short 5.8 step at the start and then 120 feet of 5.0 to reach the chains. **PITCH 9:** An easy pitch climbs up and right into a depression. Halfway up, move to the left side of the groove and continue. The chains are difficult to spot. **PITCH 10:** Easy corners work up and turn the overlap and cedar bush on the left side of an obvious big block (5.8). **PITCH 11:** Step to the right from the belay and climb over the lap (5.8 PG). Sustained 5.10 climbing works up the middle of the face to the Balcony Bivy.

**PITCH 12:** Start in a depression 15 feet left of the rings. The whole pitch is wonderful 5.10- on excellent rock. Chains are above and on the right. **PITCH 13:** Scramble left across ledges, then up the giant right-facing corner. Work the crack until the edges step right (5.9) to narrow ribs. A crux move left reaches the anchor. **PITCH 14:** Climb the water streak above the anchor (5.10-) until flakes and features work up and left to a shallow dihedral. **PITCH 15:** Smear up the corner until a bolt marks the sequence out

right. Climb up a second corner a bit before a cruxy move to the right (5.10) to an edge. Continue up and right until a 5.9+ sequence leads farther right, to an edge. Finally, move up and around to the left side of an obvious feature (5.10-) and the belay.

**PITCH 16:** Underclinging the little crack above the anchor and move across the slab to reach small flakes and cracks. Two bolts mark a short crux (5.10+), and the pitch soon finishes on a small ledge. **PITCH 17:** Step right and pass a bolt to reach a horizontal dike. Tricky 5.10 moves cling to the right edge of the block, and finally a 35-foot traverse right leads to a blocky-loose belay ledge. **PITCH 18:** Climb the obvious flake past breaks and overlaps (5.6) until more flakes and blocks lead up and right to a narrow belay stance. Some parts are a little loose. **PITCH 19:** Step out right (5.9) to reach the obvious flake edge. Climb the flake (5.8) until an undercling works the 4- to 6-inch crack. Slither over the roof and shuffle 20 feet left on the ledge to reach the chains. **PITCH 20:** Work up the groove (5.10c A0 or 5.11-) and make a couple of A0 grabs as needed. Soon it's easier, then knobs and edges (5.8) appear on the left. Chains are on a sloping stance. **PITCH 21:** Climb left and around small corners (5.8 PG) to reach a clean crack in a right-facing corner. Make a tricky transition (5.9) left into another crack and work up to the anchors. **PITCH 22:** Hard moves above the belay work to the right (5.9) into a corner and a short crack. Continue up a short slab with a bolt to a short vertical black wall with thin cracks. Move up (5.10-) and over; 5.7 cracks and blocks finish the adventure!

### DESCENT

Rappel the route using two ropes. From the anchors at the top of the second pitch, it's possible to rappel to climber's right and reach the ground or snow in one rap.

*David Whitelaw working hard hand-drilling on* **Slab Daddy,** *pitch 15* (Photo by Zack Krupp)

# 25. THE HOLY GREYELL: GRADE III, 5.10⁺

**TIME:** 1 day. **GEAR:** include #4 and #5 Camalots if taking the left-hand variation on pitch 6. This route, near the "nose" of the Illusion Wall, takes an incredible line, probably the first line ever attempted on the buttress. It is on the steepest part of the feature, requiring generally more gear placing than on many Darrington lines. This route is a great mix of slabs, flakes, knobs, and cracks and even offers two choices at pitch 6. Begin in the bivy site and to the right of the huge corner-roof feature visible from the road.

## APPROACH, GRADE III

Follow the approach for *Slab Daddy* (Climb 24), and continue past the *Slab Daddy* turnoff another mile until the old roadbed stops at the largest of the seasonal creeks that cross the old road. This was the old parking area back in the day; a bicycle is not useful beyond here. In the spring, there may be enough water in the side creek to make crossing difficult. Usually a few short steps upstream on the left lead to a thoughtful jump across to a big boulder; the rest of the 50-foot scramble across the creek is less engaging.

Immediately upon reaching the other side, find a path leading downhill to Squire Creek and an easy crossing on a large log. From the far side of the log, walk upstream on a gravel bar about 100 feet and then turn up an obvious trail-creek wash. In a short distance, cairns mark a place to leave the gravel wash on the right and continue on the mostly obvious track up and somewhat left to reach the lowest slabs.

At this point, a huge tree just below an obvious 3rd-class approach slab marks a feasible bivouac location for those who enjoy a night out. Scramble up the slab, taking care if it's wet or dirty, and exit at a lip near the top that usually has a short section of fixed line attached to a bolt. Continue via bits of trail and scramble routes to work your way up the main weakness to a large natural water pool on the right side of the drainage. From there, continue up and left across ledges and boulders and aim for the big prow of the Illusion Wall to the left. Another small but workable bivy site at the very base of the wall also marks the start of the route.

*Squire Creek Wall from the southwest:* Skeena *(III, 5.8) (A) is 12 pitches; and* Concerto Inc. *(III, 5.9) (B) is 15 pitches. These routes are not described in the text but are well worth doing. (Photo by John Scurlock)*

## SELECTED HISTORY

**1985** Illusion Wall, *Engineers Route*. II, 5.8. Party unknown.

**1986** Crow Quill Buttress. II, 5.9. Chris Greyell, David Whitelaw.

**1998** *Not Fred Beckey's*. IV, 5.9 A1. Chris Christensen and friends.

**2009** Illusion Wall, *The Holy Greyell*, FA. III, 5.10+. Chris Greyell, Mark Hannah

**2009** *Slab Daddy*, FA. V, 5.11-. David Whitelaw, Bill Enger, Dan Dingle.

**2010** Illusion Wall, *Excalibur*. FA. III, 5.10+. Chris Greyell, Darryl Kralovic.

**2011** *Oso Rodeo*. V, 5.10+. David Whitelaw, Bill Enger, Jim Shokes.

**2011** Illusion Wall, *The Page*. III, 5.11-. Mike Dobie, Ian Geddes, Brandon Workman.

**2011** Illusion Wall, *Schizophrenic*. III, 5.11-. Chris Greyell, Darryl Kralovic.

**2012** *Skeena26*. III, 5.8. David Whitelaw, Bill Enger, Yale Lewis.

## ROUTE

**PITCH 1:** Climb the obvious crack (5.7) that zigzags halfway up the first slab. When the crack ends, move right and reach a steep crack (5.8) that ends at the anchor. **PITCH 2:** Climb up the right-facing corner crack, then pass several bolts up and left to a left-facing corner crack (5.8). After that, follow more bolts up a slab to the belay ledge. **PITCH 3:** Climb left and work over the huge right-facing corner. Three modern bolts reach an old relic bolt from Chris Greyell's 1980 explorations. From this bolt, follow a line of six more bolts and pass the route's 5.10d crux. **PITCH 4:** Climb up past ten bolts on a knobby 5.8-5.9 slab for the entire pitch to the top of a small pillar. **PITCH 5:** Start out on a right-trending ramp, which reaches Chris's "eye-popping" detached flake. Plug in your biggest cam where it fits. From the flake, step back onto the wall and left to find a short layback crack (5.9) that takes you to a line of eight bolts that traverses left, then up to a right-facing corner. Follow the corner another 50 feet (5.9), then step right to a semi-hanging belay. **PITCH 6:** From the belay, move up past a bolt and a flake to a long left-facing crack. Follow this crack to the "big reach" left (5.9), then over an overlap,

past two more clips. Reach a hanging belay from one bolt and gear. **VARIATION:** Pitches 6-7 can be bypassed by climbing two 5.9 pitches up big cracks somewhat out to the left of the original line. **PITCH 7:** Start up the classic finger crack on the headwall. The crack goes from small to thin fingers (5.10a), then vanishes. Pass three more bolts (5.10c) and reach a comfy ledge. **PITCH 8:** Work left, then follow cracks of least resistance (some 5.8) up and right to some cedars. Belay above at a bolted anchor. **PITCH 9:** Climb the crack system above (5.8), then detour left over a small roof and back to the right again on a ramp with a bolt. Finish with more overlaps and the last anchor. Walk to the top of the Illusion Wall from here.

## DESCENT

Rappel the route with two 60m ropes.

# WHITEHORSE MOUNTAIN    6840'

## PROMINENCE: 2160'

## NORTHWEST SHOULDER, SO-BAHLI-AHLI GLACIER; EAST FACE, HIRST-LARSON

To local American Indians, the mountain (So-Bahli-Ahli) warned of coming storms by tossing tufts of fog from the summit. Whitehorse offers lush forest, alpine beauty, and modest elevation. Notable for its steep local relief, the north face rises 6000 feet in less than 2 miles! The mountain has two summits: the Main (southwest) Summit (6840 feet) and the Northeast Peak (6563 feet).

The postcard-perfect view from Darrington likely was irresistible to local resident Nels Bruseth, who made the first ascent from town and back in a day. Visit the Nels Bruseth Memorial Garden by the Darrington Ranger Station to learn more about this legendary Renaissance man.

## LAND MANAGER

Boulder River Wilderness, Mount Baker-Snoqualmie National Forest, Darrington Ranger District. Northwest Forest Pass or interagency recreation pass required for parking. Free self-registered wilderness permit required for day or overnight trips.

*Nearing the So-Bahli-Ahli Glacier on Whitehorse Mountain (Photo by Sky Sjue)*

## 26. NORTHWEST SHOULDER, SO-BAHLI-AHLI GLACIER: GRADE II, 5.2

**TIME:** 1–2 days. **GEAR:** Some rock gear and a rope are helpful on the Main (southwest) Summit's rocks. The best season is June to October. The upper portion of the mountain's Northwest Shoulder route was pioneered in 1909 by Nels Bruseth. In a classic one-day scramble outing, he reached Lone Tree Pass at 4973 feet, continued to the summit, and was home again by dark.

A great training workout with a total elevation gain of 7000 feet, the route traverses steep alpine slopes while ascending toward High Pass at 6030 feet. From there, a short trek across the So-Bahli-Ahli Glacier gets you close. If conditions for the main summit scramble look daunting, the 6600-foot snow dome east of the main summit is a worthy alternative.

### APPROACH, GRADE II

From Interstate 5 near Arlington, take exit 208 and drive east on State Route 503 toward Darrington. Continue for about 25 miles and turn right onto Mine Road, also shown on some maps as 387th Avenue. In about 0.5 mile park near the bridge (which sits at 512 feet elevation) over Moose Creek.

After safely parking your vehicle, start walking up the road. Stay left at each of the next two forks in the road and keep an eye out for where the road crosses Furland Creek. Shortly beyond the creek, reach the Neiderprum Trailhead; it's marked on the right with a sign that reads "Neiderprum Camp," 1.75 miles from the bridge. Hike up the Neiderprum Trail No. 653 for approximately 2 miles to reach the 3000-foot level. In early to midseason, you will leave the trail here.

*Whitehorse Mountain from the northeast: northwest shoulder, So-Bahli-Ahli Glacier* (Photo by John Scurlock)

So-Bahli-Ahli Glacier

to Lone Tree Pass & Neiderprum Trail

*Whitehorse Mountain from the northwest: northwest shoulder, So-Bahli-Ahli Glacier* (Photo by Steph Abegg)

## ROUTE

From the trail, make a rising traverse to the south (left) through the trees for another 0.5 mile to reach a wide couloir, which is hopefully snow-filled till midseason. Hike up the couloir to Lone Tree Pass at around 4973 feet, then go left and traverse the southern slopes east, losing about 500 feet to near a small lake.

Make a long, ascending trek east and eventually reach big open slopes. Slog up the hillside-gully to reach High Pass at 6030 feet. Crossing the pass reaches the So-Bahli-Ahli Glacier.

Hike up the glacier to the snowy ridge, then continue up the ridge to a bergschrund near the highest rocks. The 'schrund may not present difficulty in early season, but it forms a daunting moat later. The final bit to the Main (southwest) Summit is an exposed but short rock scramble.

## DESCENT

Descend by the same route.

## 27. EAST FACE, HIRST-LARSON: IV, AI 4

**TIME:** 2–3 days. **GEAR:** pins, nuts, and cams to 3 inches; ice screws. Winter in and around Whitehorse Mountain can offer the combination of mixed rock, snow, and ice necessary for classic alpine climbing. The huge relief and low elevations here make the necessary conditions rather hard to guess at, but they do happen!

The imposing east face in winter was revealed to the climbing community by aerial photographer John Scurlock starting in about 2002. John published pictures of Whitehorse on his website in February 2005, and a year later Peter Hirst and Rolf Larson made this landmark climb. The route is recommended by both climbers, but still awaits a repeat.

Another classic winter snow and ice climb resulting from Scurlock's images was the spectacular northeast face of nearby Three Fingers, by Dave Burdick and John Frieh in February 2007.

## APPROACH, GRADE III+

From Interstate 5 near Arlington, take exit 208 and drive east on State Route 530 for 32 miles to Darrington. After entering the town, continue for about 0.5 mile and then turn right onto the Mountain Loop Highway (Forest Road 20). In another 0.5 mile, turn right at the Red Top Saloon onto Darrington Avenue. Follow the avenue until it exits town, passing a sign for a fish hatchery on the right. In another 0.5 mile, turn left at the T intersection onto Squire Creek Road. Pass some scattered homes and follow a few switchbacks as the gravel road leads up alongside Squire Creek. From the gravel road, look for a crossing for Squire Creek just opposite its confluence with Buckeye Creek, and park (1100 feet).

Start walking, traversing up and right into Buckeye Basin somewhere around 2150 feet. This isn't straightforward, and winter conditions vary. Avalanche chutes lead to the upper basin and start of the route.

*Rolf Larson on the east face of Whitehorse Mountain* (Photo by Peter Hirst)

Main Summit

Northeast Peak

to Buckeye Basin

*Whitehorse Mountain from the east: east face,* **Hirst-Larson (Photo by John Scurlock)**

## ROUTE

The route climbs the major chimney-gully weakness directly to the ridge below the Main (southwest) Summit. From the bergschrund, the first-ascent party climbed about seven 200-foot (60m) pitches before simul-climbing about four pitches of steep snow to the summit. The climbing was a mixture of good névé, water ice, and snow-ice. Cruxes included a couple of short but fine sections of vertical to slightly overhanging snice. Protection and belays were reported as good to adequate.

## DESCENT

Down-climbing and two rappels lead down the south face and southeast ridge. The first-ascent party rappelled the first east-side descent gully they came to, though both climbers suspected they could down-climb the next gully to the south. Several rappels were made before arriving back at camp late in the afternoon.

## SELECTED HISTORY

**1909** Northwest Shoulder. II, 4th class. Nels Bruseth.

**1936 MAY** So-Bahli-Ahli Glacier, Direct. Joe Halwax, Granville Jensen, George McGowan, Marion Marts.

**1953 FEBRUARY** FWA. Pete Schoening and partners.

**1956 MAY** Southeast Ridge. II, 4th class. Kenn Carpenter, David Collins, Tom Williams.

**1970 JUNE** East Ridge. II, 5.3. Ben Guydelkon, Ron Miller.

**2006 FEBRUARY** East Face. IV, AI 4. Peter Hirst, Rolf Larson.

# PTARMIGAN TRAVERSE

### PTARMIGAN TRAVERSE HIGH ROUTE

This is the classic North Cascades traverse. Winding its way from Cascade Pass to the Suiattle River, this high route crosses lonely alpine gardens and sparkling snowfields amid great vistas with high mountain lakes and glaciers. While the summits are optional, experience and comfort with alpine terrain is a prerequisite for safety. Experience with navigation and mountain weather is essential.

Mid-July through about September is considered prime time. Most years the time window is rather short, but still

*Looking south from the Spider Mountain-Mount Formidable Col on the Ptarmigan Traverse* (Photo by Jim Nelson)

the Ptarmigan has been done during all seasons, including winter. In fact, one-day trips north to south are not out of the question for experienced backcountry skiers when conditions are right. Once the winter snows melt, there is a well-worn path connecting the glacier sections.

The trip can be done in either direction, although north to south seems to be more popular. Most parties now start or exit via Downey Creek rather than Sulphur Creek, which was used by the original Ptarmigans in 1938.

The history is the really interesting thing about this traverse. It was a legendary tour de force that the Cascades have not seen since. During the summer of 1938, Bill Cox, Ray Clough, Tom Myers, and Calder Bressler hadn't been able to find jobs, and a complete traverse of the Cascade crest was a dream they all shared. Parties had reached the crest at two points along the line, storming up valleys guarded by brush and canyons, but most of the country was unknown, barely mapped and never visited. The following account is five days of the thirteen-day adventure from "Ptarmigans and Their Ptrips" by Harvey Manning, published in the 1958 *Mountaineer Annual:* For more Ptarmigan Traverse history, see Johannesburg Mountain and Boston Peak in the Cascade Pass Area chapter.

**DAY 1:** *At Darrington the Ptarmigans filled out forms for campfire permits and after scanning them the ranger, who had lived and worked all his life in rough country, announced with almost tearful sincerity that their proposed route was utterly and absolutely impossible for members of the human race. In the words of Calder Bressler, whose story of the trip is freely rendered hereafter:"We had considerable respect for his judgment, but we thought we would find out for certain. . . . The first day out of Seattle we rattled in the Model A up the Suiattle River Road to Sulfur Creek, and after saddling up our exceedingly heavy packs tramped along that foul-smelling valley as far as there was trail, and then thrashed a little distance more, spending the night on an island in the middle of the creek.*
**DAY 2:** *Next morning we struck directly upward out of the valley, toiling through brush, timber, and meadows for seven and a half hours. At about 7000 feet on the*

*shoulder below the southwest peak of Dome we found snow for cooking our gruel and made camp.*

The story continues eight long days later:

**DAY 11:** *Before starting we shared out all the remaining salami for it had long since passed its reasonable life expectancy. Cox gulped down his ration, but the rest of us, famished though we were, could stomach only small portions. A sample was enough, and all of us but imperturbable Cox were ill and burped our way down the Stehekin to camp at Bridge Creek.*
**DAY 12:** *Next morning we met some hikers from Seattle who told us they had cached some food up the Agnes Trail and freely gave us full property rights. The vision speeded our steps, but 22 miles later we were disillusioned to find the cache consisted almost entirely of Jell-O. A quart apiece gave our shrunken stomachs enough solace to allow sleep.*
**DAY 13:** *The thirteenth and last day we stormed over Suiattle Pass, down Miners Ridge, down the Suiattle valley, stirring the volcanic dust into great choking clouds that required us to walk at intervals of 100 yards. As always the final mile was interminable, but at last we spied the Model A, and with one more breath of Sulfur Creek fumes we were on our way back to civilization and our first meal deserving of the name since Cascade Pass.*

Editorial comment is scarcely needed. Anyone who knows the country will marvel at thirteen days of such sustained energy. It is likely that the original Ptarmigan Traverse, which included climbing thirteen summits, has not seen a repeat to this day!

### LAND MANAGER
Glacier Peak Wilderness, Mount Baker-Snoqualmie National Forest, Darrington Ranger District. Northwest Forest Pass or interagency recreation pass required for parking; free self-registered wilderness permit required for day and overnight trips. The northern couple of miles (north of Cache Col) is within North Cascades National Park, Marblemount Wilderness Information Center; permit required year-round for overnight trips within the park.

# 28. PTARMIGAN TRAVERSE HIGH ROUTE

**TIME:** 5–8 days; while 1-day trips are becoming increasingly popular, 5–8 days is the norm. This famous route is almost entirely snow, glacier, and exposed off-trail travel. The route can be done in either direction, but the description given here is from north to south.

## APPROACH
Start with leaving a shuttle car at the Downey Creek Trailhead. From Interstate 5 near Arlington, take exit 208 and drive east on State Route 530 for 32 miles to Darrington. From Darrington, continue on SR 530 north about 8 miles and turn east onto Suiattle River Road (Forest Road 26). Continue on FR 26 about 19 miles to the Downey Creek

Trailhead at 1415 feet. Leave the shuttle car, then return to SR 530.

Drive north on SR 530 for 19 miles to Rockport on the North Cascades Highway (SR 20). Drive east on SR 20 for 8 miles to Marblemount. From the east end of downtown Marblemount, where SR 20 turns north, turn east onto Cascade River Road. Immediately cross the Skagit River and continue east 23 miles for about an hour to the road end and the Cascade Pass Trailhead at about 3600 feet. The road, which is paved for about 10 miles before becoming gravel, enters North Cascades National Park at about 16 miles; there are some narrow and steep sections near the end. The road typically opens to the Cascade Pass parking lot by the end of June or into July. Follow the Cascade Pass Trail as it gains elevation slowly with more than thirty switchbacks before reaching Cascade Pass (5400 feet) in 3.7 miles.

*Looking south from the summit of Mount Formidable, early March 2006: Ptarmigan Traverse High Route* (Photo by Sky Sjue)

## ROUTE

Leave the maintained trail at Cascade Pass and continue to the southwest, up Mixup Arm on a well-worn trail. At about 6000 feet, the path fades and the way traverses several steep snow slopes with cliffs below. At about 6200 feet, a ridge crossing leads to what remains of the Cache Glacier. Continue to traverse, then climb the glacier to Cache Col at 6960 feet, where there are bivy sites. This is the first available campsite, other than camping on the glacier at around 6300 feet. Still better camping is not far away at Kool Aid Lake (6100 feet). This is a strenuous day for people shouldering a multiday pack, with 3500 feet of elevation gain followed by 1000 feet of loss.

From Kool Aid Lake, an obvious path traverses alpine gardens, small streams, and slabs to the base of a small cliff band. A short but steep snow slope (dirt later) climbs to a path across the "Red Ledges" and so to easier terrain at about 6300 feet. The path continues south, traversing talus, slabs, and streams before reaching the Middle Cascade Glacier at around 6600 feet. Forge a route up the glacier and head for the Spider Mountain–Mount Formidable Col

### SELECTED HISTORY

**1938 JULY** FA. Calder Bressler, Ray Clough, Bill Cox, Tom Myers.

at 7380 feet. From the col's eastern notch, descend the gully (usually snow) several hundred feet to the unnamed glacier on the south side of Formidable. This gully begins steeply and may require rappels or belays. Start a descending traverse and aim for a promontory at about 6500 feet. Pleasant walking continues down to Yang Yang Lakes, where there is lovely but buggy camping.

From the lakes, faint paths climb to the southwest and finish on steep heather, which gains the ridge at about 6500 feet. Walk south on the gentle ridge crest with the Cascade River and Skagit River drainages on the right. When approaching Le Conte Mountain, leave the crest and make a descending traverse across the glaciers on the northeast side of the crest. Traverse below a buttress at about 6500 feet, then join the greater portion of the LeConte Glacier

*Looking southeast toward Dome Peak. Goosestep Pinnacle is right of center on the ridgeline to Spire Point and German Helmet is in the left foreground: Ptarmigan Traverse High Route* **(Photo by John Scurlock)**

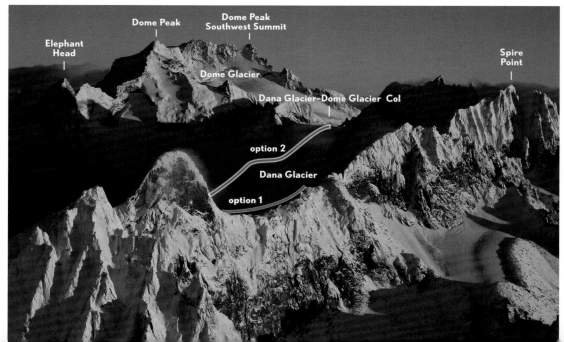

at about 6600 feet. Often the western edge of the glacier is straightforward, but late in the season detours to the east may be necessary. The area between about 6800 feet and 7000 feet can become a jumble as the season advances. This is certainly roped glacier-travel terrain.

Cross to the west of the divide at the LeConte-Sentinel Col (7300 feet) and traverse across and down to the South Cascade Glacier at around 6800 feet. (Alternatively, traverse the west side of Sentinel Peak to reach the glacier at about 6800 feet.) Cross the upper South Cascade Glacier, aiming for the pass at 6840 feet and a bit west of Lizard Mountain. From the pass, a moderately steep gully leads toward White Rock Lakes and camping at 6194 feet.

From the lakes begin a long traverse toward the Dana Glacier. You have two options upon reaching the glacier. **OPTION 1:** The western portion of the glacier leads to a small col just southeast of Spire Point at 7800 feet. From this crossing, descend the southwest slopes to Cub Lake at 5338 feet and join the obvious path near Itswoot Ridge at 6200 feet. This is the original Ptarmigan route and a bit more direct. **OPTION 2:** Ascend the eastern portion of the glacier to the Dana Glacier–Dome Glacier Col at 7800

feet. This is a good choice if you want to summit Dome Peak. From Dome Glacier, traverse west and cross Itswoot Ridge at 6200 feet to join the path leading to Cub Lake.

The path continues around the north side of Cub Lake, then climbs to a pass at 5900 feet, which accesses the upper Bachelor Creek meadows. The path down Bachelor Creek is mostly obvious, with the exception of a short bit at around 4600 feet where it crosses to the north side of the creek. Another trouble spot may be between 3600 feet and 3800 feet when winter avalanches often make a mess of the trail. The Bachelor Creek Trail ultimately joins the Downey Creek Trail No. 768 at 2400 feet, then continues 6 more miles to the Downey Creek Trailhead at 1415 feet.

# DOME PEAK 8920'

### PROMINENCE: 3040' [24]

### DOME PEAK TRAVERSE
Dome Peak anchors one end of the world-famous Ptarmigan Traverse (Climb 28). This massive mountain is similar in

*Dome Peak from the west* (Photo by John Scurlock)

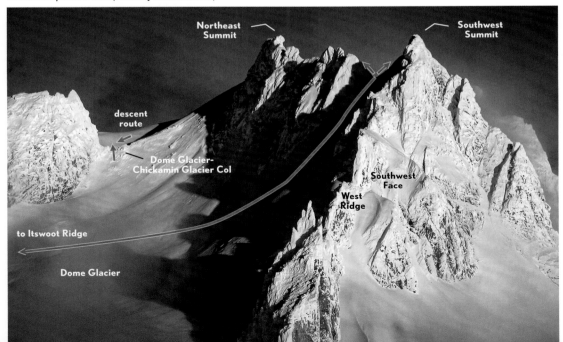

scale to nearby behemoth Bonanza Peak, and the full massif includes many summits, crags, and one of the largest glaciers in the North Cascades. With above-average rock quality, these peaks have much to offer alpine climbers. The journey into Dome Peak is long, well traveled, and scenic. Starting at the valley bottom and working up through old-growth forest, the long approach spans classic meadows, a small alpine lake, scree, snowfields, and finally the glacier and upper mountain.

### LAND MANAGER

Glacier Peak Wilderness, Mount Baker-Snoqualmie National Forest, Darrington Ranger District. Northwest Forest Pass or interagency recreation pass required for parking. Free self-registered wilderness permit required for day or overnight trips.

## 29. DOME PEAK TRAVERSE: GRADE II⁺, 5.4

**TIME:** 2-4 days. The mountain has two primary summits: the higher northeast peak and the pointy southwest peak (8880 feet). Follow in the tradition of the Ptarmigans and climb them

### SELECTED HISTORY

**1936 JULY** Southwest Summit, West Ridge. II, 5.0. Forest Farr, Norval Grigg, Donald Blair, Bob Hayes.

**1936 AUGUST** Dome Peak, Chickamin Glacier. III. George Freed, Erick Larson.

**1938 JULY** Both summits. II+. Calder Bressler, Ray Clough, Bill Cox, Tom Myers.

**1994 MARCH** FWA. Fred Beckey, Laurel Black, Paul Gonzales.

**2009 JULY** Southeast Face, *Gran Torino*. IV, 5.9. Mike Layton, Wayne Wallace.

**2011 SEPTEMBER** Southeast Face, *Indian Summer*. III, 5.10. Nate Farr, Tim Halder.

both! The southwest peak can be climbed via its west ridge or by the north face directly from the Dome Glacier.

### APPROACH, GRADE III+

From Interstate 5 near Arlington, take exit 208 and drive east on State Route 530 for 32 miles to Darrington. From Darrington, drive SR 530 north for about 8 miles

*Dome Peak from the east* **(Photo by John Scurlock)**

and turn east onto Suiattle River Road (Forest Road 26). Continue on FR 26 about 19 miles to the Downey Creek Trailhead at 1415 feet. There are 6.5 miles of maintained trail, 8.5 miles of unmaintained, and 4760 feet of elevation gain.

Follow the Downey Creek Trail No. 768 along the east side of Downey Creek and in 0.5 mile cross into the Glacier Peak Wilderness. Continue through forest to reach Six-Mile Camp in 6.5 miles from the trailhead, at Bachelor Creek (2440 feet). Locate and follow the unmaintained Bachelor Creek Trail east along the north side of Bachelor Creek. At 9.5 miles, the trail crosses the creek at around 4100 feet and leads into a brushy area, where it turns sharply left (east) and follows the stream; alternatively, stay on the north side of the stream before crossing and rejoining the main trail at around 4450 feet. The trail switchbacks steeply before reaching the Bachelor Creek meadows (5400 feet) at 11 miles. Now travel south, crossing the ridge at a small pass (5900 feet) and descend to Cub Lake (5338 feet) and campsites at 14 miles. Beyond Cub Lake, the trail climbs northeast another mile to Itswoot Ridge at 6200 feet.

## ROUTE

From Itswoot Ridge at 6200 feet, follow a long traverse east across snow and talus, eventually climbing to the north end of the Dome Glacier at 7400 feet. Dome's southwest peak can be climbed directly from the glacier or around on the south side of the west ridge: The direct route crosses the bergschrund, followed by 45-degree snow to the ridge between Dome's peaks. From the ridgetop, a pitch of low-5th-class rock and a bit of scrambling leads to Dome's southwest summit. From the col between Dome's peaks, the traverse to the northeast peak's main summit is made by scrambling east, mostly along the south side of the crest. Continue scrambling with occasional bits of 5th class and finish near the crest with a short crack pitch.

## DESCENT

From the northeast peak, descend north to the Dome Glacier-Chickamin Glacier Col at 8560 feet and follow the Dome Glacier route back to Itswoot Ridge and out.

# GUNSIGHT PEAKS 8198'

**PROMINENCE: 518'**

### GUNRUNNER TRAVERSE

News of Gunsight's superb rock reported in the 1938 *Mountaineer Annual* by Agnes Dickert did not escape notice. Eager to confirm the news, budding alpinist Fred Beckey made his first of many trips to the area shortly thereafter.

*Blake Herrington on Gunsight's northwest peak, beginning the* **Gunrunner** *traverse of Gunsight's four peaks* (Photo by Dan Hilden)

This is a quiet little place with an approach that keeps the riffraff at bay. The climbs of the four main peaks are rather short, but several have become recognized as classics. The east face of the main (middle) peak was climbed in 1979, the west face of the north peak in 1986. A second route on the main peak's east face was established in 2006, following a rockfall that destroyed the 1979 route.

Traversing the four main peaks must surely be a delight. Starting with the northwest peak makes the most sense and is a great climb by itself (the *Cascade Alpine Guide* calls it the "northeast peak," but more accurately it's the northwest peak). The long north ridge of this north-northwest peak looks attractive and reported to be third and fourth class on good rock. What a location!

### LAND MANAGER
Glacier Peak Wilderness, Mount Baker-Snoqualmie National Forest, Darrington Ranger District. Northwest Forest Pass or interagency recreation pass required for parking. Free self-registered wilderness permit required for day or overnight trips.

## 30. GUNRUNNER TRAVERSE: GRADE IV, 5.10

**TIME:** 3–5 days. **GEAR:** medium rack to 4 inches, ice axe, crampons. The best season is June–September. Allow a full day from high camp and expect a full program of cracks, knobs, slabs, and ridgetop thrills. The *Gunrunner* begins with several pitches of beautiful crack and corner climbing on the northwest peak before continuing south over the three higher Gunsight Peaks. There are about eighteen belayed pitches with several rated at 5.9. Most pitches are low to mid-5th class, however. Look for the names Beckey, Craig, and Thompson rumored to be inside a still-intact tiny summit register on North Gunsight Peak.

### APPROACH, GRADE IV
Follow the approach to Itswoot Ridge for Climb 29, Dome Glacier Traverse. From Itswoot Ridge, follow the Dome Glacier route nearly to the top of Dome Peak, where there are a couple of tent sites. From near the Dome Glacier-Chickamin Glacier Col at 8560 feet, find a route

*The Gunsight Peaks from the north* (Photo by John Scurlock)

through the large crevasses at the top of the Chickamin Glacier. A descent of about 1500 feet east leads to the Gunsight Peaks, below the south side of the northwest peak at about 7400 feet.

## ROUTE

Begin with hand cracks and climb toward the crest of the west ridge. Continue near the crest and finish in a chimney for six-eight pitches. The fourth pitch has well-protected face climbing leading to an exposed roof on golden rock.

The first-ascent party continued along the main Gunsight ridge, simul-climbing and making one short pendulum (A1) on the north peak, which can be easily avoided. From the namesake Gunsight Notch, climb the main peak up a 5.9 dihedral on the east side of the crest. Descend the main peak with rappels, following the ridge crest and over the top of a tower to ascend the south peak.

Two rappels north lead to the Blue Glacier, and from there a traverse south to the Blizzard Peak-Gunsight Col at 7650 feet. Cross the col to the Chickamin Glacier and return to camp and out.

## SELECTED HISTORY

**1938 JULY** Main Peak. II, 5.0. Agnes Dickert, Lloyd Anderson, Lyman Boyer.

**1940 JUNE** North Peak (8160 feet). II, 5.6. Fred Beckey, Robert Craig, Will Thompson.

**1940 JUNE** South Peak (8080 feet). II, 5.0. Fred Beckey, Robert Craig, Will Thompson.

**1951 SEPTEMBER** Northeast Peak (8040 feet). II, 4th class. Gibson Reynolds, Philip Sharpe.

**1979 JULY** Main Peak, East Face. III, 5.9. Gary Brill, Gordy Skoog.

**1986 AUGUST** North Peak, West Face. III, 5.11. Carl Diedrich, Jim Nelson.

**2006 JULY** South Peak, South Ridge. II, 5.7. John Frieh, Blake Herrington.

**2006 AUGUST** Main Peak, East Face. III, 5.10+. Martins Putelis, Sol Wertkin.

**2007 JULY** South Peak, East Face. II, 5.10. Blake Herrington, Dan Hilden.

**2007 JULY** *Gunrunner Traverse*. IV, 5.10. Blake Herrington, Dan Hilden.

*The Gunsight Peaks from the southwest* (Photo by Steph Abegg)

# CASCADE PASS AREA

## BUCKINDY RANGE

### BUCKINDY-SNOWKING TRAVERSE

Tucked into a remote corner of the North Cascades, the rugged Buckindy Range is a hidden gem. This subrange of greenschist between Glacier Peak and Cascade Pass represents an array of alpine challenges that rewards with commanding central views and lies in close proximity to many of the other giants of the North Cascades: Glacier Peak, Snowking Mountain, and the central portion of the Ptarmigan Traverse. The Buckindy Range could genuinely be considered a sort of "mini Pickets Range" characterized by long and arduous approaches, isolation, and challenging alpine problems.

There are numerous ways to approach the Buckindy Range, as well as several exit points. Among the many possible starting and exit points are Illabot Creek Road, Snowking Trailhead, Sonny Boy Ridge, and Green Mountain Trailhead—or as a variation and addition to the Ptarmigan Traverse. The shortest approaches are via Chaval, Snowking, or Green Mountain, and any of the approaches take two days. Once you reach the Buckindy group, expect challenging routefinding, glacier travel, and, above all, isolation.

An ideal way to tour the Buckindy group is to make it a variation of the Ptarmigan Traverse. Remote and seldom done, this strenuous but rewarding option travels through terrain relatively untouched by humans and offers unique views of the range. Expect very few signs of human visitation.

### LAND MANAGERS

Glacier Peak Wilderness, Mount Baker-Snoqualmie National Forest, Darrington Ranger District. Northwest Forest Pass or interagency recreation pass required for parking; free self-registered wilderness permit required for day or overnight trips. North Cascades National Park, Marblemount Wilderness Information Center; permit required year-round for overnight trips within the park.

## 31. BUCKINDY-SNOWKING TRAVERSE

**TIME:** 5-7 days; total distance about 45 miles, mostly cross-country; about 16,000 feet total elevation gain without climbing any peaks. The summits of the Buckindy group are between 7000 and about 7500 feet in altitude and harbor surprisingly large glaciers for mountains of their stature. Snow conditions dictate the best time of year to do these climbs; July and August seem to be the best. During these summer months, wildflowers are at their peak, glaciers aren't broken up enough to make travel cumbersome, and weather is reliable. Most of this traverse lies within the Glacier Peak Wilderness, but most of day one (Cascade Pass Trailhead to Cache Col) lies within North Cascades National Park.

### APPROACH

This traverse begins at the Cascade Pass Trailhead at about 3600 feet: see the approach for Climb 28, Ptarmigan Traverse High Route. It finishes at the start of the Kindy Ridge-Snowking climbers trail, 10 miles down Cascade River Road from the Cascade Pass Trailhead. It can work well to park at the endpoint trailhead and hitchhike up the road 10 miles to the Cascade Pass Trailhead to start this loop traverse. Or leave a shuttle car at the endpoint trailhead: From the North Cascades Highway (State Route 20) at Marblemount, drive to the east end of downtown where SR 20 turns north, and continue east on the Cascade River Road. Immediately cross the Skagit River and continue on Cascade River Road 13 miles to spur Forest Road 1570, which crosses to the south side of the Cascade River, and follow it to just beyond the river crossing, at about 1200 feet. Then drive to the starting-point trailhead and park.

### ROUTE

Follow the route for Climb 28, Ptarmigan Traverse High Route, as far as the South Cascade Glacier. Cross the South Cascade Glacier to the west at about 6300 feet, and ascend a couloir to a notch just southwest of Point

7188; this point can also be passed on its east. Contour and descend the ridge separating the South Fork Cascade River from Slim Lake and cross a forested notch at about 5000 feet, then ascend toward Point 5967, where good camping can be found.

From Point 5967 continue to the west, generally staying north of the ridge crest. Continue contouring on snow or talus to reach a basin north-northwest of Mount Bruseth at 6400 feet and then ascend to a notch at the head of Kindy Creek (about 6600 feet). Continue west from the Kindy Creek basin and contour on talus to reach a forested rib north of Tara Peak (6723 feet), which is an eastern sub-peak of the Buckindy massif. Good camping with running water may be found here when snow is present. If exiting via Green Mountain, one option is to camp at the 7000-foot notch separating Horse and Kindy Creeks, just east of the main summit of Mount Buckindy.

From a camp on the forested rib below Tara Peak, continue west through the basin north of Buckindy. A 50- to 100-foot (15m–30m) rappel may be required to get down off this rib into the adjacent basin to the west. Make a long traverse west of the Kindy Creek cirque below the unnamed glacier on the north side of Mount Buckindy.

Continue northwest across the Kindy Creek cirque and cross a prominent rock rib at 5500 feet, aiming for the northeast ridge of Peak 7160, also known as Snowqueen (or Mutchler). A key talus and heather ramp tops out on the northeast ridge and leads to within 500 feet of the summit on 3rd- or 4th-class terrain. An alternative is to gain Snowqueen's shoulder at 6000 feet. Scramble easy terrain to Snowqueen's west summit ridge.

From Snowqueen, traverse the unnamed glacier north to Snowking Mountain while staying high to avoid slab problems southeast of Snowking's summit. Descend from the

*Mount Buckindy from the northwest; the actual summit is hidden behind the point marked.* (Photo by John Scurlock)

*Snowking Mountain from the north* (Photo by John Scurlock)

base of Snowking's summit block and down the east ridge to the Snowking climbers trail located on Kindy Ridge east of and above Cyclone and Found Lakes. From the 4800-foot saddle on the ridge, the trail descends forest to the abandoned road at 2200 feet. Expect this route to be dry from the glacier to about 2000 feet after about midsummer. The road crosses the Cascade River and reaches the main Cascade River Road a couple miles west of Mineral Park Campground and 10 miles from the Cascade Pass Trailhead.

# JOHANNESBURG MOUNTAIN 8200'

## PROMINENCE: 1560'

## NORTHEAST RIB

It is hard to grasp the complexities of Johannesburg's 5000-foot north face, especially when viewed from the valley bottom where foreshortening distorts and hides the mountain's secrets and hidden passages. Observe the wasteland from avalanches a stone's throw from the car. The rock walls of

Cascade River schist and the hanging glaciers of this beast are on full view as the road traverses the upper valley. Witness the power of gravity as the mountain sheds its winter snowpack all summer long.

Joberg has long been notorious for epic battles and unplanned bivouacs. That the mountain is easily underestimated is demonstrated in the story of its first ascent, told by Calder Bressler in the 1958 *Mountaineer Annual:*

*Climbing over Cache Col on day eight we dropped down to Cascade Pass and leaving our packs at a good campsite south of the pass set out for the peak we called Elsbeth, now named Johannesburg. We traversed the talus beneath the Triplets gaining altitude gradually, traversed and climbed most of the north face of Cascade Peak, arriving at last on the col between Cascade and Johannesburg. By now it was late in the afternoon, but any qualms we might have had were dispelled by the mountain goat which appeared suddenly to guide us. Climbing the cliff west of the col we followed the goat, who kept at a uniform distance of 200 feet, leading us to the summit at 6 pm.*

*Though now we had a few second thoughts, and moved with all possible speed it was dark before we regained the col. Rather weary and desperate we attempted to descend the hanging glacier that drops away on the north side of the col, and none of us came away from that evening with any love for clawing around on steep ice by flashlight. We were finally stopped by a gaping crevasse that spanned the entire width of the narrow ice torrent and gave it up as a bad job. Back over the col we groggily struggled and bivouacked in a sparse meadow on the south slope, huddling all night over a small twig fire, scorching our hands and faces while other portions of the anatomy froze. At first light we carefully conducted our stiff bones the long way to Cascade Pass, circling on the south side of Triplets and descending a snow finger between Triplets and Mixup to our camp. The remainder of that day we spent dozing and swatting horseflies.*

Harry Majors reports that in a letter to Betty Manning dated July 30, 1957, Bill Cox wrote, "The 1938 Ptarmigan party found a mining monument on top of Johannesburg."

## LAND MANAGER

North Cascades National Park, Marblemount Wilderness Information Center. Permit required year-round for overnight trips within the park.

## 32. NORTHEAST RIB: GRADE IV⁺, 5.7

**TIME:** 1-2 days. **GEAR:** small rack to 3 inches; crampons useful on exposed heather. This climb is on the eastern of two parallel ribs that join at the snow ridge on the northeast rib, a long route on a mountain that is often underestimated. The route is often done in two days with a planned bivouac high on the peak.

## APPROACH

On the North Cascades Highway (State Route 20) at Marblemount, drive to the east end of downtown where SR 20 turns north and continue east on Cascade River Road. Immediately cross the Skagit River and continue east 23 miles to the road end and the Cascade Pass

*Daniel Jeffrey enjoys one fine bivy on Johannesburg Mountain's northeast rib.* **(Photo by Tom Sjolseth)**

Trailhead in about an hour, at about 3600 feet. The road is paved for the first third and then becomes gravel, with some narrow and steep sections near the end; the road typically opens to the Cascade Pass parking lot by the end of June or into July.

From the Cascade Pass parking lot, walk back down the road a short way to the first road bend. Leave the road and cross the stream at 3500 feet to begin.

## ROUTE

Ascend the moraine or snow slopes toward the Cascade-Johannesburg Couloir and aim for a good route through the initial cliff band at around 3900 feet. Gullies, slabs, and bushes lead to a seasonal snow patch. The next 1000 feet involve steep bushwacking, including slide alder, which leads to a higher snow patch between the eastern rib (1951) and western rib (1957). Climb heather and rock near the eastern rib to where the two ribs join at a snow arête near 7200 feet and the bivy site. This section varies between 3rd and 4th class, is exposed, and may include some 5th class depending on routefinding. The snow arête and hanging glacier are often straightforward but will have seasonal challenges. From the ridgetop, a short rock scramble reaches the summit.

*Wayne Wallace, and Sergio Verdina on the summit of Johannesburg Mountain* (Photo by Tom Sjolseth)

*Johannesburg Mountain from the north* (Photo by Steph Abegg)

## DESCENT

Follow the east ridge east across ledges mostly below the south side of the ridge crest. From the east end of the ridge, descend several hundred feet until able to trend north near a seasonal snow patch. Continue north and up and over a rocky shoulder before continuing down gullies toward a heather bench directly above the Cascade-Johannesburg Col. The entire face can be mostly down-climbed with good conditions, and there are a number of rappel stations as well. From the C-J Col, two descent options are available.

**OPTION 1:** To the north down the C-J Couloir is tempting, but it's dependent on snow conditions and one's experience on steep snow. **OPTION 2:** More common is a long traverse east, crossing the ridge near Mixup Peak. Begin with a traversing descent to about 5800 feet below the Triplets' south ridge. Then work up to Mixup's north ridge and cross at about 7300 feet. Steep heather, 3rd-class slabs, and gullies lead toward the north edge of the Cache Glacier near the Ptarmigan Traverse "trail" at about 6000 feet. A steep traverse slogs across Mixup Arm, then heads down to Cascade Pass and a trail of many switchbacks.

## SELECTED HISTORY

**1934 JULY** Northeast Summit. Dan O'Brien, Hermann Ulrichs.

**1938 JULY** East Ridge. III+, 4th class. Calder Bressler, Bill Cox, Ray Clough, Tom Myers.

**1949 JULY** West Summit (8065 feet), West Route. III, 4th class. Charles Cehrs, Bill Elfendahl, Dave Lind, Tom Miller, Jay Todd.

**1951 JULY** Northeast Rib. IV, 5.6. David Harrah, Tom Miller.

**1957 JULY** Northeast Rib, Western. IV, 5.3. Stan Curtis, Ned Gulbran, Michael Hane, Rowland Tabor.

**1963 AUGUST** Northeast Face. IV+, 5.4. Dave Beckstead, Don Gordon, Jim Stuart.

**1965 JULY** Northeast Face. IV+, 5.7. Hans Baer, Alex Bertulis, Jack Bryan, Frank Tarver.

**1967 AUGUST** Northeast Face. IV+, 5.6. Scott Davis, Al Givler, Doug McGowan.

**1971 AUGUST** Southeast Arête. III, 4th class. Claude Garrod, Leon Slutsky.

**1971 AUGUST** South Face. III, 4th class. Julian Ansel, Claude Garrod, Mickey Schurr, Leon Slutsky.

**1973 JULY** Northeast Face. IV+, 5.6. Dave Anderson, Don Brooks, Julie Brugger, John Teasdale.

**1981 FEBRUARY** East Ridge, FWA via C-J Couloir. Robert Deltete, Dave Seman.

**1984 FEBRUARY** Northeast Rib, 1957 route, FWA. Bill Pilling, Steve Mascioli.

**1985 JULY** North Face, West Summit. IV, 5th class. Mark Desvoigne, Dallas Kloke.

**1985 DECEMBER** Northeast Face. IV. Mark Bebie, John Stoddard.

**1986 FEBRUARY** Northeast Couloir. IV. Peter Keleman, Josh Lieberman.

**2005 AUGUST** North Face, West Summit. IV. Loren Campbell, Jens Klubberud.

# BOSTON PEAK                8894'

## PROMINENCE: 854' [26]

### BOSTON-SAHALE TRAVERSE

Boston Peak is the centerpiece for the North Cascades' largest glacier, the Boston. Along with its neighbors Forbidden Peak and Mount Buckner, these three important peaks form the ridgeline of this massive glacial cirque. It is truly one of the grandest views and difficult to see in its entirety.

The first ascent of Boston Peak was made on day ten of the original Ptarmigan Traverse. It was climbed on a traverse of Sahale, Boston, and Mount Buckner's north face—quite a day out, considering both Boston and Buckner were unclimbed, and only one day had elapsed since their Johannesburg climb, which had included a night out.

Why are Forbidden and Boston designated "peaks" and Buckner a "mount"? Considering that all three are connected by the same ridgeline, the two lower summits then become subpeaks of the higher Mount Buckner. While there appears to be good logic to the method, it is not always followed. Nearby Mount Torment is nearly 700 feet lower than its neighbor Forbidden Peak but still titled a mount.

### LAND MANAGER

North Cascades National Park, Marblemount Wilderness Information Center. Permit required year-round for overnight trips within the park. Hard-sided food storage canisters required June 1–November 15 when camping in Boston Basin.

## 33. BOSTON-SAHALE TRAVERSE: GRADE II+

**TIME:** 1–2 days. Our suggested route approaches from Boston Basin, eliminates Buckner, and then descends the Sahale route to Cascade Pass for a classic loop trip. This traverse loop combines a short but exciting glacier climb to the prominent summit of Boston Peak, followed by an ascent of Sahale and one of the North Cascades' signature hikes back down Sahale Arm.

### APPROACH, GRADE III

On the North Cascades Highway (State Route 20) at Marblemount, drive to the east end of downtown where SR 20 turns north and continue east on Cascade River Road. Immediately cross the Skagit River and continue east 22 miles to the small pullout area (3200 feet) directly opposite the spectacular northeast face of Johannesburg Mountain; park here.

Sharkfin Tower

Mount Logan

Boston Peak

Sahale Mountain

Sahale Glacier

to Sahale Arm & Cascade Pass

Quien Sabe Glacier

from Boston Basin

*Moonrise over Boston Peak from the southwest* (Photo by John Scurlock)

The Boston Basin climbers trail begins in forest before climbing steeply through an open area starting at about 3800 feet. Continue through timber for several hundred yards before traversing west and crossing Midas and Morning Star Creeks. Expect some brush and stream-crossing problems during snowmelt. Beyond the crossings, a pleasant trail switchbacks through beautiful old-growth forest. Upon entering Boston Basin at about 5500 feet, a branch of Boston Creek can present a difficult crossing when running high. Crossing a couple hundred feet higher where the stream is braided leads to the lower bivy area at 5640 feet.

## ROUTE

From the lower bivy site in Boston Basin, slabs and snow lead to the northern end of the Quien Sabe Glacier at 7500 feet, below the distinctive Sharkfin Tower. The glacier steepens near 8000 feet where a bergschrund is the only remaining obstacle to the Boston-Sahale Col at 8600 feet.

Starting with Boston Peak, from the col follow the ridge crest north, passing subsummit bumps on the left (west) side and very near the crest (3rd class). A short down-climb from the subsummit leads to the top of the Boston Glacier at about 8750 feet. A traverse north on the snow below Boston's east face leads to a moat and an exposed ledge. Follow the ledge north, then leave it before it narrows down. Climb up and across Boston's upper east face to a chimney (3rd class). Above the chimney, gain the ridgetop and follow it south to the summit.

**DESCENT OF BOSTON:** Down-climb the ascent route or make three 75-foot (24m) rappels to the east, then return to the Boston-Sahale Col.

**TRAVERSE TO SAHALE:** From the Boston-Sahale Col, the ridge to Sahale includes a short 4th-class step and a bit of snow climbing in early season. From a notch about 20 feet below the Sahale summit block, a couple of 5th-class moves reach the small summit.

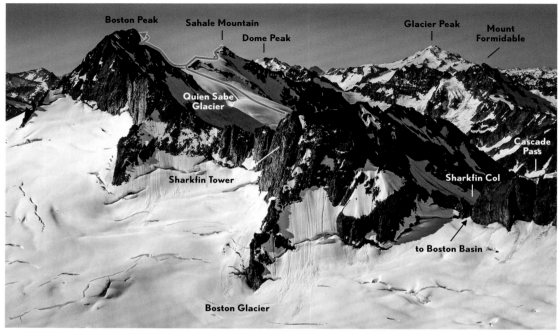

Boston Peak, Sahale Mountain, Dome Peak, Glacier Peak, Mount Formidable, Quien Sabe Glacier, Cascade Pass, Sharkfin Tower, Sharkfin Col, to Boston Basin, Boston Glacier

*Boston Peak from the north* (Photo by John Scurlock)

**DESCENT OF SAHALE:** From the small notch below the top of Sahale, descend to the south. The terrain here is 3rd-class slabs and ledges with loose stones and no good options for pro. A rappel is a good way to cross this area. A second rappel anchor is commonly found lower and toward the west.

Once off the slabs, begin a descending traverse west on talus or snow to reach the Sahale Glacier at about 8200 feet. From there, descend the western end of the glacier with a steep section leading to campsites below the glacier at about 7600 feet. From the lower end of the camping area,

find the trail a bit to the west and then head straight down. The track leads down and around the east end of Sahale Arm and continues down to Cascade Pass, with lengthy switchbacks leading to the trailhead. About a mile of road walking leads to the Boston Basin Trailhead.

# MOUNT BUCKNER                                      9112'

### PROMINENCE: 3032' [14]

#### NORTH FACE
The north face of Mount Buckner ranks up there with Mount Shuksan as one of an elite group of snow and ice climbs in the Cascades. It is a beautiful and classic face on one of the elusive "nine-thousanders." The volcanoes have longer routes, but without the rugged alpine character of Buckner. There are great views to Forbidden Peak, the Eldorado ice cap, and the whole stunning panorama of Cascade Pass

## SELECTED HISTORY

**1897 AUGUST** Sahale Peak, FA. II. John Charlton, Albert Sylvester.

**1938 JULY** Boston Peak, FA. II+. Calder Bressler, Ray Clough, Bill Cox, Tom Myers.

peaks. Expect a genuine feeling of remoteness and commitment while trudging across the Boston Glacier en route to this classic snow face.

The route was first climbed in a day by the Ptarmigans. A two- to three-day ascent from Sahale Glacier Camp is more common today. Note that the climb can also be approached from Boston Basin over Sharkfin Col or from the Boston-Sahale Col. Whether you include the summits of Sahale and Boston along the way or not, climbing from Boston Glacier and returning via Horseshoe Basin is a classic alpine tour.

## LAND MANAGER
North Cascades National Park, Marblemount Wilderness Information Center. Permit required year-round for all overnight trips within the park.

## 34. NORTH FACE: GRADE III

**TIME:** 1-3 days. The original route on the face no longer holds snow through the summer. The North Couloir climbed in 1967 holds snow longer and is worth a look when evaluating conditions.

## APPROACH, GRADE II
On the North Cascades Highway (State Route 20) at Marblemount, drive to the east end of downtown where SR 20 turns north and continue east on Cascade River Road. Immediately cross the Skagit River and continue east another 23 miles to the road end and Cascade Pass Trailhead in about an hour, at about 3600 feet. The road is paved for the first third and then becomes gravel, with some narrow and steep sections near the end; the road typically opens to the Cascade Pass parking lot by the end of June or into July. There is 3900 feet of elevation gain on 6 miles of trail to reach Sahale Glacier Camp at 7600 feet.

The Cascade Pass Trail gains elevation slowly with more than thirty switchbacks before reaching Cascade Pass at 5400 feet. From the pass, the trail climbs more steeply to Sahale Arm at 6200 feet, followed by a long slog to campsites below the Sahale Glacier at 7550 feet.

## ROUTE
Climb the Sahale Glacier before traversing east and gaining Sahale's south ridge at about 8400 feet. Third-class scrambling just east of the ridge crest leads to a small notch about 50 feet below Sahale's summit. From this notch, the

*Mount Buckner from the north* (Photo by John Scurlock)

North Couloir
1967

1938 route

Ripsaw Ridge

Boston Glacier

to Boston Peak
& Sahale Glacier

to Sharkfin Col

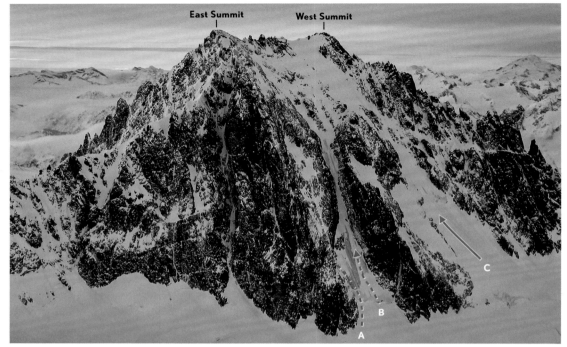

*Mount Buckner from the north in early December: (A) North Face, East Summit route, 2005, (B) North Couloir route, 1967, (C) North Face route, 1938 (Photo by John Scurlock)*

## SELECTED HISTORY

**1901** Southwest route. II, 3rd class. Lewis Ryan, Washington State Geological Survey.

**1934 JULY** Northeast Summit. Dan O'Brien, Hermann Ulrichs.

**1934 JULY** South Ridge. II, 4th class. Donald Blair, Norval Grigg, Art Winder.

**1938 JULY** North Face. II+. Calder Bressler, Ray Clough, Bill Cox, Tom Myers.

**1967 AUGUST** North Couloir. II+. John Holland, Walter Gove, and friends.

**2003 FEBRUARY** Southwest Face, FWA. Sean Courage, Tim Matsui, Andreas Schmidt.

**2004 FEBRUARY** North Couloir, FWA. Corey Bloom, Ross Peritore, Sky Sjue.

**2005 FEBRUARY** North Face, East Summit. III+. Peter Hirst, Rolf Larson.

**2006 AUGUST** Full Southeast Ridge. IV, 5.8. Blake Herrington, Gordy Skoog.

ridge connecting with Boston Peak leads northeast, losing a bit of elevation at first. Follow the ridge crest north, passing subsummit bumps on the left (west) side very near the crest (3rd class). Finally, a short down-climb from Boston's subsummit leads to the top of the Boston Glacier at about 8750 feet. Descend the glacier until you can traverse east toward Buckner's north face. As the face begins to melt out by midseason, a section of rock climbing is often necessary at about midheight before the West Summit is reached. (A bit farther east, the North Couloir offers a more continuous snow climb if conditions on the western route are unfavorable.)

### DESCENT

From the West Summit, descend to the southwest via gullies and scree into Horseshoe Basin. Once off the mountain, begin traversing west at about 6800 feet and onto a wide ledge system below the Davenport Glacier at about

6600 feet. Skirt cliffs and look for a short gully at approximately 6550 feet. Scramble (3rd and 4th class) 200 feet to reach alpine slopes leading up and west back to Sahale Glacier Camp.

# FORBIDDEN PEAK        8815'

## PROMINENCE: 1053' [30]

### NORTH RIDGE; TORMENT-FORBIDDEN TRAVERSE

Forbidden can be a frightening peak, friendly one minute and threatening the next. Fast-forming weather combined

*Historic photo of the great Don Gordon on the 1958 first ascent of Forbidden Peak's East Ridge.* (**Photo by Ed Cooper**)

with a challenging descent have benighted many parties through the years. The mountain also has wonderful climbing and a striking classic shape. Three distinct sharp ridges converge at a tiny summit to form a classic glacier-carved pyramid. With ideal conditions, the climb is over much too quickly, and for many the peak is well worth return visits.

One member of the first-ascent party, Fred Beckey, returned to pioneer routes up both the east and north ridges, as well as up the extremely elegant northwest face. Four great routes each have their own delights, and yet each is distinctly Forbidden in character. The north-ridge party considered it the finest alpine climb in the range at the time. Of course, Fred had not yet teamed up with Ed Cooper. Together, Ed and Fred pioneered some great climbs, including two on Forbidden.

We feature the north ridge here for its length and variety of climbing, which can be divided into three sections: The lower ridge is quite narrow and exposed, with some loose rock. The middle section forms a snow arête where the northwest face of the north ridge abuts the ridge. The final third is pure joy, with easy climbing, solid rock, and moderate exposure. The north ridge also provides a good look at the notorious east-ledges descent route.

Because Forbidden is steep on all sides, there is no simple descent route. Several options are popular, each with its own positive and negative considerations. Previous experience on the mountain, seasonal conditions, and location of other parties should all be considered when choosing the descent.

Just about any climb in the Cascade Pass area has a lot going for it in terms of sheer alpine ambiance and atmosphere. The Torment-Forbidden Traverse is a route that has gone from curiosity to classic in recent years. The first-ascent party made the traverse in classic style, using no bivy gear on their two-day ascent. Ed Cooper, who has made a number of first ascents in the region, calls this route one of his favorites in an area famous for quality climbs. "I thought it would be a great mountaineering adventure, and it was," said Cooper, forty-three years after the first ascent. "I had seen this long ridge during previous trips that same year. Our gear was primitive; we did not take sleeping bags. . . . We knew that we would spend the night up there and actually looked forward to the experience. Despite a cold night, it was a splendid trip."

**LAND MANAGER**

North Cascades National Park, Marblemount Wilderness Information Center. Permit required year-round for all overnight trips within the park. Hard-sided food storage canisters required June 1–November 15 when camping in Boston Basin.

## 35. NORTH RIDGE: GRADE IV, 5.5

**TIME:** 1–2 days. More accurately this is a northeast ridge, but for simplicity it's known as the north ridge. This is a long route, with a technical approach, technical climbing off the beaten path, and a technical descent. The lower third of the ridge can be climbed directly or bypassed. Bypassing the lower ridge can add variety by climbing 45-degree snow or ice above the Forbidden Glacier. The lower ridge has spectacular sections and short sections of loose rock, with a few blocks perched on the crest.

The first-ascent party described the rock as "very good almost everywhere, with excellent belay points." The party of three made their climb from a camp in Boston Basin and

back down again without a bivouac. Spending the night out on the north side of the mountain also has great appeal.

**APPROACH, GRADE III**

Follow the approach for Climb 33, Boston-Sahale Traverse, and then follow the Boston-Sahale route to the northern end of the Quien Sabe Glacier at 7500 feet, below the distinctive Sharkfin Tower.

**ROUTE**

From the north end of the Quien Sabe Glacier at 7500 feet, head toward Sharkfin Col, the lowest col directly above. From the highest snow, a few moves of mid-5th class reach a protected belay stance, followed by loose 3rd-class scrambling to the col at about 7760 feet. From the col, a 100-foot (30m) rappel reaches the Boston Glacier moat. Descend Boston Glacier to the north, passing below a rock buttress at about 7000 feet. Continue a long rising traverse to the very end of Forbidden's lower north ridge at about 7600 feet. There are nice bivy sites here and access to the Forbidden Glacier. To climb the lower north

*Forbidden Peak from the northeast: (A) North Ridge, (B) Torment–Forbidden Traverse* (Photo by John Scurlock)

*Forbidden Peak from the south* (Photo by John Scurlock)

ridge, start just south of the first high point on the north end of the ridge.

**OPTION:** To bypass the lower ridge, make a short descent onto the Forbidden Glacier and continue south, reaching the beginning of the large snow patch abutting the ridge on its northwest face. Seasonal bergschrund conditions will determine route choice, and dry conditions may involve rock climbing. About 500 feet of snow or ice climbing on the northwest face leads to the north ridge.

The north ridge route continues on 3rd class to the final arête, where a prominent ledge leads down and around a corner on the left, connecting with the east ledges. The final 300 feet follows very close to the ridge crest and leads directly to the summit.

## DESCENT

**WEST RIDGE:** This involves a combination of down-leading and short rappels to access the top of the West Ridge Couloir. The WRC can be simple with good snow conditions, but it becomes more difficult throughout the summer. In later season, a popular alternative to the WRC is to continue down the ridge just a little bit farther (west) until a series of indistinct and somewhat loose gullies can be rappelled. Expect chossy anchors and tattered webbing.

Whether descending the WRC or the gullies immediately west, be mindful of rockfall from climbers above. The Park Service recently chopped anchors here, and fatalities have occurred. After reaching the unnamed remnant glacier, it is a short way on snow and slabs to the Boston Basin campsites at 6200 feet.

**EAST LEDGES:** Reach these ledges, which traverse low across the northeast face, with five straightforward 80-foot (25m) rappels right from the summit. The key is to descend low enough to reach the correct ledge system. Alternatively, climb back down the north ridge about 300 feet to a prominent ledge that connects the north ridge to the northeast ledges—look for it on the ascent; this is a good option for those familiar with the east ledges.

The traverse ledges are 3rd class, exposed, and without good protection. The route stays low, traversing across the face, crossing several ribs, eventually reaching a chimney-gully. The chimney is 4th class, about 100 feet high, leading to the east ridge immediately west of a prominent gendarme at the end of the ridge.

Once on the ridge, descend a scree slope eastward to a rocky rib. Descend the 3rd-class rib to about 7800 feet, above a gully leading toward the unnamed remnant glacier. Descend the loose gully. From the glacier it is straight downhill to the upper Boston Basin bivy sites.

# 36. TORMENT-FORBIDDEN TRAVERSE: GRADE IV–V, 5.7

**TIME:** 2–3 days. **GEAR:** small rack; snow and glacier gear for 40-degree snow. The best season is June to September. Although there are few technical challenges on this long course, it requires comfort on both rock and snow. It is physically demanding, and routefinding difficulties are to be expected. This is a committing climb with technical descents. These components add up to an appealing package with generally sound rock and awesome bivy spots. Fast parties cruise the route without a high bivy, and rapid ascents are not uncommon.

## APPROACHES

**BOSTON BASIN, GRADE III:** Follow the approach to Boston Basin for Climb 33, Boston-Sahale Traverse, to the lower bivy sites at about 5640 feet. From below the lower bivy sites the trail leads north across the basin to the grassy moraine. From the top of the moraine at about 6200 feet the trail continues north across the basin, reaching the

*Liz Daley (in yellow) and Juya Ghanaie on the north ridge of Forbidden Peak* (Photo by Alasdair Turner)

upper bivy sites at about 6400 feet. From the upper Boston bivy sites at 6200 feet, traverse west, passing below the spur ridge separating Boston Basin from Taboo Basin. Scramble alongside a waterfall coming off the eastern end of the Taboo Glacier (3rd–4th class) and cross slabs westward. Ascend the Taboo Glacier, aiming for a hidden gully leading to a small notch (7440 feet) below the south ridge of Torment.

**TORMENT BASIN, GRADE III:** This route is less traveled but has a worn path much of the way. Plan for the initial 3500 feet to be dry! Follow the approach for Climb 37, East Ridge, Eldorado and Inspiration Glaciers, driving Cascade River Road to just less than 1 mile beyond the parking area for Eldorado Peak. The unmarked trail begins a short way beyond where the road crosses to the north side of the Cascade River at about 2350 feet.

The path is just past the bridge and climbs steeply through forest, encountering some brush at about 4600 feet. Above the forest, pass through patches of talus, heather, and a few bushes as you continue up to the small snowfield below Torment's south face. Aim for the small notch (7440 feet) below the south ridge.

*Lowell Skoog near Point 8100 on the Torment-Forbidden Traverse (Photo by Carl Skoog)*

## SELECTED HISTORY

### FORBIDDEN PEAK

**1940 JUNE** West Ridge. III, 5.3. Lloyd Anderson, Fred Beckey, Helmy Beckey, Jim Crooks, Dave Lind.

**1950 JULY** South Face. III, 5.7 A2. Bill Fix, Pete Schoening.

**1952 JUNE** North Ridge. IV, 5.6. Fred Beckey, Jack Schwabland, Don Wilde.

**1958 MAY** East Ridge. III, 5.8. Fred Beckey, Don Gordon, Ed Cooper, Joe Hieb.

**1958 JULY** Torment-Forbidden Traverse. IV–V, 5.7. Ed Cooper, Walter Sellers.

**1959 JULY** Northwest Face. IV, 5.7. Fred Beckey, Ed Cooper.

**1968 AUGUST** South Face Direct. III+, 5.8 A2. Jim Langdon, Jim McCarthy.

**1969 FEBRUARY** West Ridge, FWA. Alex Bertulis, Bill Sumner, Pete Williamson.

**1977 JULY** South Face. III+, 5.9. Jim McCarthy, Craig McKibben.

### MOUNT TORMENT (8120')

**1946 AUGUST** Southwest Face. III, 5.5. Jack Schwabland, Herb Staley.

**1958 JUNE** Northwest Ridge. III, 5.6. Tom Miller, Franz Mohling.

**1958 JULY** South Ridge. II+, 5.5. Ed Cooper, Walter Sellers.

**1960 JULY** North Ridge. III, 4th class. Ed Cooper, Jim Kurtz.

**1961 JUNE** Northwest Glacier. III. Joan Firey, Joe Firey, Tony Hovey, Don Keller.

*Forbidden Traverse from the southwest* (Photo by John Scurlock)

## ROUTE

From the south-ridge notch at 7440 feet, climb a short crack, followed by ledges down and left to an alcove below a steep gully. Climb the low-angle dihedral immediately west of the gully for 100 feet of low 5th class. The next two pitches climb up and leftward on OK rock (mid-5th class), eventually becoming 3rd class and reaching a prominent notch on the south ridge.

From this notch, ledges traverse the entire southeast face. From these ledges, 3rd- and 4th-class climbing leads quickly to the summits of Torment from about halfway across. Continue traversing the southeast-face ledges down to Torment's east ridge. The first two high points on the ridge east of Torment's summit can be passed on either side or directly: the north side is very alpine and may include snow or ice; the south side options can be fast, but they lack much of the alpine character.

The first high point east of Torment (8100 feet) can be climbed directly or bypassed. To pass on the north, make a short rappel to reach a portion of the Forbidden Glacier; from the eastern edge of the glacier, carefully find a route onto the rock, where ledges lead up and around the north side of Point 8100. To pass the point on the south, a mix of sandy ledges and 4th-class rock, descend ledges on Torment's southeast face that lead to other ledges traversing east; regain the crest just east of Point 8100.

Beyond is the classic snow traverse leading to Point 8200. Gaining Point 8200 gets you back on rock again and climbing near the ridge crest.

Beyond 8200 feet, the routefinding is straightforward, staying near the crest all the way to Forbidden. The climbing is fun—and exposed! Forbidden's west ridge is the perfect finish. The rock quality on the west ridge is some of the best in the region. The ridge steepens about halfway up with a short 5.6 step. Stay on the crest for the full experience!

## DESCENT

Follow the descent options for the preceding climb, returning to the Boston Basin Trailhead. To return to the Torment Basin approach's start, walk 2 miles down Cascade River Road.

# ELDORADO PEAK                8868'

## PROMINENCE: 2188' [28]

### EAST RIDGE, ELDORADO AND INSPIRATION GLACIERS

A very popular summit in the heart of the North Cascades, Eldorado is a great introduction to the range. This is a technically easy climb with a grand finish along the exposed and narrow summit snow ridge. As with many peaks, the approach is a big portion of the climb. And a beautiful approach it is! Ascending through old forests of hemlock, followed by silver fir and, finally, subalpine mountain hemlock, it is a quiet hike through filtered light, leading to a promise of shining peaks.

Rising from the southern edge of a huge ice sheet, Eldorado Peak is the gateway to a vast alpine area. The region is defined by expansive glaciers, moderate scrambles, and some of Washington's highest peaks, including Primus, Klawatti, Austera, Dorado Needle, and others. There is much to do here!

The Eldorado Creek approach is the most direct path to Eldorado and the surrounding peaks. There are a couple of less-traveled approach routes also worth knowing about. The Sibley Pass-Triad cross-country route from the Hidden Lake Trail is also very scenic and only a bit less direct. There are inspirational views to Marble Creek, Early Morning Spire, Dorado Needle, and the vast expanse of the McAllister and Klawatti Glaciers. To the east are Logan, Goode, Buckner, and others. To the south are the peaks of the Ptarmigan Traverse.

In addition to the route described here, there are two classic technical routes on Eldorado's western aspect above Marble Creek. The west arête offers a rock climb with a spectacular section among towers, followed by scrambling. For something different, the north couloir is a classic but conditional mixed climb. Watch for ice and mixed conditions starting in late November. This rugged side of the mountain is on full display at several roadside locations near Rockport.

### LAND MANAGER

North Cascades National Park, Marblemount Wilderness Information Center. Permit required year-round for all overnight trips within the park. Hard-sided food storage canisters required June 1–November 15 when camping in the Eldorado cross-country zone.

*The McAllister Glacier (foreground), Eldorado (left) and Dorado Needle (right) from the north* (Photo by John Roper)

## 37. EAST RIDGE, ELDORADO AND INSPIRATION GLACIERS: GRADE II

**TIME:** 1-2 days. The best season is June to September. The actual climbing route is short, with snow and glacier travel.

### APPROACH, GRADE III

On the North Cascades Highway (State Route 20) at Marblemount, drive to the east end of downtown where SR 20 turns left (north) and continue straight (east) on Cascade River Road. Immediately cross the Skagit River and drive 19 miles to a parking lot with bathroom on the right at about 2160 feet. This is a classic North Cascades approach, much of it on a steep climbers trail, with a good amount of talus and at least 3400 feet of elevation gain to the lowest tent sites, starting at about 5600 feet.

To cross the Cascade River, find the most-traveled crossing. The ranger issuing permits in Marblemount may provide current beta. Once across the river, find a path going uphill before you reach Eldorado Creek. The path on the west side of Eldorado Creek climbs steeply through forest to a dry talus field at about 4000 feet. At the top of the first talus field, a steep path through slide alder leads to more talus or snow. Locate a path along the right (east) edge of

### SELECTED HISTORY

**1933 AUGUST** East Ridge. II. Donald Blair, Norval Grigg, Arthur Wilson, Art Winder.

**1951 AUGUST** West Face. III. Dwight Baker, Pete Schoening.

**1969 AUGUST** West Arête. III, 5.7. Richard Emerson, Walter Gove.

**1981 MARCH** FWA. Don Goodman party.

**1986 OCTOBER** North Couloir. III, mixed. Dan Cauthorn, Bill Pilling.

**1988 MARCH** West Arête, FWA. Kit Lewis, Bill Liddell.

the talus. When the path fades near boulders, continue up and eventually traverse east to a stream below small waterfalls at about 5200 feet. Cross the stream and follow the switchbacks through the trees to an open basin with tent sites starting at about 5600 feet.

The way continues up slabs and steep heather to the ridge dividing Eldorado Creek from Roush Creek. Find a 3rd-class gully descending west into Roush Creek. The correct gully is identified by a large boulder just below the crest. Once in the Roush drainage, hike north over slabs and moraine toward the southeast edge of the Eldorado

*With views to the southeast, Mark Bunker enjoys the Eldorado area on skis. Visible behind him are (left to right) Goode, Buckner, Forbidden, Boston, and Sahale, with Torment below Boston.* (Photo by Colin Haley)

*Eldorado Peak from the northwest* (Photo by John Scurlock)

Glacier. Slog the glacier to a flat area at 7500 feet and continue north to the base of Eldorado's east ridge and several small bivy sites at 7800 feet. Additional sites are a bit higher.

## ROUTE

From bivy sites near the base of Eldorado's east ridge, begin on the north side of the ridge along the southern edge of Inspiration Glacier. Snow followed by scree or more snow leads to the final snow slope at about 8400 feet. Climb to the narrow, exciting, and very exposed snow arête and follow it south to the summit rocks.

## DESCENT

Descend the climbing route.

*Eldorado Peak from the northeast* (Photo by John Scurlock)

# SKAGIT AREA/STATE ROUTE 20

## SNOWFIELD PEAK        8347'

### PROMINENCE: 2907' [87]

**NEVE GLACIER**

Snowfield is the highest of a small group of peaks surrounding the Neve and Colonial Glaciers and immediately south of Diablo Lake. The Neve is a significant North Cascades glacier with lobes flowing both east (Neve Creek) and west (Ladder Creek). The Colonial Glacier is insignificant, but the waterfalls above and below the glacier are spectacular.

A long, high ridge extends east from Snowfield Peak with seldom-climbed subsidiary summits, including the Distal Phalanx (7615 feet), Mantis Peak (7614 feet), and Styloid Peak (6972 feet). More popular and accessible are the peaks closely west and north, including the Horseman (8080 feet), the Horseman's Pack (8152), the Needle (8040 feet), Cats Ear (7560 feet), Colonial Peak (7771 feet), Paul Bunyans Stump (7480 feet), Pinnacle Peak (7360 feet), and Pyramid Peak (7182 feet).

Despite close proximity to the highway, Snowfield is hidden behind Colonial and Pyramid Peaks. Both Colonial and Pyramid have impressive alpine faces. That they are fully on display from the highway makes them difficult to ignore. These are serious alpine faces, usually climbed in winter, and they have great history. The variables of winter mixed climbing guarantee adventure every time.

Fun fact: Colonial Creek Falls is the fifteenth-highest waterfall in the world, second-highest in North America, and possibly the highest waterfall in the continental United States. While up close Colonial Creek Falls is fairly impressive, this is not a globally significant waterfall by any metric other than height. It's visible from the North Cascades Highway—look for it.

**LAND MANAGER**

North Cascades National Park, Marblemount Wilderness Information Center. Permit required year-round for all overnight trips within the park.

## 38. NEVE GLACIER: GRADE II, 3RD CLASS

**TIME:** 2 days. Except in early season, the route will be dry between Pyramid Lake and the Colonial Glacier. This classic and straightforward glacier climb has a notorious approach. The broad Neve Glacier is ringed with a number of attractive rock summits in addition to Snowfield itself. Summit views to the south of the McAllister Cirque and Austera Towers region are exceptional.

### SELECTED HISTORY

**SNOWFIELD PEAK**

**1931 AUGUST** Neve Glacier. II. William Degenhardt, Herbert Strandberg.

**1979 MARCH** FWA. Joe Catelani, Al McGuire, Kurt Hanson.

**COLONIAL PEAK**

**1931 JULY** West Ridge. II. William Degenhardt, Herbert Strandberg.

**1968 JULY** East Ridge, Northeast Gully. III, 5.3. Dallas Kloke, Scott Masonholder.

**1973 JUNE** Northwest Face. III, 5.6. Dallas Kloke, Bryce Simon.

**1986 FEBRUARY** North Face. IV. Mark Bebie, John Stoddard, Mark Twight, Monte Westlund.

**PYRAMID PEAK**

**1931 JULY** II. William Degenhardt, Herbert Strandberg.

**1987 MARCH** North Face. III, WI 3. Bob Cotter, Jim Ruch.

**2003 FEBRUARY** East Face. III+. Coley Gentzel, Chris Koziarz, Robert Rogoz.

**2010 FEBRUARY** Northeast Face. III+, WI 5 A0. Rolf Larson, Wayne Wallace.

**CATS EAR**

**1979 MARCH** FWA. Joe Catelani, Al McGuire, Kurt Hanson.

**1982 SEPTEMBER** East Buttress. II, 5.7. Anton Karuza, Reece Martin.

*Snowfield Peak from the north* (Photo by John Scurlock)

## APPROACH, GRADE III

On the North Cascades Highway (State Route 20) at Marblemount, continue east for 23 miles to the Pyramid Lake Trailhead (1150 feet), 1 mile or less east of the Gorge Lake Bridge. About 2 miles on trail, followed by a steep and rough climbers trail, with 4900 feet of elevation gain to Colonial Glacier campsites at 6000 feet.

Hike the Pyramid Lake Trail about 2 miles to Pyramid Lake. From the south side of the small lake, find the unmaintained climbers path.

This path leads to a bench on the forested ridgeline at about 4350 feet. Point 4555 feet can be passed to the west and is followed by a couple of brushy 3rd-class steps once back on the ridge. Follow the ridge nearly to the base of Pyramid Peak at about 5800 feet, and traverse south to campsites near a new lake created by the melting Colonial Glacier.

## ROUTE

Ascend the Colonial Glacier south to the pass immediately west of Point 7505. This pass at 6850 feet leading to the Neve Glacier is also an alternate campsite. From the pass, a short descent of about 200 feet reaches the Neve Glacier. Ascend the glacier, gaining the west ridge of Snowfield at about 7750 feet. Find a gully leading to a notch, followed by a short down-climb. Third-class scrambling leads to the top.

## DESCENT

Down-climb the ascent route.

# BACON PEAK                    7061'

## PROMINENCE: 2501'

### DIOBSUD GLACIER

One of a group of peaks south of the Baker River and west of the Pickets, Bacon is a gentle nontechnical peak composed of Shuksan Metamorphic Suite with massive sprawling glaciers on three sides: the Noisy Creek Glacier on the northwest, the Green Lake Glacier on the north, and the Diobsud Glacier on the east. The mountain is often climbed as part of a multiday traverse from either the south or north with Bacon Peak closer to the southern end. The most popular entry-exit points into the area are the Anderson Butte Trailhead (south) or the Baker River Trailhead (north).

Shorter are two routes from the depths of Bacon Creek from the east. The first was pioneered in the '60s by members of the Trail Blazers, a highly successful fish-stocking club, who followed the "porkbelly" ridge between the east

and west forks of Bacon Creek. The second route was blazed by Steph Abegg and Tom Sjolseth in 2012. Both "shortcut" routes from Bacon Creek are brutal and seldom traveled. This is classic North Cascades country of virgin forests, mountain lakes, glacier-adorned peaks, and no hiking trails.

### LAND MANAGER

North Cascades National Park, Marblemount Wilderness Information Center. Permit required year-round for all overnight trips within the park.

## 39. DIOBSUD GLACIER: GRADE II

TIME: 1–2 days. This route uses a direct approach from Bacon Creek that is currently recommended as a snow climb, probably before Memorial Day. The viability of this approach as a summer route remains unknown; it may involve additional challenges once the spring snow cover is gone.

*Bacon Peak from the southeast* (Photo by John Scurlock)

*Bacon Peak from the southeast: Diosbud Glacier route* (Photo by John Scurlock)

## APPROACH, GRADE III+

On the North Cascades Highway (State Route 20) at Marblemount, continue east for 5 miles to Bacon Creek. Turn left (north) onto Forest Road 1060, following the east side of Bacon Creek north 2-3 miles, then turn left onto FR 1065 and cross to the west side of Bacon Creek. Follow FR 1065 a short way to spur FR 1064 on the right, leading north to about 1000 feet in elevation, a likely place to start. There is 3300-4700 feet of elevation gain to potential campsites near 4300 feet and 5700 feet in the upper Falls Creek drainage, plus an additional 600-700 feet of elevation gain due to up-and-down loss.

Walk the abandoned road as it switchbacks up the hill before traversing south. Leave the road at one of two spots: the first is more direct, leaving from about 1400 feet before a stream; the second follows the road to a less steep area to begin the climb. Reach a forested ridge at around 3100 feet and follow the ridge up and over a couple of bumps to its end at 4800 feet. Descend about 500 feet to a flat area with potential campsites in the Falls Creek drainage, then head southwest to a gully (rock slabs without snow) and climb it to higher campsites just below the eastern edge of the Diobsud Glacier at 5700 feet.

## ROUTE

The climb-hike to the summit via the Diobsud Glacier is a straightforward glacier walk without obstacles. Views north to Mount Shuksan and east toward the Pickets include some of the least-traveled valleys and ridges of the North Cascades. Mount Baker graces the view west.

## DESCENT

Descend the climbing route.

## SELECTED HISTORY

Without technical challenges, the mountain has very little recorded climbing history. An International Boundary party was in the area in 1905 and very likely explored Bacon Peak.

*Mount Triumph from the south as the day dawns: the northeast ridge is the right skyline.* **(Photo by Steph Abegg)**

# MOUNT TRIUMPH 7240'

## PROMINENCE: 1720'

### NORTHEAST RIDGE

A very significant and commanding peak despite its modest height, Mount Triumph is a classic granodiorite Chilliwack Batholith horn, much like Forbidden, with steep faces between three prominent ridges meeting at the summit. Triumph offers a nice variety of alpine rock climbs, as well as the original scramble route first climbed in 1938. Joan Firey, one of the northeast ridge first-ascent party, reported in the 1966 *Mountaineer Annual*: "It proved to be a classic alpine ridge offering a fine variety of class three and four climbing and a few safety pitons." The east and north faces are particularly notable, with both offering challenging alpine rock climbs. The northeast ridge splits these two faces, providing a perfect moderate route.

Both Triumph and close neighbor Mount Despair offer tantalizing views of the Picket Range across Goodell Creek. The creek's headwaters include the northern aspects of Mount Triumph and Mount Despair, the southern aspects of Mount Fury and Mount Terror, and much more. From valley bottom to ridgetop, these are among the most rugged cirque walls in the range.

In the early part of the twentieth century, the famous North Cascades surveyor, Lage Wernstedt, was clearly impressed with the mountains in this part of the Cascades. It was Lage who bestowed the names Triumph, Despair, Fury, Terror, and Challenger to some of the most notable mountains.

## LAND MANAGER

North Cascades National Park, Marblemount Wilderness Information Center. Permit required year-round for all overnight trips within the park.

*Rolf Larson enjoys some great climbing on Mount Triumph's east face.* (Photo by Eric Wehrly)

# 40. NORTHEAST RIDGE: GRADE III, 5.7

**TIME:** 2 days. **GEAR:** small rack to 3½ inches. The ridge has more vegetation than higher peaks, but the rock is mostly good. The climb is a combination of scrambling and mid-5th-class climbing, some of it quite exposed.

## APPROACH, GRADE III

On the North Cascades Highway (State Route 20) at Marblemount, continue east approximately 11 miles and turn left (north) onto Thornton Lakes Road. The road is in poor condition and not good for low-clearance vehicles. Follow it 5 miles to the Thornton Lakes Trailhead at about 2700 feet. There are 5.3 miles of trail, a steep scramble, and 3900 feet of elevation gain to reach the 5760-foot col above Thornton Lakes.

The Thornton Lakes Trail traverses above Thornton Creek on a former logging road, then climbs to tree line through old-growth forest. At 5100 feet the trail crests a ridge with views of Triumph and the way ahead. The trail then descends 500 feet to designated campsites at the lowest of the three Thornton Lakes and continues to the middle lake at 4700 feet.

From the northwest end of the middle lake, the route to the 5840+-foot col is steep and scrappy, with talus, 3rd-class slabs, and a few bushes. There are several bivy sites at the col and a few more near Triumph's unnamed eastern glacier, all with amazing views of both the Crescent Creek and Terror Creek Cirques.

## ROUTE

From bivy sites near the 5840+-foot col, traverse slabs leading to the snowfield below the steep east face. This snowfield is mostly gone by late season but may stick around for a few years yet. From the north end of the snowfield, 4th-class slabs, ledges, and scree lead to the ridge crest at a low notch estimated to be at 6100 feet. (From this notch, a route leads to the 1987 North Face/Rib route.)

The lower section of the northeast ridge has a couple of short steps but is otherwise 3rd class. Where the ridge narrows, exposed low 5th class leads past two small towers. Beyond the narrow section, the ridge steepens, leading to a steep wall considered the crux. Several options exist, but

*Mount Triumph from the north: (A) Northeast Ridge, (B) North Face/Rib* (Photo by John Scurlock)

climbing the wide crack (5.7) and corner above is popular; farther north is about 5.6. Another pitch of mid-5th class leads to a major notch. From the notch either climb direct or find an exposed trail traversing south, leading to 3rd-class heather and the top.

**DESCENT**

Descending the route with a combination of 100-foot (30m) rappels and down-climbing is the most popular option. Certainly, the original scramble route and south ridge are reasonable options, depending on strategy.

## SELECTED HISTORY

**1938 JULY**   West route. II, 4th class. Lloyd Anderson, Lyman Boyer, Dave Lind, Sigurd Hall.

**1965 AUGUST**   Northeast Ridge. III, 5.6. Natalie Cole, Joan Firey, Joe Firey, Frank Tarver.

**1969 JULY**   Northwest Ridge. II, 5.3. Joan Firey, Joe Firey, Peter Renz, Frank Tarver.

**1972 JULY**   South Ridge. II+, 5.6. Lou Dangles, Doug Martin, John Streich, Bill Sumner.

**1981 AUGUST**   North Face, Central Rib. V, 5.10. Bob Crawford, Pete Doorish.

**1985 AUGUST**   East Face. III, 5.9. Alex Cudkowicz, Pete Doorish.

**1985 AUGUST**   North Face, Eastern Rib. IV, 5.6. Alex Cudkowicz, Pete Doorish.

**1986 MARCH**   West route, FWA. Mark Bebie, Lowell Skoog, Brian Sullivan.

**1987 JULY**   North Face/Rib, west start. V, 5.10. Bryan Burdo, Yann Marrand.

**2005 FEBRUARY**   Northeast Ridge, FWA. Dan Aylward, Colin Haley.

**2015 AUGUST**   East Face, *Memento Mori*, Tom Thomas Route. IV, 5.9+. Rolf Larson, Eric Wehrly.

# THE PICKET RANGE

North of the Skagit River the North Cascades crest becomes a sharp ridgeline for 7 miles. This is the Picket Range, twenty-five or thirty summits rising above a narrow ridge remarkably constant in height. The ridge supports nine magnificent glacier-carved cirques and can be considered the culmination of the range. The area is known for its serious alpine climbing objectives, as well as for the spectacular traverses linking these rugged alpine cirques.

## WESTERN ACCESS POINTS AND HIGH ROUTES

**A. GOODELL CREEK-TERROR CREEK:** southern access to Terror Creek Cirque (aka Terror Basin).

**B. TERROR CREEK CIRQUE:** From the east end of Terror Basin, a high traverse of Stetattle Creek Cirque provides access to the southern end of McMillan Creek Cirque. This is a good but technical route that may include rappelling. Exiting Terror Basin to the west from Mount Degenhardt requires navigating a long cliff band known as the Barrier that can be crossed high from the upper west end of the Terror Glacier at about 7500 feet or low from below the west end of the Terror Glacier at about 6100 feet; for the lower crossing, ledges lead west into a gully, followed by more exposed traversing west and up, gaining the Barrier's top at about 6300 feet. Both high and low crossings involve very exposed 3rd-class climbing and are more difficult to navigate from above (west to east) than from below (east to west); this is especially true for the lower crossing. This high traverse begins closely below Little Mac Spire at about 7200 feet and traverses exposed ledges at 7000 feet to reach Stetattle Ridge, which is then descended to the 6320-foot col, giving access to the east end of McMillan Cirque.

**C. GOODELL CREEK-STUMP HOLLOW:** southern access to Crescent Creek Cirque.

**D. THORNTON CREEK-TRIUMPH PASS-JASPER PASS-PIONEER RIDGE:** southwest access to Pickell Pass, which connects Goodell Creek Cirque with the *Picket Creek* Cirque.

**E. BACON CREEK-BERDEEN LAKE-MYSTERY RIDGE:** southwest access to Jasper Pass-Pioneer Ridge and Pickell Pass.

**F. BACON PEAK-GREEN LAKE-BERDEEN LAKE:** one approach through the rugged area west of the Pickets.

*Tom Sjolseth on Pioneer Peak with the Trail Blazer Cliff Lawson Memorial Summit Register placed by Dan Sjolseth in 2003; the Northern Pickets are in the background.* (Photo by Steph Abegg)

**G. BAKER RIVER-BLUM LAKES-MYSTERY RIDGE:** western access to Jasper Pass-Pioneer Ridge and Pickell Pass.

**H. RUTH CREEK-HANNEGAN PASS-EASY RIDGE:** western access to Perfect Pass, which connects the Baker River Cirque with the Little Beaver-Challenger Glacier Cirque.

## EASTERN ACCESS POINTS AND HIGH ROUTES
**I. SOURDOUGH RIDGE-ELEPHANT BUTTE:** eastern access to the south end of McMillan Creek Cirque.

**J. BIG BEAVER-ACCESS CREEK:** eastern access to Mount Fury, the southern end of Luna Cirque, or Picket Pass. From Picket Pass, options include McMillan Creek Cirque to the south or Goodell Creek Cirque and Pickell Pass to the northwest.

**K. BIG BEAVER-BEAVER PASS-EILEY WILEY:** northeast access to the Challenger Glacier and either Luna Creek Cirque or Picket Creek Cirque.

**L. LITTLE BEAVER CREEK-WHATCOM PASS:** northern access to Whatcom Peak and the Challenger Glacier.

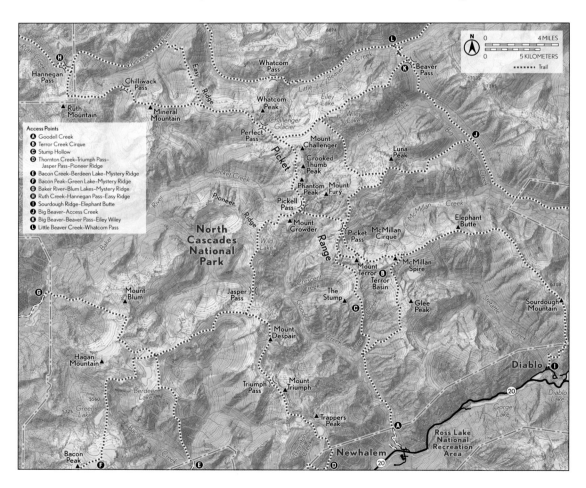

## SELECTED HISTORY

### NORTHERN PICKETS

**1936 SEPTEMBER**  Mount Challenger (8207 feet). Philip Dickert, Jack Hossack, George McGowan.

**1938 SEPTEMBER**  Mount Fury, East Peak (8280 feet). Bill Cox, Will Thompson.

**1938 SEPTEMBER**  Luna Peak (8311 feet). Bill Cox, Will Thompson.

**1940 JULY**  Crooked Thumb Peak (8124 feet). Fred Beckey, Helmy Beckey.

**1940 JULY**  Phantom Peak (8000 feet). Fred Beckey, Helmy Beckey.

**1958 AUGUST**  Mount Fury, West Peak (8292 feet). Vic Josendal, Maury Muzzy, Phil Sharpe, Warren Spickard, Roe (Duke) Watson.

**1962 JULY**  Mount Fury, Southeast Peak (7757 feet). Don Keller, Irene Meuleman.

**1962 AUGUST**  Mount Crowder (7082 feet). Jack Ardussi, Cal Magnusson, Don Mech, Don Schmechel.

**1968 JULY**  Swiss Peak (7988 feet). Andy Carson, Martin Epp, Ernst von Allman.

**1970 JULY**  Ghost Peak (8000+ feet). Carla Firey, Joan Firey, David Knudson, Peter Renz.

**1980 JULY**  Spectre Peak (7999 feet). Peter Jewett, Stuart Ferguson, John Roper, Reed Tindall.

**1989 DECEMBER**  Luna Peak, FWA. Jim Burcroff, Russ Kroeker, Paul Michelson, John Roper, Silas Wild.

**2005 JULY**  Fury-Challenger Traverse. V, 5.7. Josh Kaplan, Wayne Wallace.

**2013 JULY**  Little Mac–Challenger Traverse. VI, 5.10. Jens Holsten, Chad Kellogg.

*The Northern Pickets and the amazing Goodell Creek valley. Sean Martin near the summit of Mount Despair on day 3 of an 8-day Pickets Traverse beginning at the Thornton Lakes Trailhead, and finishing at Ross Lake via Big Beaver. Visible behind him are: Whatcom Peak (1), West Challenger (2), Middle Challenger (3) Mount Challenger #2 (4), Mount Challenger #1 (5), Crooked Thumb (6), Phantom Peak (7), Cub Scout Salute (8), Apparition & Spectre Peak (9), Swiss Peak (10), Mount Fury, West Peak (11), Mount Fury, East Peak (12), Luna Peak (13). (Photo by Tom Sjolseth)*

# THE PICKETS

## PICKET FENCE TRAVERSE (14 SUMMITS)

Nearly 3 miles long and named for the strong resemblance to a picket fence, this sharply serrated ridgeline of about twenty major and minor peaks and towers of Skagit and biotite gneiss spans the entire Terror Creek and Crescent Creek Cirques on the south and McMillan Creek Cirque on the north, each peak challenging and a worthy objective individually.

The eastern third of the traverse climbs above Terror Basin, which confusingly does not include Mount Terror: Terror sits on the ridge above Crescent Creek Basin farther west. The Terror Creek Cirque includes six peaks: three McMillans, Inspiration, and the Strandberg Pyramid. Mount Degenhardt shares both southern cirques, with its southern footings separating Terror Basin from Crescent Creek Basin. Degenhardt's northern footings also descend to a low elevation, nearly dividing the McMillan Cirque in two.

When describing the peaks in the Terror Basin, Herbert Strandberg reported in 1932 that "these peaks seem to have only two dimensions; width and height. These would offer most difficult climbing, in fact we might, without much danger of contradiction, say that these peaks are impossible to climb."

An obvious and intriguing line, the ridgetop traverse of the Southern Pickets is likely the longest technical rock climb in the North Cascades. It's doubtful that the first-ascent party was the first to consider such an obvious challenge. Wayne Wallace (www.waynewallace.wordpress.com) wondered, "Is it possible to find a world-class climbing adventure here in the North Cascades? I decided the trick was to be creative, pursuing link-ups, traverses, and other variations on the enchainment theme enabling grand tours along summits all day—or all week!"

The first traverse was done in a bold lightweight style, with everything in the pack carefully considered and debated. The challenge of the many unknowns provided opportunity for

*Southern Pickets above McMillan Cirque from the northeast: (1) Little Mac Spire, (2) east McMillan Spire, (3) West McMillan Spire, (4) Inspiration, (5) Strandberg Pyramid, (6) Mount Degenhardt, (7) Mount Terror, (8) The Blob, (9) East. Twin Needle, (10) West Twin Needle, (11) Himmelgeister Horn, (12) Ottohorn, (13) Frenzel Spitz. Climbs from the McMillan Cirque are among the finest alpine climbs in the Cascades. (Photo by John Scurlock)*

a mostly beta-free climb, an experience still available in the North Cascades.

## LAND MANAGER

North Cascades National Park, Marblemount Wilderness Information Center. Permit required year-round for all overnight trips within the park.

# 41. PICKET FENCE TRAVERSE (14 SUMMITS): GRADE VI, 5.10

**TIME:** 4-5 days. **GEAR:** small rack to 3 inches. Because retreat is a relatively short affair from pretty much anywhere along the route, the commitment factor is low considering the length for a full traverse. Importance of finding snow patches for water suggests early summer rather than later. While there is no shortage of bivy sites, a few stand out. The best sites have snow close by for water and a flat space large enough for a small tent.

The first-ascent party climbed fourteen primary peaks plus a number of smaller summits and pinnacles, including the Blip and Dusseldorferspitz. New ground climbed on the first traverse included the east ridges of the Blob, East Twin Needle, and Himmelgeister Horn. This section holds the most exhilarating climbing, as well as the most difficult pitches. Expect lots of very exposed climbing on mostly good rock, but ranging from very good to poor.

## APPROACH, GRADE III+

On the North Cascades Highway (State Route 20) at Marblemount, continue east for 15 miles to the west end of Newhalem (milepost 120) and turn north directly across from Goodell Creek Campground. Drive north about 1 mile to the south end of Upper Goodell Creek Campground and a small pullout at 600 feet.

Follow the unmarked Goodell Creek Trail on an overgrown logging road 3.5 miles to just before Terror Creek at about 1650 feet, where there is a small campsite and the start of the well-worn path to Terror Basin. Expect this approach to be dry beyond the Goodell Creek Trail after about midsummer. This well-traveled route to Terror Basin is considered a "short" Pickets approach with 3.5 miles of trail, a climbers path, and 5600 feet of elevation gain.

*Wayne Wallace (with pack) leading on the East Twin Needle on day three of the Picket Fence Traverse* (Photo by Mark Bunker)

From the Goodell Creek Trail campsite, a well-traveled climbers path climbs steeply east through open forest much of the way. Beyond about 4000 feet, the path makes short traverses north as necessary to pass cliffy areas. Breaking out of the forest around 4800 feet, the way continues up, traversing north and connecting heather benches. Ascend and traverse to about 6200 feet, where a crossing of the west ridge of Glee Peak (7160 feet) can be made. A steep descent north (scree or snow) reaches a large flat camping area in Terror Basin at 5800 feet.

## ROUTE

With most of the east ridges being steeper than the west, the first-ascent party made their traverse from east to west starting with **LITTLE MAC SPIRE:** From the 5800-foot camping area, reach Little Mac on a high traverse at about 6200 feet. The south-face route follows ledges and a 5th-class ramp, followed by two pitches through a steeper section (5.7–5.8) and finishing with a 4th-class gully. Descend with a 100-foot (30m) rappel.

**EAST MCMILLAN SPIRE:** From the Little Mac–East Mac Col, follow 4th-class with short 5th-class sections to the crest of the east ridge. Ascend mid-5th class up the south-face summit block, finishing on the ridge. Descend west on 3rd class.

**WEST MCMILLAN SPIRE:** Pass a gendarme on the north and descend a bit across the southeast face to a 4th-class section onto the southeast face. Ledges connected with 5th-class sections up to about 5.7; climb the face, finishing on the left. Descend 3rd-class terrain west. A bivy site on the West McMillan–Inspiration Towers Col likely has snow.

**INSPIRATION PEAK:** The ridge narrows with five small towers before reaching Inspiration's classic east ridge. The first tower can be climbed directly, and the other four can be navigated around with minimal 5th class. The east ridge, first climbed in 1958, delivers three exposed pitches up to 5.9. Pitch 3 climbs a hand crack (5.9), avoiding the wide crack to its right. Descend west with up to a half dozen short rappels.

**PYRAMID PEAK:** 3rd-class terrain leads to a notch below Strandberg Pyramid's east ridge/face, where three pitches up to 5.8 ascend to the top. Pitch 2 climbs a short chimney to the right of a roof. Descent is 3rd class.

**MOUNT DEGENHARDT:** Climb a gully, finishing with 4th class. Descent includes a rappel. Continue west on the south side of the ridge.

*Colin Haley, Mark Bunker, and Wayne Wallace on top of the Frenzel Spitz at the west end of the Southern Pickets; in three days they climbed thirteen peaks along the Picket Fence ridge line. On their way out, they climbed The Stump as well, for a total of fourteen peaks.* (Photo by Mark Bunker)

# SELECTED HISTORY

## SOUTHERN PICKETS

**1931 AUGUST** Mount Degenhardt (8000+ feet). William Degenhardt, Herbert Strandberg.

**1932 AUGUST** The Stump (6819 feet). William Degenhardt, Herbert Strandberg.

**1932 AUGUST** West Peak (7000+ feet). William Degenhardt, James Martin, Herbert Strandberg.

**1932 AUGUST** West Twin Needle (7936 feet). William Degenhardt, James Martin, Herbert Strandberg.

**1932 AUGUST** Mount Terror (8151 feet). William Degenhardt, James Martin, Herbert Strandberg.

**1940 AUGUST** Inspiration Peak (7880+ feet). Fred Beckey, Helmy Beckey.

**1940 AUGUST** West McMillan Spire (8000+ feet). Fred Beckey, Helmy Beckey.

**1951 JUNE** East McMillan Spire (7992 feet). David Collins, Don Gordon, Paul Salness.

**1951 JUNE** The Strandberg Pyramid (7960+ feet). David Collins, Don Gordon, Paul Salness.

**1951 SEPTEMBER** The Blob (7840+ feet). Pete Schoening, Philip Sharpe.

**1961 SEPTEMBER** Himmelgeister Horn (7880+ feet). Ed Cooper, Glen Denny, Joan Firey, Joe Firey, George Whitmore.

**1961 SEPTEMBER** Dusseldorferspitz (east of Himmelgeister). Ed Cooper, Glen Denny.

**1961 SEPTEMBER** Ottohorn (7840+ feet). Ed Cooper, Glen Denny, Joan Firey, Joe Firey, George Whitmore.

**1961 SEPTEMBER** Frenzel Spitz (7440+ feet). Ed Cooper, Glen Denny, Joan Firey, Joe Firey, George Whitmore.

**1968 JULY** East Twin Needle (7840 feet). Larry Clark, Joan Firey, Joe Firey, Peter Renz.

**1969 JUNE** Little Mac Spire (7600 feet). Mike Heath, Bill Sumner.

**1973 JULY** The Blip. Jim Lucke, Gary Mellom, John Roper.

**1976 MARCH** West McMillan Spire, FWA. Mike Colpitt, Jaerl Secher-Jensen.

**1981 MARCH** East McMillan Spire, FWA. Rick Nolting, Dane Waterman.

**1984 JULY** The Turret (easternmost summit of the Blob). Russ Kroeker, John Roper, Silas Wild.

**1994 JANUARY** Mount Degenhardt, FWA. Dave Creeden, Sam Grubenhoff, Silas Wild.

**2003 FEBRUARY** Inspiration Peak, FWA. Colin Haley, Forrest Murphy.

**2003 JULY** Little Mac–Frenzel Spitz Traverse. Mark Bunker, Colin Haley, Wayne Wallace.

**2004 FEBRUARY** The Stump, FWA. Colin Haley.

**2017 JULY** Honk (west of Beep). Mark Bunker.

**2017 JULY** Beep (west of Ottohorn). Keith Luther, Seth Pollack.

**MOUNT TERROR:** A bivy site below the east ridge of Terror likely holds snow. Terror's east ridge, more face than ridge, can be climbed in three pitches. The first pitch begins with twin cracks above a ledge, the crux pitch (5.8+). Descent includes rappels of the summit structure, followed by scrambling, followed by two rappels to the Terror-Blob Col.

**THE BLOB:** A marvelous peak with many intriguing routes in addition to the ridgetop traverse. Its south buttress (IV, 5.10) was climbed in 2006 by Mike Layton and Erik Wolfe. The west summit has space for a bivy close to a snow patch that generally remains through midsummer. From the Terror-Blob Col, make a loose descent south to a chossy 4th-class gully leading around to the south side of the east face. Climb four to five pitches (up to 5.8) to the notch on the west side of the first tower. From the notch, the route follows on or near the ridgetop westward. The easiest way to reach the higher east summit is to traverse onto the south side of the ridge. From the east summit, a rappel followed by one short pitch (up to 5.8) reaches the Blob's lower (west) summit. The descent is 3rd class; pass the Blip and continue to the first Twin Needle.

**EAST TWIN NEEDLE:** Climb the southeast ridge in three pitches, two at 5.8, followed by the airy summit pitch that moves left under an overhang (5.10). Descend via 4th class that leads to a 100-foot (30m) rappel.

*Southern Pickets peaks of Crescent Creek Cirque from the west: Honk (1), Frenzel Spitz (2) Ottohorn (3), Himmelgeister Horn (4), West Twin Needle (5), East Twin Needle (6), West Blob (7), The Blob (8), Mount Terror (9)* **(Photo by John Scurlock)**

**WEST TWIN NEEDLE:** Traverse across the southeast face (3rd class). Descend west via 3rd class.

**HIMMELGEISTER HORN:** Four pitches are on or near the east ridge crest. Pitch 2 climbs to the right of the ridge crest with face climbing and small gear (5.10). Pitch 3 passes the Dusseldorferspitz tower. Descent begins with a rappel or scramble, followed by four or five 100-foot (30m) or less rappels to the Himmelgeister Horn-Ottohorn Col.

**OTTOHORN:** Climb it on 3rd-class terrain.

**FRENZEL SPITZ:** While the first ascent was made after descending to the Mustard Glacier, it is also possible to make a scrappy traverse from the Himmel-Otto Col across the north side of Ottohorn to reach the southwest ridge of Frenzel Spitz. Three pitches (5.4, 5.7, 5.8) follow the southwest ridge.

## DESCENT

The descent route depends on where the traverse is finished. If finishing with Ottohorn and Frenzel Spitz, descend from the Ottohorn-Himmelgeister Horn Col into Crescent Creek Basin and out via Stump Hollow; see the approach for North Buttress (Climb 42) on Mount Terror. The 2003 first-ascent party climbed the Stump on their way out.

# MOUNT TERROR                          8151'

**PROMINENCE: 1911'**

## NORTH BUTTRESS

The Southern Pickets' eastern cirque is arguably one of the Cascades' greatest walls of rock and snow. When appraising the McMillan Cirque for classic climbs, several lines stand out among many: the tremendous north buttress of East McMillan Spire on the east end and, dead center, the Skagit gneiss north buttress of Mount Terror.

In the late 1950s, when several summits in the Picket Range were still unclimbed, any climb from McMillan Cirque would be new territory. In 1961, following a strenuous approach via Stetattle Creek, a party of four found themselves on the Degenhardt Glacier below the north buttress of Mount Terror. Being the first team to consider a climb from the cirque, they also chose one of the most daunting lines.

Ed Cooper recounted the experience in the 1962 *Mountaineer Annual*: "We found the climbing enjoyable beyond description. Steep weathered granite offered excellent firm holds and we made rapid progress, for the most part unroped, until we found a fair bivouac halfway up the face. We anchored in with pitons for an airy night far above the glaciers, and reached the summit early the next morning having encountered only one class 5 pitch."

In the following seventy years of exploration, most of the major features were climbed; there are a dozen classic routes, all serious climbs, all classic North Cascades to be enjoyed. With the exception of Mount Terror itself, climbs from the McMillan Cirque are rare and beta is scarce.

*Mike Swayne, Ed Cooper, and Charlie Bell on top of Mount Terror, July 1961. The North Buttress of Mount Terror was the first of the great alpine climbs in the McMillan Cirque.* (Photo by Dave Hiser)

*Alan Kearney on day 3 of East McMillan Spire's Direct North Buttress, September 2008* (**Photo by Erik Johnson**)

### LAND MANAGER

North Cascades National Park, Marblemount Wilderness Information Center. Permit required year-round for all overnight trips within the park.

## 42. NORTH BUTTRESS: GRADE III, 5.7

**TIME:** 3 days. **GEAR:** small rack to 3 inches. Following a line of least resistance, the original party climbed west of the buttress crest. A mostly direct line was climbed solo by John Stoddard in 1984, as described in the 1985 *American Alpine Journal:* "After reaching the base of the original route, I traversed ledges several hundred feet left to gain the steeper, more compact left buttress. From here mid-5th-class climbing followed the clean, solid rock of the crest to a notch at one-third height. Above, a sharp prow guarded by overhangs on both sides blocked the route, forcing a rappel down and right to ledges. I then found a route up the narrow face dividing the two buttresses, which led me back to the crest above the prow. Another long, spectacular section on the arête led to a false summit below the west peak, with difficulties to 5.7 on slightly looser rock."

### APPROACH, GRADE III+

On the North Cascades Highway (State Route 20) at Marblemount, continue east for 15 miles to the west end of Newhalem (milepost 120) and turn north directly across from Goodell Creek Campground. Drive north about 1 mile to the south end of Upper Goodell Creek Campground and a small pullout at 600 feet. This well-traveled route to Terror Basin is considered a "short" Pickets approach, with 3.5 miles of trail, a climbers path, and 6000 feet of elevation gain; expect this approach to be dry beyond the Goodell Creek Trail after about midsummer.

Follow the unmarked Goodell Creek Trail on an overgrown logging road 3.5 miles to just before Terror Creek at about 1650 feet, where there is a small campsite and the start of the well-worn path to Terror Basin.

A faint but improving path angles up toward Terror Creek, aiming for a good crossing spot at about 2000 feet. The forested slope above Terror Creek is steep and cliffy, and locating the path at the beginning is helpful. Continue generally straight up to the crest of Barrier

*Mount Terror from the northeast: North Buttress* (Photo by John Scurlock)

Ridge at about 3800 feet. Remember this spot if return-ing the same way.

Follow the brushy ridge until tree line, where open alpine slopes lead through Stump Hollow to the pass east of the Stump (Pinnacle Peak on some maps) at 6200 feet. Descend from the pass a couple hundred feet into Crescent Creek Basin, where talus and snowfields traverse the basin north to small tent sites below the south face of Mount Terror at 6330 feet.

## ROUTE

From the high campsites, traverse west across Crescent Creek Basin, finding the entrance to a narrow gully lead-ing to the Himmelgeister Horn–Ottohorn Col at 7450 feet. The gully is straightforward with snow, loose but reasonable without, and time-consuming during times of transition. From the col a rappel or two reaches the Mustard Glacier. Descend the Mustard Glacier until able to traverse east below the Twin Needles. Expect crevasses and technical challenges after about midsummer most years.

Traversing slabs below a snow patch leads to the but-tress crest a couple hundred feet above the toe. The but-tress crest steepens abruptly at a small notch at intersecting ledges. Face climbing (5.7) near the crest eliminates the rappel mentioned by Mr. Stoddard on his bold on-sight solo ascent. There are many pitches of easy climbing before more 5th-class climbing works over and around a lower summit. Scramble the terrain on the south side of the west ridge to gain the summit.

## DESCENT

From the summit, descend the south side of the west ridge, passing below the false summit. Lower-3rd-class ledges lead to a 100-foot (30m) rappel above the Blob-Terror notch. Descending the Blob-Terror gully to Crescent Creek Cirque calls for attentive care, especially when there is no snow in the gully. Careful rope management, party coordination, and several rappels are helpful in navigating this loose and narrow gully safely.

## SELECTED HISTORY

### MOUNT TERROR

**1932 AUGUST** West Ridge. II+, 4th class. William Degenhardt, James Martin, Herbert Strandberg.

**1961 JULY** North Face. III+, 5.5. Charles Bell, Ed Cooper, David Hiser, Mike Swayne.

**1970 JULY** East Ridge. II+, 5.6. Carla Firey, Joan Firey, David Knudson, Peter Renz.

**1977 FEBRUARY** West Ridge, FWA. Paul Ekman, Roy Farrel, Joan Firey, Joe Weiss.

**1984 JULY** North Buttress, Central Rib. IV, 5.7. John Stoddard.

**2013 JULY** South Rib. III, 5.9. Rolf Larson, Eric Wehrly.

### MCMILLAN CIRQUE

**1962 JULY** Mount Degenhardt, Degenhardt Glacier. III+. Joan Firey, Joe Firey, Tony Hovey, Ken Hunich, Don Keller, Irene Meulemans, John Meulemans.

**1966 JULY** West McMillan Spire, North Face. III+, 5.6. Fred Beckey, Jerry Fuller.

**1974 JULY** The Blob, North Couloir and Buttress. III+, 5.0. Carla Firey, Joe Firey, Joan Firey, David Knudson, Frank deSaussure, George Wallerstein.

**1976 SEPTEMBER** East McMillan Spire, North Face. IV, 5.7 A1. Doug McNair, Bryce Simon.

**1977 JUNE** Inspiration Peak, North Face. IV+, 5.9. Alex Bertulis, Sergei Efimov, Mark Fielding.

**1986 JUNE** The Pyramid, North Rib. IV, 5.6. Carl Skoog, Lowell Skoog.

**1986 JULY** East McMillan Spire, North Buttress. V, 5.9. Rachel Cox, Peter Keleman.

**1996 JULY** Inspiration Peak, North Buttress. IV, 5.10. Dana Hagin, Alan Kearney.

**2008 SEPTEMBER** East McMillan Spire, Direct North Buttress. V, 5.10. Erik Johnson, Alan Kearney.

# TWIN NEEDLES      7936'

## PROMINENCE: 616'

### THREAD OF ICE

West Twin Needle (the higher summit) and East Twin Needle (7840 feet) are but two of the many summits along the great Southern Pickets ridgeline. Easily over-looked, they show fierce, classic needlelike profiles when viewed from both the north and southeast. The twin gneiss buttresses at the north end of the great McMillan Cirque call out.

The elegant eastern buttress, attempted and still unsolved, rises a good 1600 feet above the Mustard Gla-cier. John Roper, connoisseur of mountain nomenclature and prolific climber of unclimbed summits, termed it *Thread of Gneiss* and the adjoining snow gully *Thread of Ice*. These two enchanting lines are perhaps best viewed from Picket Pass.

*Wayne Wallace on the East Twin Needle* (Photo by Steph Abegg)

The Crescent Creek Cirque includes everything from Mount Degenhardt to Ottohorn on the main ridgeline plus a couple of outlier peaks at either end of the cirque. The main summits collectively acquired the name Crescent Creek Spires in the '60s. The outlier peaks—the Stump at the southwest end and West Peak at the northwest end—are prized for their position and views.

**LAND MANAGER**
North Cascades National Park, Marblemount Wilderness Information Center. Permit required year-round for all overnight trips within the park.

# 43. THREAD OF ICE: GRADE III, 5.8

**TIME:** 3 days. This is the slender north-facing gully located between the East and West Twin Needles. With good snow conditions, this is a moderate climb with a great alpine feel. Good snow conditions are important for any gully climb, and cool temperatures are preferred as well. While it's difficult to speculate the best season for this route, the first-ascent party found good conditions in June.

**APPROACH, GRADE III+**
Follow the approach for North Buttress (Climb 42) on Mount Terror. There is 6000 feet of elevation gain to the camp in Crescent Creek Basin at 6330 feet. Camping at the pass east of the Stump ridge before dropping into Crescent Creek Basin is also a good early-season strategy for this climb.

**ROUTE**
From the west end of Crescent Creek Basin, climb the gully leading to the Himmelgeister Horn-Ottohorn Col. The gully is mostly straightforward when snow-filled, with chock stone or moat obstacles later. Some years it melts out completely. From the col, one or two rappels are common to reach the Mustard Glacier. Descend about 1200 feet into McMillan Cirque until it's possible to traverse below Himmelgeister Horn and West Twin Needle. Enter the gully between the East and West Needles.

The gully narrows after a few hundred feet, becoming narrower and steeper for the upper half. The gully tops out at the Eye Col notch between the East and West Twin

*Steph Abegg enjoys perfect conditions on the Twin Needles'* **Thread of Ice. (Photo by Wayne Wallace)**

Needles. The climb of East Twin Needle begins a bit to the right with a 5.7 hand crack, followed by 5th-class climbing to an exposed summit. For West Twin Needle, begin a short distance below the Eye Col with an ascending traverse across the south face. The climbing is 3rd-4th class with a nice mid-5th-class finish on the west ridge.

*Twin Needles from the north: The Blob (1), East Twin Needle (2), West Twin Needle (3), Himmelgeister Horn (4), Frenzel Spitz (5), Ottohorn (6) (Photo by John Scurlock)*

## DESCENT

From either summit, return to the Eye Col's south gully. Descend the gully south into Crescent Creek Basin with a combination of down-climbing and rappels. Leave the main gully after a few hundred feet, moving into a broad gully system to the west.

### SELECTED HISTORY

**1932 AUGUST**  West Twin Needle, South Face. II+, 4th class. William Degenhardt, James Martin, Herbert Strandberg.

**1968 JULY**  West Twin Needle via Mustard Glacier. III, 5.0. Larry Clark, Joan Firey, Joe Firey, Peter Renz.

**1968 JULY**  East Twin Needle, West Ridge. II+, 5.7. Larry Clark, Joan Firey, Joe Firey, Peter Renz.

**1981 AUGUST**  West Twin Needle, Southeast Face. II+, 5.0. Russ Kroeker, John Roper.

**2009 JUNE**  North Couloir, *Thread of Ice*. III, 5.7. Steph Abegg, Wayne Wallace.

## MOUNT FURY                                    8292'

### PROMINENCE: 1280' [101]

#### EAST FURY-WEST FURY TRAVERSE

Orthogneiss Mount Fury, the showpiece of the Luna Creek Cirque, epitomizes the grand alpine wilderness of the Picket Range. Most prominent is East Fury's 3000-foot north buttress, flanked by hanging glaciers below twin snowfields merging to an elegant snow arête at the top. With a half mile of 3rd- and 4th-class climbing, the Fury traverse is time-consuming and tedious, requiring constant vigilance all the way out, and on the return. This is not the shortest route to Fury's summit, but rare views of the country west of the Pickets provide incentive.

While Fury's north and east aspects are well known, the south and west faces are more mysterious. Hidden away at the end of Goodell Creek, West Fury's southwest arête, otherwise known as Mongo Ridge, rises 4000 feet

*Prolific peak bagger Fay Pullen on West Fury with the Southern Pickets behind* (Photo by Tom Sjolseth)

in a series of towering gendarmes and sobering notches. This is one of the largest bastions of rock in the North Cascades, located in an immense cirque with several ridges of similar scale.

An alternate route to West Fury traverses the south face from Picket Pass. This route, while more straightforward, has issues too. The shortest route would be through the Himmelgeister Horn-Ottohorn Col from Crescent Creek Basin, but it would be faster only for climbers comfortable on technical terrain.

Both routes are multiday affairs. West Fury is one of the least accessible peaks in the Cascades. Because it's difficult to access and a few feet shy of making the Top 100 list, solitude is almost guaranteed here. Although only a few feet lower, East Fury sees many yearly visitors, while West Fury, a mere half mile away, sees fewer ascents.

## LAND MANAGER

North Cascades National Park, Marblemount Wilderness Information Center. Permit required year-round for all overnight trips within the park.

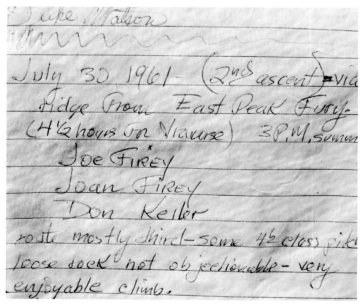

*Summit register entry on West Fury* (Photo by Tom Sjolseth)

## 44. EAST FURY-WEST FURY TRAVERSE: GRADE IV, 5.6

**TIME:** 4-5 days. Most of the climbing is 3rd-4th class with a few exposed areas of low 5th. Expect a fair bit of loose rock, but it's solid on the short 5th-class sections.

### APPROACH, GRADE IV

On the North Cascades Highway (State Route 20) at Marblemount, continue east for 38 miles to mile marker 134 (59 miles west of Winthrop) at the Ross Dam Trailhead (2120 feet). Plan on 16.5 miles of trail hiking, or 10.5 miles of trail hiking if using the water taxi to Big Beaver Landing—make prior arrangements for the water taxi with the Ross Lake Resort (see Resources).

If not using the water taxi, walk down to Ross Lake, cross the dam, and hike the Ross Dam Trail 6 miles to the Big Beaver Trail junction at Big Beaver Landing, 1600 feet.

From Big Beaver Landing, follow the Big Beaver Trail up Big Beaver Valley, passing active beaver ponds and an ancient cedar grove at about 3 miles. There are spectacular McMillan Creek views at 7 miles; reach Luna Camp at 9.5 miles. Leave the trail a little over 1 mile beyond Luna Camp, across from the Access Creek valley, at about 2500 feet.

Scout a safe place for crossing Big Beaver Creek, or have current beta from the Park Service. A good route for the lower valley is on the north side of Access Creek, then cross to the south side when it gets brushy at about 3700 feet. A faint trail leads to nice camping at the head of the valley (4350 feet). Ascend talus or snow south from the valley end, and gain Luna Peak's southeast ridge at about 5900 feet. Continue up the ridge to Point 6720 and follow a long traverse and climb to Luna Col at 7190 feet, where there are limited tent sites. Nice campsites are also available farther along the McMillan Cirque-Luna Cirque ridgeline leading to Fury.

*Mount Fury from the east* (Photo by John Scurlock)

## SELECTED HISTORY

### WEST FURY
**1958 AUGUST**  Northwest Ridge. III+. Vic Josendal, Maury Muzzy, Philip Sharpe, Warren Spickard, Roe (Duke) Watson.
**1961 JULY**  Traverse from East Fury. IV, 5.0. Joan Firey, Joe Firey, Don Keller.
**1980 JULY**  Southeast Face to East Ridge. III, 5.0. Stuart Ferguson, Peter Jewett, John Roper, Reed Tindall.
**2003 JULY**  South Face. III. Roger Jung.
**2004 FEBRUARY**  South Face, FWA. III. Roger Jung.
**2006 AUGUST**  Southwest "Mongo" Ridge. VI, 5.10. Wayne Wallace.
**2014 SEPTEMBER**  Southwest Face. III+, 5.6. Matt Aukland, Tom Sjolseth.

### EAST FURY (8280')
**1938 SEPTEMBER**  Fury Glacier. III+, 5th class. Bill Cox, Will Thompson.
**1940 JULY**  Fury Glacier, upper couloir variation. III+. Fred Beckey, Helmy Beckey.
**1958 JULY**  Southeast Glacier from Luna Lake. III. Tim Kelley, Dale Kunz, Tom Miller, Franz Mohling.
**1962 JULY**  North Buttress. IV+, 5.0. Fred Beckey, Dan Davis.
**1968 AUGUST**  Northeast Face. IV. Andy Carson, Martin Epp, Ernst von Allman.
**1980 JULY**  Fury Finger. 5.6. Stuart Ferguson, Peter Jewett, John Roper.

*Mount Fury from the southwest* (Photo by John Scurlock)

## ROUTE

From the Luna Col campsites farther west, follow on or near the McMillan Cirque–Luna Cirque ridgeline south, then west, leading to East Fury. The ridge route passes the first high point to the west and continues over several high points before leaving the ridge at a 7000-foot col. The ridge has short sections of 3rd and 4th class but is mostly much easier. Drop off the ridge south until it's possible to traverse west to Fury's Southeast Glacier at about 6400 feet. Ascend the glacier, which now has a small rock band near the top, then climb a snow slope that becomes icy before reaching East Fury's summit.

To continue to West Fury, descend East Fury's southwest slope, aiming for the East Fury–West Fury Col or below it. This slope holds snow in early summer and becomes dry later. From the col, traverse west near the ridge crest or stay below it to the south, crossing several rock ribs and gullies, on the way to West Fury's summit.

## DESCENT

Descend the climbing route.

# MOUNT CHALLENGER     8207'

## PROMINENCE: 607'

## CHALLENGER GLACIER

Anchoring the north end of the Picket Range, a massive glacier terminates the main Picket ridgeline at quartz diorite-Chilliwack Batholith Mount Challenger. The Challenger Glacier reaches nearly to Challenger's summit and stretches from Perfect Pass on the west to Wiley Ridge on the east. This broad glacial cirque lives on a high bench above the Little Beaver Valley, with an eastern lobe connecting with the Luna Cirque Glaciers. Closely west of the mountain's main peak are about a half dozen lower summits that separate the Challenger Glacier from the West Challenger Glacier. A good crossing route between these two glaciers is the 7600-foot col between West and Middle Challenger.

Challenger is a high ridgeline from which the broad Challenger Glacier flows. With great position, the main summit located at the east end of the Challenger ridge sits at the apex of three great cirques: Luna Cirque to the southeast, Picket Creek Cirque to the southwest, and the Challenger Glacier Cirque to the north. While the main peak sees the most traffic, all of Challenger's summits are nice objectives.

## LAND MANAGERS

Mount Baker-Snoqualmie National Forest, Mount Baker Ranger District; Ross Lake National Recreation Area, North Cascades National Park, Marblemount Wilderness Information Center. Northwest Forest Pass or interagency recreation pass required for parking; free self-registered wilderness permit required for day or overnight trips. North Cascades National Park, Marblemount Wilderness Information Center; permit required year-round for all overnight trips within the park.

*Mount Challenger's Main Summit and South Summit (right) from the north* (Photo by John Scurlock)

## 45. CHALLENGER GLACIER: GRADE II, 5.5

**TIME:** 3–6 days. This is a short climb with a nice finish, following a lengthy approach. The glacier travel is straightforward most of the year, but may involve technical snow or ice climbing near the summit as the glacier transitions through the summer. The final rock pitches are well protected on good rock.

### APPROACHES, GRADE IV

There are no good shortcuts to reach Challenger, and all the popular approaches require roughly the same level of time and effort.

**FROM THE EAST:** From Ross Lake to Big Beaver to Wiley Ridge is a bit more than 6000 feet of elevation gain (as well as 700 feet of loss) to the east end of the Challenger Glacier near 6700 feet. Follow the approach for Climb 44, East Fury–West Fury Traverse, to Luna Camp on the Big Beaver Trail at about 2500 feet. From Luna Camp, continue on the Big Beaver Trail another 3.5 miles to Beaver Pass at 3600 feet.

Beginning about 0.3 mile south of the Beaver Pass Shelter, ascend the forested slope and aim for the 5700-foot bench just above tree line at the east end of Wiley Ridge. Traverse steep alpine slopes on the south side of Wiley Ridge, going as low as 5600 feet to stay below cliff bands. After about 1 mile, the terrain eases considerably near

*Chad Kellogg on Mount Challenger on the eighth morning of a south to north ridgetop traverse of the Pickets* (Photo by Jens Holsten)

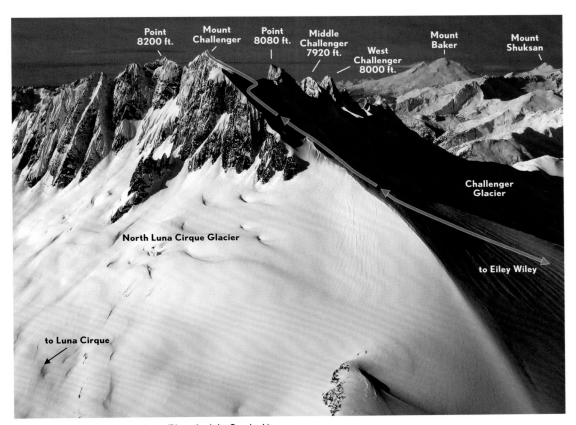

*Mount Challenger from the northeast* (Photo by John Scurlock)

meadows and ponds. There is no shortage of great camp-sites between here and the Challenger Glacier. Open terrain leads past Eiley Lake, Wiley Lake, and Point 7374 (aka Big Beaver Peak), followed by a descent to reach the east end of the Challenger Glacier at about 6720 feet. A rock island a short way up the glacier has adequate tent sites.

**FROM THE NORTH:** From Ross Lake to Little Beaver to Whatcom Pass to Perfect Pass, traversing the east side of Whatcom Peak via Whatcom Glacier, there is about 5600 feet of elevation gain and 1000 feet of loss. Follow the approach for East Fury–West Fury Traverse (Climb 44), to the Ross Dam Trailhead, and take the water taxi to Little Beaver Creek at 1600 feet—make prior arrangements for the water taxi with the Ross Lake Resort (see Resources).

Follow the Little Beaver Creek Trail for 17 miles up the creek valley to reach Whatcom Pass at 5200 feet. From above Whatcom Pass, traverse the east side of Whatcom Peak, which requires losing about 600 feet of elevation, followed by crossing rock slabs below the Whatcom Glacier and around Whatcom Peak to Perfect Pass (6280 feet) at the western edge of the Challenger Glacier. There are several tent sites at Perfect Pass, as well as higher, and also along the glacier's western edge at about 6800 feet. Another option from Whatcom Pass is to climb over the top of Whatcom Peak and down to Perfect Pass; it is more direct but also involves climbing several hundred feet of very exposed 3rd class while carrying a multiday pack.

## SELECTED HISTORY

**1936 SEPTEMBER** Challenger Glacier. II, 5.5. Philip Dickert, Jack Hossack, George McGowan.

**1961 JULY** South Ridge. II, 5.0. Joan Firey, Joe Firey, Don Keller, Tony Hovey, Frank deSaussure.

**1962 JULY** Southeast Spur. II+, 5.6. Jack Ardussi, Roger Jackson, Stan Jensen, Cal Magnusson, Steve Marts, Don Mech, Don Schmechel, Bob Swanson.

**1968 JULY** East Spur. II+, 5.6. Andy Carson, Martin Epp, Ernst von Allman.

**1977 FEBRUARY** Challenger Glacier, FWA. Jeff Davis, Dennis Mullen, Dave Tucker.

**FROM THE WEST:** From Hannegan Pass to Easy Ridge to Perfect Pass, expect 6300 feet of elevation gain and 3800 feet of loss to reach the west end of the Challenger Glacier at 6300 feet near Perfect Pass; add another 1000 feet of gain and loss if using the low crossing of the *Imperfect Impasse*. The approach begins from Interstate 5 at Bellingham; take exit 255 to the Mount Baker Highway (State Route 542) and follow it east 46 miles to Forest Road 32. Continue on FR 32 for 5.3 miles to the Hannegan Pass Trailhead at 3110 feet.

Hike the Hannegan Pass Trail No. 674 for 9 miles up and over Hannegan Pass (5066 feet) to a ford of the Chilliwack River a bit east of Easy Creek at about 2625 feet. From the river, follow the abandoned Easy Ridge Trail as it climbs to tree line, then continues along the ridge and over 6613-foot Easy Peak.

Perfect Pass appears close, but you must first make a long descent to about 5200 feet, below Whatcom Peak, to reach the infamous *Perfect Impasse*. A real routefinding challenge, this high crossing involves exposed 4th-class climbing, followed by unprotected slabs. With a good snowpack it can be possible to cross on snow; the nontechnical lower crossing of the imposing slot is 1000 feet lower. Once across the impasse, the climb to Perfect Pass (6280 feet) is straightforward. There are tent sites near Perfect Pass and also nice sites at 6800 feet on the ridge south of the pass. From Perfect Pass, access to the Challenger Glacier can be made by a traverse of steep snow (early season) or rock slabs from above the pass to the south. It is also possible to reach the glacier with a rappel or two from immediately east of the pass.

### ROUTE

Once on the Challenger Glacier, make a long traverse to the east end of the glacier. The glacier steepens near the summit, where a bergschrund can be skirted to the west or climbed through. Above the 'schrund, a short snow arête leads to a 45-foot rock pitch. Scrambling then completes the route.

### DESCENT

Descend the route, including one 45-foot (15m) rappel.

# MOUNT BAKER AREA

## LINCOLN PEAK           9080'

**PROMINENCE: 720' [16]**

Lincoln Peak, one of the Black Buttes—several glacially eroded remnants of a prior stratovolcano from the mid-Pleistocene (500,000 years ago)—is just west of the much younger current summit of Mount Baker. The steep walls of suspect andesite rock have discouraged climbing activity on the Black Buttes, with the exception of winter or winter-condition ascents.

Lincoln Peak is notorious for being the most challenging peak of Washington's 100 highest mountains with 400 feet or more of prominence. When the Bulger climbing group

*Michal Rynkiewicz nearing the summit of Lincoln Peak* (**Photo by Daniel Coltrane**)

organized their list of Washington's highest peaks, it was decided that subpeaks of volcanoes must have 800 feet of prominence to be included on their Bulger List. Omitting Lincoln Peak created a friendlier list of peaks, achievable for more people.

While the southwest face is the route used for almost all ascents, the peak's northwest face is irresistible when it is iced up. Winter conditions make sense for the Black Buttes, providing exciting opportunities for technical climbing. The area's western location and proximity to Mount Baker attract the full dose of moist Pacific storms: nearby Mount Baker Ski Area recorded 1140 inches of snow in the 1998-99 season.

## LAND MANAGER

Mount Baker Wilderness, Mount Baker-Snoqualmie National Forest, Mount Baker Ranger District. Northwest Forest Pass or interagency recreation pass required for parking. Free self-registered wilderness permit required for day and overnight trips.

## 46. NORTHWEST FACE, WILKES-BOOTH ROUTE: GRADE IV, AI 4

**TIME:** 1–2 days. Lincoln Peak was first climbed via its Southwest Face in midsummer, and the climbers reported "none of us would care to repeat the climb or to recommend it." Subsequent ascents have chosen to climb the Southwest Face route earlier in the summer in order to be on snow rather than rock. The ascent is fairly committing, requiring 2000 feet of exposed snow climbing, followed by 2000 feet of down-climbing on exposed snow. Good conditions are essential! Remarkably, the first ascent of the *Wilkes-Booth Route* was made in a strenuous one-day push.

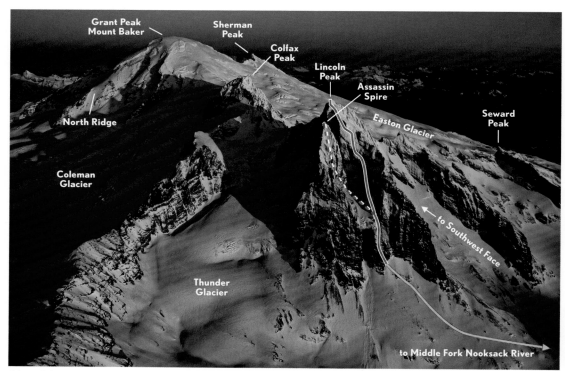

*Mount Baker and the Black Buttes from the west* (Photo by John Scurlock)

*Lincoln Peak from the west: (A) Assassin Spire route, 2010; (B)* Wilkes-Booth, *2015; (C) Southwest Face route, 1956* **(Photo by John Scurlock)**

## APPROACH, GRADE III

The southern approach from the Middle Fork of the Nooksack described here, is more direct and often used for Lincoln Peak climbs; this approach is best in early season when snowpack covers the slide alder. From the North Cascades Highway (State Route 20) at Sedro-Woolley, drive SR 9 north 14 miles to Mosquito Lake Road and follow it 9 miles to Middle Fork Nooksack River Road (Forest Road 38) on the right. Continue on FR 38 about 12 miles to just before its end at 2400 feet. There is about 3000 feet of elevation gain on the approach hike.

Walk the unmaintained, overgrown road above Rankin Creek to the road's end in an old clear-cut at about 4100 feet. Head uphill through the clear-cut and pass a couple of small lakes. There is a good camp at about 6100 feet, about 1 mile south of Lincoln Peak's west face.

**OPTION:** You can also approach from the north via the Heliotrope Ridge Trailhead (see Northwest Face, Cosley-Houston [Climb 47], on Colfax Peak). The northern approach was used by the first-ascent party, although the Nooksack approach is more often used for Lincoln Peak climbs.

## ROUTE

At the base of the peak (6400 feet), begin in a gully where two 100-foot (30m) ice pitches with vertical steps lead through the initial rock band. Easier climbing is followed by a pitch of glacier ice to reach the hanging-glacier amphitheater shared by both Assassin Spire and Lincoln Peak. Above the glacier, several ice flows form over the rock bands. The first-ascent party chose the fattest flow about midface, finding excellent ice conditions. A 230-foot (70m) pitch with

vertical steps was followed by a second pitch with less vertical. Snow climbing above the ice leads to the southwest ridge, followed by snow and rime up and over a false summit to attain a final technical pitch to the top.

## DESCENT

The southwest face, the standard route on the peak, is the logical descent route, although conditions could affect that decision. With good snow cover, the southwest side is essentially a snow climb. Once through the X-Couloir gully, a traverse south skirts the rock band at the bottom of the face. The lower rock band can also be rappelled midface where there is an ice flow in a gully.

# COLFAX PEAK 9440'

## PROMINENCE: 400' [9]

### NORTHWEST FACE, COSLEY-HOUSTON; NORTHWEST FACE, POLISH ROUTE

Colfax is the highest of the Black Buttes immediately west of Mount Baker. Remnants of ancient eruptions, these features were named by Edmund Coleman on the first ascent of Baker. Coleman was impressed with the views of Colfax and Lincoln looming in and out of the swirling clouds: "Thousands of feet above the snowfield rose on every side black, jagged, splintered precipices."

After the name of Lincoln was given to the more impressive of the two, Colfax was named for Lincoln's congressional friend and ally Schuyler Colfax. The peak's broad north

*Kathy Cosley with her '70s era "ice tools" above the crux on Colfax Peak (Photo by Mark Houston)*

face sits above the popular Coleman Glacier summit route, merging with Mount Baker at the Colfax-Baker Col. The northwest face, almost 1000 feet high, is home to several of the Cascades' finest alpine climbs.

Conditions for these climbs are ever changing, offering a unique experience every time. The difficulty grades vary widely and are given here only as a rough guideline. Despite the fickle nature of snow and ice conditions for alpine climbing, Colfax has proven to be a good bet with its high elevation and reasonable approach.

### LAND MANAGER

Mount Baker Wilderness, Mount Baker-Snoqualmie National Forest, Mount Baker Ranger District. Northwest Forest Pass or interagency recreation pass required for parking. Free self-registered wilderness permit required for day and overnight trips.

# 47. NORTHWEST FACE, COSLEY-HOUSTON: GRADE IV, WI 4

**TIME:** 1-2 days. **GEAR:** protection for both snow and ice; include some rock gear for lean conditions. Conditions vary greatly from year to year, but look for this route to be climbable from about November to May. Late autumn or during low-snowpack winters, when the trailhead access is drivable, are good times to consider this climb.

This was the first route completed on the northwest face, and while it is moderate compared to adjacent routes, it should not be underestimated. Both of the technical crux steps are very steep. Enough ice to make it climbable can form quickly, and even one strong storm can produce the magic. Early season or with lower snowpack, the ice steps tend to be longer and more technical. With a heavy snowpack, the crux steps become shorter and less difficult.

*Roger Strong enjoys running laps on the* **Cosley-Houston** *route on* **Colfax Peak.** **(Photo by Colin Haley)**

## APPROACH, GRADE II

From Interstate 5 just north of Bellingham, take exit 255 to the Mount Baker Highway (State Route 542) and drive east about 34 miles to the Glacier Public Service Center. Turn right onto Glacier Creek Road (Forest Road 39) and continue 8 miles to the Heliotrope Ridge Trailhead on the left at 3700 feet. There is 4700 feet of elevation gain on the approach hike.

Hike the Heliotrope Ridge Trail No. 677, which breaks out of the forest after about 2 miles at about 5000 feet. Reach the western portion of the Coleman Glacier at about 6200 feet and ascend the glacier southeast to the bergschrund at the bottom of the face at 8400 feet.

## ROUTE

The route starts just above the bergschrund with a low-angle ice ramp that leads to the base of the crux pillar. The pillar is short and steep before it reaches a snow gully that trends up and right. The ramp leads to another pitch of ice and more of a curtain. It's possible to pitch this route in many different ways; between two and four pitches complete the main difficulties. Above the curtain, follow the gully system up and right to a tighter exit gully, which brings you to the summit.

## DESCENT

From the summit, walk to the south, down, then left and down on the crest. Continue up and over a false summit-gendarme on its right side. Scramble down the ridge crest, then drop onto the right side of the ridge (the Deming Glacier side) via a narrow chute. From there it's easy walking to the Coleman Glacier-Deming Glacier Col at 9000 feet.

*Colfax Peak (in April 1982) from the northwest;* (A) Kimchi Suicide Volcano, (B) Polish Route, (C) Cosley-Houston, (D) Ford's Theatre (Photo by Mark Houston)

*Roger Strong on the first pitch of the* Polish Route *(Photo by Doug Hutchinson)*

## 48. NORTHWEST FACE, POLISH ROUTE: GRADE IV, WI 6

**TIME:** 1–2 days. **GEAR:** protection for both snow and ice; also include some rock gear for lean conditions. Conditions on the face vary greatly from year to year, but look for this route to be climbable from about November to May. A striking slender line of ice, this is the plumb line on the steepest part of the northwest face. The route had seen attempts, but no one had been willing to challenge a free-hanging dagger until Robert Rogoz climbed past the crux with a partner who then asked to descend. Fifteen years passed before the climb was completed to the summit for the first ascent. Five more ascents in the following months confirmed the quality of the climb, earning it a place on many to-do lists.

### APPROACH, GRADE II
Follow the approach for the preceding climb.

### ROUTE
The route starts just above the bergschrund. Conditions dictate the difficulty. Depending on conditions, cross the bergschrund and make a mixed traverse left to reach the first pitch of ice. A full pitch of WI 4 leads to a snow slope below the upper wall. The crux is the dagger above, which may connect with the lower curtain on rare occasions. The ice stays steep above the dagger, followed by another pitch of ice, before reaching the upper snow slope. More ice leads through a much shorter rock band, followed by snow to the top.

### DESCENT
Follow the descent for the preceding climb.

## SELECTED HISTORY

**1921** Colfax Peak. II. David Anderson, Clarence Fisher, Paul Hugdahl.

**1958 MAY** Northeast Face. II+. Ed Cooper, Fergus O'Conner.

**1982 APRIL** Northwest Face. III, WI 4+. Kathy Cosley, Mark Houston.

**1986 JUNE** West Ridge. III. Bob Richards, Scott Schmidt.

**2000 OCTOBER** Northwest Face, *Polish Route* (incomplete). Robert Rogoz, Piotr Kasprzycki.

**2015 JANUARY** Northwest Face, *Polish Route* (complete), FWA. III+, WI 6. Braden Downey, Will Hinckley.

**2015 APRIL** Northwest Face, *Kimchi Suicide Volcano*. III+, M5R, WI 4+. Colin Haley, Sarah Hart.

**2015 APRIL** West-Northwest Face, *Ford's Theatre*. III, WI 4+. Dana Bellows, Andrew Fabian.

# MOUNT BAKER 10,781'

**PROMINENCE: 8881' [5]**

### EASTON GLACIER; NORTH RIDGE; NORTHEAST RIDGE

Mount Baker, with its classic cone shape and flat top, is visually prominent throughout the Puget Sound region from Seattle to Vancouver, British Columbia. Snow covered year-round and only 30 miles from Bellingham Bay, Baker receives the full force of storms from the west. Annual snowfall at nearby Mount Baker Ski Area averages 641 inches and is home to the world's highest recorded annual snowfall: 1140 inches. The result is ten glaciers containing more snow and ice than all the other Cascade volcanoes combined (except Rainier).

*Sunrise on Mount Baker: looking west with the mountain's shadow cast across the Salish Sea* (Photo by Alasdair Turner)

*Descending the upper Deming Glacier, on the Coleman-Deming route on Mount Baker* (Photo by Alasdair Turner)

Currently dormant, the andesite stratovolcano has a long history of volcanic activity going back well over a million years. Earlier cones built from eruptions and lava flows have long since eroded and been carried away by ice-age glaciers. The bulk of the current Mount Baker was built up over a 20,000-year period that began about 35,000 years ago. The volcano has had significant eruptive periods as recently as the nineteenth century, and increased thermal activity in 1975-76 serves as a reminder that the current state of inactivity is historically temporary. Scientists who study the volcano's history consider it active.

The first person known to show interest in reaching the mountain's summit was an Englishman living in Victoria, British Columbia. Edmund Coleman was successful on his third try, reaching the summit from the northwest via the now-classic Coleman Glacier route. Coleman and his party used roped glacier-travel methods learned in the Alps, and his ascent was likely the first use of crampons (then called "creepers") in North America.

Today the mountain is hugely popular with outdoor enthusiasts and a great resource to the climbing community. Climbing schools and clubs find it an ideal training ground for gaining snow- and glacier-climbing experience, presenting many of the same challenges as Mount Rainier—weather, navigation, avalanches, crevasses—but without the acclimatization burden necessary for Rainier's additional height.

### LAND MANAGERS
**EASTON GLACIER ROUTE:** Mount Baker National Recreation Area and Mount Baker Wilderness, Mount Baker-Snoqualmie National Forest, Mount Baker Ranger District; **NORTH RIDGE AND NORTHEAST RIDGE ROUTES:** Mount Baker Wilderness, Mount Baker-Snoqualmie National Forest, Mount Baker Ranger District or Glacier Public Service Center. Northwest Forest Pass or interagency recreation pass required for parking. Free self-registered wilderness permit required for day and overnight trips.

# 49. EASTON GLACIER: GRADE III

**TIME:** 1–3 days. The outing is often done in two days, but with good snow conditions, one-day ascents work well too. Soft snow conditions can slow the pace significantly, as well as increase the risk of crevasse falls. A good understanding that snow conditions vary widely, both seasonally and daily, serves climbers well. This route is not really recommended as a beginner's climb; mountaineers will want enough experience to be comfortable ascending and descending on steep snow. For those with adequate experience and fitness, this is a good climb.

## APPROACH, GRADE II

On the North Cascades Highway (State Route 20) at Sedro-Woolley, drive to the Mount Baker Ranger District office, then follow SR 20 east for 16 miles and turn left (north) on the Baker Lake Highway (Forest Road 11).

Continue 12 miles and turn left on FR 12. Travel 3.6 miles to the junction with FR 13; stay right to follow FR 13 an additional 5.3 miles to the Park Butte Trailhead at 3364 feet. There is about 6000 feet of elevation gain on the approach hike.

Follow the Park Butte Trail No. 603 past the Scott Paul Trail junction in about 100 feet, staying on the Park Butte Trail through Schriebers Meadow. At 1.5 miles the trail crosses Rocky Creek, which can be challenging during periods of heavy runoff. A bit farther, the trail switchbacks up through the trees and passes a second junction with the Scott Paul Trail; keep left on the Park Butte Trail. Continue on the Park Butte Trail to reach Morovitz Meadows (4600 feet) at about 3 miles from the trailhead. At the next junction, go right on the Railroad Grade Trail No. 603.2. Designated campsites can be found at Railroad Camp (4850 feet) about 4 miles from the trailhead, High Camp (5600 feet), and Sandy Camp (5900 feet).

*Mount Baker from the southwest* (Photo by John Scurlock)

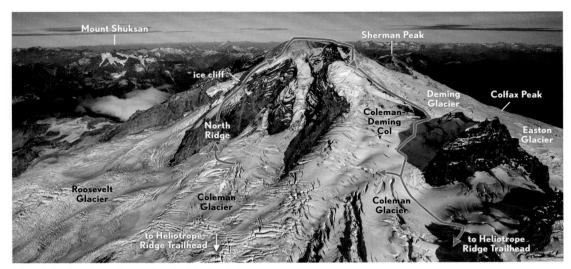

*Mount Baker from the northwest* (Photo by John Scurlock)

## ROUTE

From Sandy Camp, the route keeps west of the Easton Glacier's western moraine. The route is mostly snowfields until it reaches the glacier at around 6800 feet. As with many large glaciers, the exact route varies from year to year but generally ascends to the northeast toward Sherman Peak. Somewhere around 9400 feet, the Easton merges with the Deming Glacier and passes west of Sherman Crater, which was created when a large hydrovolcanic explosion took place in 1843. The route steepens at 10,200 feet before reaching the summit ice cap a few hundred feet higher. A trek east across the ice cap leads to the highest point, now known as Grant Peak.

## DESCENT

Descend the ascent route.

## 50. NORTH RIDGE: GRADE III⁺, AI 3

**TIME:** 1–3 days. This was the first of several classic routes on the mountain's steep northwest aspect. The approach is via Heliotrope Ridge; early explorers mistook the local valerian for the vanilla-scented heliotrope, but the name stuck. The route climbs through the upper ice cliffs at a spot least exposed to collapsing icefalls. Climbing through the ice cliff, the first-ascent party found it necessary to chop footholds, and even a few handholds, for several rope lengths on blue ice. Climbing with only one ice axe each, they used six primitive pound-in ice pitons for belays and protection.

## APPROACH, GRADE II

Follow the approach for Northwest Face, Cosley-Houston (Climb 47) on Colfax Peak, hiking the Heliotrope Ridge Trail No. 677 about 2 miles to a trail junction at about 5000 feet. Follow the right branch as it ascends the Hogsback Moraine to numerous campsites below the Coleman Glacier at around 6000 feet. The left branch also leads to the lower Coleman Glacier, but the right branch is the more common path to the Coleman-Deming summit route.

## ROUTE

The route to the north ridge leaves the Coleman-Deming route by heading to the east side of the Coleman Glacier. The original ascent gained the upper ridge crest from the east (Roosevelt Glacier) side, but starting from the western side of the ridge has become more popular.

From the Coleman Glacier flats at about 8200 feet on the west side of the north ridge, climb a 45-degree snow face to the ridge crest. The ridge crest leads to the ice cliff, where two to four pitches of ice climbing from 60 to 85 degrees depends on conditions. Above the technical section, find a way around a few crevasses to reach the summit plateau.

## DESCENT

Walk to the southwest end of the summit ice cap and descend the west side of the Deming Glacier. The upper snow-ice slope is fairly steep for several hundred feet; it's mislabeled as the "Roman Wall" on the USGS map, but the actual Roman Wall is the rock wall west of the upper Deming. Continue down the Deming or along its snow-free western edge to the Coleman-Deming Col at 9000 feet. Large crevasses generally develop through the season on the Coleman Glacier

*Mount Baker from the north* (Photo by John Scurlock)

on the north side of the saddle. Once through this section, the route traverses west below the Black Buttes and is less problematic.

## 51. NORTHEAST RIDGE: GRADE III

**TIME:** 1–3 days. This was the third route climbed on the mountain, pioneered by Mighty Joe Morovits, the jolly hermit of Baker Lake. Morovits was a self-educated miner and mountain guide who made early ascents of Mount Baker and the first ascent of Mount Shuksan. He also made accurate observations about the lahar mudflows of the mid-nineteenth century and their effects on the Boulder, Park, and Morovits Creek valleys.

Joe's ascent of the Northeast Ridge was his first of several guided climbs of Mount Baker, managed before acquiring an ice axe. When his six companions were unwilling to continue beyond Pumice Stone Pinnacle (the

Cockscomb), Joe continued to the summit by cutting foot notches in the ice with his rifle. Joe's descent was even more harrowing as he crept down backward, feeling blindly below with his toes for the indentations he'd made in icy-hard snow.

With modern climbing equipment and favorable snow conditions, the Northeast Ridge is a classic intermediate climb with a beautiful high-country approach. The adjoining Park Glacier Headwall offers classic technical ice climbing after about midsummer.

### APPROACH, GRADE III

From Interstate 5 just north of Bellingham, take exit 255 to the Mount Baker Highway (State Route 542) and drive east 34 miles to the Glacier Public Service Center. Continue driving SR 542 another 24 miles to the Artist Point Trailhead at 5100 feet. The final 3 miles beyond Heather Meadows do not open to vehicles until about July, depending on winter snowpack. There is 1100 feet of elevation gain to reach campsites below the East Portal.

Begin on the Chain Lakes Trail No. 682, and after 1 mile, turn left (south) on the Ptarmigan Ridge Trail No. 682.1. This trail traverses the northwest side of the Ptarmigan Ridge divide and loses a couple hundred feet before crossing to the southeast side of the divide in about 2 miles at 5300 feet. The trail keeps to the southeast side of the divide before merging with snowfields beyond Coleman Pinnacle at about 4.5 miles. The final rocky high points on the ridge are named the Portals: East, West, and Middle Portal. One good camping area is on the ridge just east of East Portal about 6 miles from the trailhead, at about 6000 feet. Additional campsites are found all the way to the top of the ridge dividing the Rainbow and Park Glaciers at 7000 feet.

**ROUTE**

From the 6000-foot campsite, a traverse around the north side of East Portal on the Sholes Glacier leads to the East-Middle Portal Col (6160 feet). From here, make a traversing descent south to reach the Rainbow Glacier. A traversing ascent of the Rainbow Glacier then leads to the Park Glacier at 7000 feet, where there is a nice alternate high camp. The Park Glacier steepens at about 9800 feet, where a bergschrund becomes more technical through the summer. Above the 'schrund, gain the northeast ridge just beyond the Pumice Stone Pinnacle at 9950 feet. A straightforward ridge walk leads to the top.

**DESCENT**

Descend the climbing route.

*Mount Baker from the northeast* (Photo by John Scurlock)

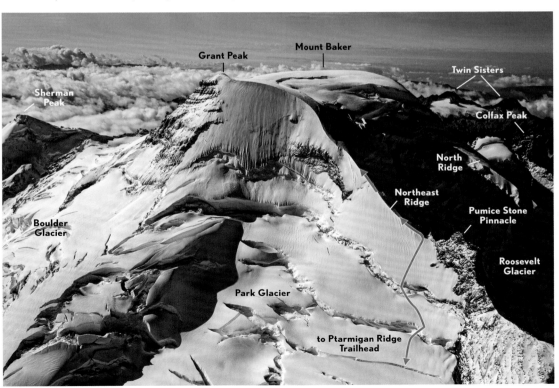

## SELECTED HISTORY

**1868 APRIL** Coleman Glacier. III. Edmund Coleman, Edward Eldridge, David Ogilvy, Thomas Stratton, John Tennant.

**1884 JUNE** Sherman Peak (10,160 feet) via Easton Glacier, FA. II+. Valentine Lowe, L. L. Bales.

**1891 AUGUST** Boulder Glacier. III. S. Bailey, Alex Beilenberg, Charles Beilenberg, J. Boen, William Lang, Sue Nevin, Robert Woods.

**1892 AUGUST** Northeast Ridge. III. Joe Morovits.

**1924 SEPTEMBER** Roosevelt Glacier. III+. Dudley Foster, Gus Fraser, Eric Fuller, Harold O'Connor, Alec Vidal, Bill Wheatley.

**1925 DECEMBER** Mount Baker, FWA. W. L. Cochran, Clarence Fisher, Louis Gilfilen, Jerry Smith.

**1948 AUGUST** North Ridge. III+. Fred Beckey, Dick Widrig, Ralph Widrig.

**1957 AUGUST** Coleman Headwall. III+. Phil Bartow, Ed Cooper, Donald Grimlund, David Nicholson.

**1958 APRIL** Coleman Headwall, western finish. III+. Les MacDonald, Henryk Mather.

**1960 JUNE** *Roman Nose*. III+. Ed Cooper, Don Ihlenfeldt, Mike Swayne, Gordon Thompson.

**1960 JULY** Northeast Ridge from west. III. Chuck Morley, John Musser, Klindt Vielbig.

**1970 JULY** Park Glacier Headwall. III+. Norman Bodine, Jim Friar, Tim Keliher.

# MOUNT SHUKSAN                9131'

## PROMINENCE: 4411' [13]

### FISHER CHIMNEYS; JAGGED RIDGE TRAVERSE

Everyone recognizes Shuksan, even if they don't know its name. The picturesque scene from Heather Meadows is seen on calendars and wall art from around the world, representing the North Cascades quite well. Fisher Chimneys is a classic intermediate route on both rock and snow, while the Jagged Ridge is a long, technical adventure where intuitive routefinding is required.

Mount Shuksan is characterized by deep cirques, ragged arêtes, and chaotic hanging glaciers. For challenging alpine terrain, no other peak covers as much real estate as Shuksan's approximately 30 square miles of mountain. The entire Northern Picket Range comes close, but for a single peak Shuksan has no equal.

Looking at a map of Shuksan reveals nearly a dozen glaciers surrounding several rocky high points. East of the main summit is the Nooksack Ridge, topped by the intimidating Nooksack Tower. A couple of miles south and east of the summit, the striking Jagged Ridge extends east for nearly a mile to Cloudcap Peak. (Cloudcap is the name bestowed by the peak's first-ascent party in 1941, acknowledging a cloud surrounding the summit while on the climb; the Forest Service adopted the name Seahpo in 1943.) The virtually unexplored Sulphide Creek Cirque south of

Jagged Ridge's crest contains three of the world's highest waterfalls.

### LAND MANAGER

North Cascades National Park, Marblemount Wilderness Information Center. Permit required year-round for all overnight trips within the park.

## 52. FISHER CHIMNEYS: GRADE III

**TIME:** 1–3 days. **NOTE:** The USGS topo map mislabels the location of several features: Fisher Chimneys top out a good way east of where labeled. Winnies Slide is just west of the U of the Upper Curtis Glacier label. Hells Highway is labeled as the Hourglass.

### APPROACH, GRADE II

From Interstate 5 just north of Bellingham, take exit 255 to the Mount Baker Highway (State Route 542) and drive east 34 miles to the Glacier Public Service Center. Continue east on SR 542 another 22 miles to the Lake Ann Trailhead at Austin Pass at 4743 feet. There is 1000 feet of elevation gain to reach Lake Ann, which was named for Anna Price, the first woman to climb Shuksan.

*Looking east across Mount Shuksan's Jagged Ridge: this ridge crowns the mountain's two great eastern cirques—the Nooksack and the Sulphide.* (Photo by John Scurlock)

Hanging Glacier

southeast ridge

south gully

to Winnies Slide

Sulphide Glacier

to Hells Highway

*Mount Shuksan from the southwest* (Photo by John Scurlock)

Follow the Lake Ann Trail No. 600 as it loses 800 feet, dropping into the Swift Creek headwaters. At 2.5 miles pass the junction with the Swift Creek Trail No. 607, continuing on the Lake Ann Trail as it climbs eastward to the 4850-foot pass just north of the lake. Campsites are near Lake Ann or east of the lake along the trail to Fisher Chimneys. There are also higher bivy sites located above the Fisher Chimneys at about 6800 feet, below Winnies Slide.

## ROUTE

From above Lake Ann, a well-traveled path leads east before switchbacking up to a stream-gully crossing and the start of the Chimneys Trail. The trail makes a long ascending traverse east to a slabby and exposed 4th-class area below a final gully. Above the chimneys, a short traverse east leads past bivy sites below a 45-degree snow and/or ice slope known as Winnies Slide. Above Winnies Slide, a short rock scramble leads onto the Upper Curtis Glacier.

A traverse south leads to the Hells Highway climb to the top of the Upper Curtis Glacier, then join the Sulphide Glacier at about 7800 feet. Traveling north on the Sulphide leads to the base of the summit pyramid at 8400 feet. The summit pyramid can be ascended by the 3rd- and 4th-class central south gully or by the southeast ridge (5.0) on solid rock. Climbing below others in the central south gully can include substantial exposure to rockfall caused by climbers on busy days.

## DESCENT

Most parties descend with care from the summit via the central gully. Hells Highway, Winnies Slide, and the upper third of Fisher Chimneys are additional areas that often require extra care and can slow the descent considerably.

# 53. JAGGED RIDGE TRAVERSE: GRADE V, 5.6

**TIME:** 2–4 days. **GEAR:** double ropes may be handy for rappels. Jagged Ridge divides Shuksan's two greatest cirques: Sulphide and Nooksack. The Nooksack is the northern cirque, a chaos of active glaciation; the southern cirque has less ice but is even more spectacular with 1800 feet more relief than the northern cirque. The Jagged Ridge Traverse begins by climbing Cloudcap Peak's Northeast Ridge. The climbing is moderate with a high commitment factor, and the volcanic breccia here is different than much of the mountain's greenschist. The scenery remains spectacular, alpine, and unique. Arrange a car shuttle for this climb by leaving one car at either the Lake Ann Trailhead or the lower ski lodge access road 1 mile below Heather Meadows.

## APPROACH, GRADE III

The route to Jagged Ridge can be approached by either a high or low option; both routes lead to Cloudcap's east ridge. Many good camping options exist between Icy and Cloudcap Peaks, and there are also a few small places along Jagged Ridge. The descent options finish on Shuksan's north side, so arrange a shuttle car or retrace the climbing route.

**HIGH APPROACH VIA HANNEGAN PASS:** This approach has amazing views of Shuksan. Follow the west approach for Climb 45, Challenger Glacier, to Hannegan Pass.

## SELECTED HISTORY

### MOUNT SHUKSAN
**1897** III. Joe Morovits. Unrecorded but understood by Claude Rusk.

**1906 SEPTEMBER** Sulphide Glacier. II+. Asahel Curtis, W. Montelius Price.

**1926 SEPTEMBER** White Salmon Glacier. III. Dorothy Pilley, I. A. Richards, Benton Thompson.

**1927** Fisher Chimneys. III+. Esther Buswell, Clarence Fisher, Paul Hugdahl, Lars Loveseth, Winnie Spieseke.

**1927 AUGUST** North Face. III+. Rex Fassett, Lisa Hanft, Benton Thompson.

**1939 SEPTEMBER** Hanging Glacier, North Face summit pyramid. IV. Andy Henning, Otto Trott.

**1941 MAY** Nooksack Glacier. III–IV. Helmy Beckey, Lyman Boyer.

**1945 SEPTEMBER** Price Glacier. III+. Fred Beckey, Bill Granston, Jack Schwabland.

**1946 JULY** Nooksack Tower. IV, 5.5. Fred Beckey, Clifford Schmidtke.

**1957 JULY** Northwest Couloir. III. Ed Cooper, Robert Working.

**1959 JULY** Jagged Ridge. V, 5.6. Tony Hovey, Irene Meulemans, John Meulemans.

**1960 AUGUST** Nooksack Ridge. III+. Fred Beckey, Ron Niccoli.

**1960 AUGUST** Nooksack Ridge to Jagged Ridge to Nooksack Cirque (west to east). V+. Les MacDonald, Gerard McGill.

**1963 JULY** Southwest Face. III, 5th class. Dave Beckstead, Donald Gordon.

**1974 JULY** Northwest Rib. III, 5.7. Pat Cruver, Dave Davis.

**1976 JANUARY** North Face, FWA. Steve Auman, Reed Tindall, Jim Wyman.

**1981 JANUARY** Price Glacier, FWA. Mark Bebie, Lowell Skoog.

**1983 FEBRUARY** Nooksack Tower, FWA. Greg Collum, Kit Lewis, Jim Nelson, Tim Wilson.

**2007 AUGUST** Northwest Arête. III+, 5.9. Darin Berdinka, Matt Alford.

**2018 JULY** Southeast Ridge. III+, 5.6. Darin Berdinka, Chris Martin.

### CLOUDCAP PEAK/SEAHPO (7441')
**1941 JUNE** Northeast Ridge. III, 4th class. Fred Beckey, Helmy Beckey.

**1967 JULY** West Ridge via Jagged Ridge. IV+, 4th class. Joan Firey, Joe Firey, Tony Hovey, Irene Meulemans, John Meulemans.

From the pass, head south about 5 miles past Ruth Mountain and Icy Peak, ascents of which can easily be included on the way to Jagged Ridge.

**LOW APPROACH:** Follow the west approach for Challenger Glacier (Climb 45), but on Forest Road 32 at 2 miles from State Route 542, turn right onto FR 34 and follow it 1 mile to its end at 2150 feet.

Follow the Nooksack Cirque Trail No. 750 on the old roadbed for 2 miles, followed by 1 mile of second-growth forest. At 3 miles the unmaintained trail enters old growth for a bit before following gravel bars along the Nooksack River to its source about 6 miles from the trailhead at 3000 feet, a stunning place to camp. From the bottom of Nooksack Cirque, ascend ground moraine, snowfields, and glacier south to reach the Icy Peak–Cloudcap Peak ridge at 6000 feet.

## ROUTE

A fairly straightforward route can be taken from the apex of the snow adjacent to Cloudcap's Northeast Ridge and then followed (4th class) all the way to the summit of Cloudcap. Enjoy a commanding view of Mount Shuksan, Baker Lake, and Mount Blum from this uniquely situated peak at the top of both Nooksack and Crystal Cirques. The descent from the summit of Cloudcap Peak is feasible to the west and to the south. Either way, multiple rappels are required. Until this route sees more traffic, expect to build anchors along the way; climbers will likely encounter little evidence of prior travel.

After descending Cloudcap Peak, traverse west and gain Jagged Ridge just beyond the spires that are just west of Cloudcap's summit. The rock on the way to the ridge crest should be no more difficult than 3rd class, except perhaps when dealing with moat issues; in early season, there will likely be few moat problems. Once on the ridge crest, scramble west over exposed terrain. The route starts along or south of the ridge crest, then crosses to the north side, and then moves back south again to eventually finish on the north side of the crest and so reach the Crystal Glacier. The final pitch before the glacier is the crux of the route (5.6). Caution is advised here as the rock is loose and it may be difficult not to climb directly above the belayer. To finish the traverse to the summit of Shuksan, traverse the

*Jagged Ridge divides Mount Shuksan's two great eastern cirques: the Nooksack and the Sulphide.* (Photo by John Scurlock)

Cloudcap Peak

*Looking back across the Jagged Ridge toward Cloudcap Peak; Franklin Bradshaw is having a very good day.* (Photo by Tom Sjolseth)

Crystal Glacier west crossing to the Sulphide Glacier just north of an 8165-foot rock outcrop. See Climb 52, Fisher Chimneys, for Shuksan's summit pyramid options, and descent.

## DESCENT

If you have a car shuttle, you have a couple of options. Fisher Chimneys (Climb 52) is a good path back to the north side of the mountain. Below Winnies Slide (before the chimneys), there is the option of descending the north side of Shuksan Arm via the White Salmon Glacier. While shorter, the White Salmon Glacier way is much less traveled, and a brushy area near the valley bottom is difficult to avoid.

# BEAR MOUNTAIN                    7931'

**PROMINENCE: 1371'**

## DIRECT NORTH BUTTRESS

Super fabled, seldom seen: the huge northern aspect of Bear Mountain is hidden away just south of the Canadian border. This was another of Fred Beckey's great projects from back in the '60s, and its capacity to awe and inspire continues to this day. Though not as big as Slesse, Bear has a huge north face that captured the attention of talented Cascade climbers throughout the '70s and '80s, when numerous other spectacular lines were established. With a long and athletic approach leading to a huge and forbidding north face, these routes on Bear Mountain are some of the most daunting and remote alpine rock climbs in the range.

**LAND MANAGERS**

North Cascades National Park, Marblemount Wilderness Information Center; permit required year-round for all overnight trips within the park. Chilliwack Lake Provincial Park, British Columbia, Canada; backcountry permit (fee) required.

## 54. DIRECT NORTH BUTTRESS: GRADE V, 5.10

**TIME:** 2–3 days. You'll need a passport for this one! The original 1967 north buttress climb reached the upper half of the buttress by connecting slabs and ledges to bypass the direct lower buttress. The full buttress, first climbed in 1980, doubled the length of a climb that was at the time considered one of the most serious in the range.

*Doug Hutchinson leading the awesome corner, on Bear Mountain's Direct North Buttress* (Photo by Jaime Bohle)

*Bear Mountain from the north: (A) Ursa Major, 1986, (B) Ursa Minor, 1986, (C) North Buttress, 1967, (D) Direct North Buttress, 1980, (E) North Face West Buttress* (Photo by John Scurlock)

## APPROACH, GRADE IV

From Interstate 5 north of Bellingham, take exit 256A and follow State Route 539 north about 13 miles to Lynden, then turn right onto Badger Road (SR 546) and drive east about 8 miles to SR 9. Turn left onto SR 9 north and drive 5 miles to Sumas and the border crossing into British Columbia, Canada. Continue north on Sumas Highway (BC Highway 11) for 2 miles to the Trans-Canada Highway (Canadian Hwy. 1) and head east on Canadian Hwy. 1 for 12 or so miles to the Chilliwack-Sardis exit. Drive south on Vedder Road, following signs to Sardis. Drive 3.7 miles south, through town, and at about 5 miles turn left (east) just before the bridge over the Chilliwack River, onto Chilliwack Lake Road. Follow this paved road 25 miles to the north end of Chilliwack Lake, and continue driving as the road turns to gravel and potholes along the east side of Chilliwack Lake. Another 4.5 miles reaches Depot Creek Road; continue less than 1 mile to the end of Chilliwack Lake Road and park at a gate at 2050 feet.

Walk along the road about 1.5 miles to the south end of Chilliwack Lake and locate the Chilliwack River Trail. Follow this trail through tremendous old-growth forest along the Chilliwack River. Once back across the border into the US in 1 mile, the trail is rarely maintained and can be difficult going.

In 4 miles from the border, reach Bear Creek at 2200 feet. Leave the trail and ascend the timbered spur to the northwest, with minimal but steep bushwhacking. At the tree line, hike through bushes for several hundred feet before coming to a meadow above Ruta Lake. Continue along the divide, then traverse the south slopes, crossing a rock rib to reach bivy sites at the 6600-foot col. A descent from the col traverses around to the east underneath the mountain at 5500 feet before reaching the edge of the small glacier below the face at about 6000 feet.

*Bear Mountain from the north: (A)* Diamond Life, *1987, (B)* Diamond Wall, *1988, (C)* North Buttress, *1967 (Photo by John Scurlock)*

## SELECTED HISTORY

**1939 AUGUST** FA. II. Calder Bressler, Will Thompson.

**1967 JULY** North Buttress, FA. IV+, 5.9. Fred Beckey, Mark Fielding.

**1977 SEPTEMBER** North Face, West Buttress, FA. IV, 5.8. Alan Kearney, Shari Kearney, Ed Newville, Jeff Thomas.

**1980 SEPTEMBER** Direct North Buttress, FA. V, 5.9 A1. Alan Kearney, Bobby Knight.

**1985 AUGUST** Direct North Buttress, FFA. V, 5.10+. Bryan Burdo, Yann Merrand.

**1986 AUGUST** *Ursa Minor*, FA. III, 5.8. Alex Cudkowicz, Pete Doorish.

**1986 AUGUST** *Ursa Major*, FA. IV+, 5.9. Alex Cudkowicz, Pete Doorish.

**1987 JULY** *Diamond Life*, FA. VI, 5.10 A0. Alex Cudkowicz, Pete Doorish, Charlie Hampson.

**1988 AUGUST** *Diamond Wall*, FA. VI, 5.10 A3. Pete Doorish, Dale Farnham.

## ROUTE

**PITCH 1:** From the toe of the buttress, begin with a chimney (5.7) or bypass on the left across slabs. **PITCHES 2-3:** Climb (up to 5.8) on less-than-great rock to a belay at the bottom of the dihedral. **PITCH 4:** Climb the corner and through the roof (5.10) to a belay at a small ledge. **PITCH 5:** Ascend this short pitch up the corner to the base of a chimney system (5.10-). **PITCH 6:** Chimney and stem on less-than-great rock (5.9). **PITCH 7:** Climb a corner (5.8), with some loose blocks at the start of the pitch. **PITCH 8:** Begin with a rightward traverse, then ascend on lower-angle terrain. **PITCHES 9-11:** Easier climbing heads below the snow patch or out left on dry rock (5.7). **PITCH 10:** Climb the steep face behind the snow patch using the leftmost of two cracks (5.10). **PITCH 11:** Another steep pitch (5.8) leads to a ledge a bit right of the 1967 Beckey-Fielding route.

**PITCH 12:** This is where the 1980 direct route joins the 1967 route. Climb the hand crack–corner just left of the buttress crest (5.9+). **PITCH 13:** Climb along the crest of the ridge (5.6). **PITCH 14:** Climb a steep wall with a crack left of the crest (5.8) to a very fine ledge. **PITCH 15:** Climb the wide crack above the chimney on great rock (5.10). It is also possible to move to the right after the chimney (5.8). **PITCH 16:** Climb near the crest on good rock (5.7) to a belay below where the ridge steepens. At this point, it is possible to tension-traverse down and right into a 4th-class gully. **PITCH 17:** Face climbing on great rock leads to a belay below twin cracks. **PITCH 18:** Climb the cracks (5.8). **PITCH 19:** Continue near the crest to the top of the buttress (5.7), a short scramble from the summit.

## DESCENT

From the summit, descend to the west and keep to the left (south). Access to the basin below is blocked by a steep rock band at 7300 feet. Stay left (south) until able to down-climb a short 3rd-class rock gully leading north and back to bivy sites at the 6600-foot col.

*Aaron Clifford on the Beckey/Fielding route on Bear Mountain* (Photo by Steph Abegg)

# MOUNT SPICKARD 8979'

## PROMINENCE: 4779' [19]

### SILVER LAKE GLACIER

Northeast of Mount Shuksan and west of Ross Lake, Mount Spickard sits among the Chilliwack Peaks; a group that include 5 of Washington's 100 highest mountains. Spickard is Number 19 on the list of mountains with at least 400 feet of prominence; nearby Redoubt is 21, while Custer and the Mox Peaks are also on the list. While Redoubt and Spickard get the most attention, the Chilliwack Peaks have everything from glacier and scrambling routes to demanding alpine rock climbs on breccias and gneiss.

The Spickard massif, with its two subsidiary summits, shares four spectacular alpine cirques with neighboring peaks. If you seek rugged wilderness terrain, any of Mount Spickard's eastern cirques can provide the goods. The mountain was named for Seattle climber Warren Spickard, who was killed in 1961 while descending from Northwest Mox Peak.

### LAND MANAGERS

North Cascades National Park, Marblemount Wilderness Information Center; permit required year-round for all overnight trips within the park. Chilliwack Natural Resource District, British Columbia, Canada; no permit required.

*The Silver Lake Cirque of peaks from the north* (Photo by John Scurlock)

*Mount Spickard from the west* (Photo by John Scurlock)

## 55. SILVER LAKE GLACIER: GRADE II, 4TH CLASS

**TIME:** 3 days. This classic Cascade route features glacier travel followed by alpine rock climbing. The route is a bit more challenging than the southwest route, but this option won't last much longer as the planet warms; the Silver Lake Glacier becomes more challenging as the season progresses. While the climbing is engaging, Silver Lake itself steals the scene. A loop traverse from Ouzel Lake could also include visits to Ag and Solitude, which are two of Spickard's subpeaks.

### APPROACH, GRADE III

Follow the approach for Direct North Buttress (Climb 54) on Bear Mountain to Depot Creek Road, located on the north side of Depot Creek, less than 1 mile from the end of Chilliwack Lake Road. Drive or walk Depot Creek Road about 1 mile to a small parking area at about 2500 feet. There is 3200 feet of elevation gain to reach the Ouzel Lake campsites.

Walk about 2 miles on the abandoned logging road to the US-Canada border, where the Depot Creek Trail continues up the valley in North Cascades National Park. In about 3.5 miles from the border, the trail reaches 300-foot-high Depot Creek Falls at about 4100 feet.

Slabs and boulders lead across the base of the falls before ascending steep forest where there are fixed hand lines at two vertical steps. The path continues on the north side of Depot Creek, avoiding patches of alder as much as possible. A large bench near 4800 feet has camping, but most climbers continue to Ouzel Lake, 5 miles from the border, at 5660 feet. The lake sits below the broad Redoubt Glacier reaching across much of Depot Creek Cirque, one of the larger glaciers in the national park.

### ROUTE

From Ouzel Lake, hike northeast up the wide gully leading to the Custer-Spickard Col at 7380 feet. The west end of the Silver Lake Glacier terminus lies just east of the col. Conditions on the glacier vary greatly depending on the

*Mount Spickard from the north* (Photo by John Scurlock)

season. Make an ascending traverse east toward the top of the glacier. With early-season snow reaching nearly to the summit, direct ascents on snow are possible. Most summer ascents finish on the northeast ridge and avoid the north face and its seasonal bergschrunds. The northeast ridge is reached from the 8500-foot col on the ridge between

## SELECTED HISTORY

**1904**  Southwest route assumed. II. Surveyor Walter Reaburn.

**1959 MAY**  Silver Lake Glacier. II+. Paul Binkert party of five.

**1960**  Northeast/Ag Peak (8824 feet). II+. Dick Culbert.

**1975**  Northwest Ridge. III, 4th class. British Columbia Mountaineering Club report.

**1980 JULY**  Southwest Peak/Solitude Peak (8405 feet). Reed Tindall, John Roper.

Spickard's main summit and its northeast peak, Ag Peak. Climbing the ridge is 3rd and 4th class, mostly following the ridge crest but with short sections on the east face.

## DESCENT

The descent from the summit involves scrambling and/or climbing down either the upper southwest or southeast ridge. If descending the southeast ridge, watch for a good place to make a descending traverse of the south face. Once below the summit rocks, descend the upper portion of Spickard's Perry Creek Glacier until able to traverse west to a lower snowfield that leads to the 8000+-foot col on Spickard's southwest ridge. Spickard's southwest peak, known as Solitude, sits on the ridge just south of this col. Cross north through the col into the Depot Creek Cirque. Now on the west side of Spickard, continue to descend this northernmost section of the Redoubt Glacier to about 7000 feet, where a descending traverse leads to the broad gully down to Ouzel Lake.

# SLESSE MOUNTAIN (BRITISH COLUMBIA)  7969'

**PROMINENCE: 2769'**

**NORTHEAST BUTTRESS**

Slesse Mountain is located in the rugged Chilliwack region a few miles north of the US-Canada border. The mountain, very prominent from the Fraser Valley near the town of Chilliwack, British Columbia, is notable for its steep local relief. In December 1956, a Trans-Canada airplane slammed into the mountain in bad weather, killing all sixty-two aboard. In the native Salish language, Slesse means "fang"—or "dark fang," in climber-speak.

On the mountain's eastern aspect, small seasonal glaciers cling to slabs below 2500-foot rock walls. Fred Beckey called the immense northeast buttress "one of the greatest rock pillars carved by the forces of nature in western North America"—a true classic, one of the great lines anywhere. First climbed in 1963, the eastern walls and buttresses now hold more than a half dozen major rock climbs, as well as several winter mixed lines.

**LAND MANAGER**

Chilliwack Natural Resource District, British Columbia, Canada. No permit required.

## 56. NORTHEAST BUTTRESS: GRADE V, 5.9+

**TIME:** 1–2 days. Upon first view, the northeast buttress is a sobering sight. No photograph can convey the anxieties experienced as one approaches a climb that was once considered among the most serious in the Cascades. Greater knowledge of the route and advances in rock-climbing standards and equipment have lessened much of the climb's mystique. Still, the number of pitches, weather concerns, and difficulty of retreat remain factors, and the Northeast Buttress should not be underestimated.

*Alex Honnold on Slesse Mountain's Northeast Buttress* (Photo by Colin Haley)

*Slesse Mountain from the northeast: (A) Southeast Buttress, 1977, (B)* Navigator Wall, 1987, *(C) East Buttress, 1977, (D) East Buttress Direct, 1993, (E) East Face 1997, (F) Northeast Buttress, 1963 (G)* Heart of Darkness, 2015, *(H) North Rib, 1972*

One decision for Slesse climbs is whether to leave a car on the west side of the mountain for a descent to Slesse Creek Road via the Slesse Mountain Trail or to use the Crossover Pass route back to Nesakwatch Road on the east side of the mountain. The west-side route via the Slesse Mountain Trail is faster but also requires time for the car shuttle or bike stash. Except for early or midsummer, expect the descent on the west side of the mountain to be dry.

A second decision is whether to climb the original direct start (5.10+) or bypass the lower eight to twelve pitches via the Pocket Glacier approach—the route described here. The Pocket Glacier sits on polished slabs perched below Slesse's towering east wall. At some point during the summer, the glacier has a tendency to slide away, with major sections crashing into the basin below. For this reason, it's best to traverse onto the glacier from the south near the east buttress or wait until after the glacier fully discharges. Once the glacier fully discharges, the underlying slabs are easily negotiated either from the east buttress or directly from below. Expect the timing of the glacier's discharge to vary a good bit from year to year. Using the glacier bypass during the breakup period should be considered very high risk and is not recommended.

The Northeast Buttress itself can be divided into three sections. The rock on the lower section is solid and glacier polished, but also has lengthy brushy sections. The direct start was used on the first ascent and is mostly protected from Pocket Glacier avalanches. The middle third of the route also presents options: the buttress crest has some of the climb's nicest pitches and is recommended; a lower-angle corner system north of the crest used on the first ascent has easier climbing but is not as well protected. The final upper buttress is pure joy, steep but with an abundance of holds.

## APPROACH, GRADE II+

Follow the approach for Direct North Buttress (Climb 54) on Bear Mountain to the start of Chilliwack Lake Road.

**SLESSE MOUNTAIN TRAIL SHUTTLE:** Drive Chilliwack Lake Road 13 miles to Slesse Creek Road 5127-07, located on the east side of Slesse Creek. Drive Slesse Creek Road south about 4 miles, or a bit farther with a high-clearance vehicle, to the Slesse Mountain Trailhead parking at 1800 feet. Leave a shuttle car or bike here.

**SLESSE MEMORIAL TRAIL TO CLIMB'S START:** Follow Chilliwack Lake Road 18.5 miles to Nesakwatch Forest Service Road on the right (south), just beyond Riverside Campground. Drive or walk the Nesakwatch Road 4 miles south to the Slesse Memorial Trailhead at 2000 feet.

The Slesse Memorial Trail crosses Nesakwatch Creek on a footbridge and follows the abandoned logging road, reaching the Memorial Plaque in 2 miles at about 3900 feet, directly across from Slesse's Northeast Buttress and the lower basin. (If climbing the direct start and not using the Pocket Glacier bypass, leave the trail near the memorial and cross the lower basin to the lower buttress.) Farther up, the trail leads in 1.5 miles to the Propeller Cairn bivy site south of the Pocket Glacier, at about 5000 feet and roughly below the South Peak's Navigator Wall.

## ROUTE

From the Propeller Cairn bivy site, traverse below the seasonal East Glacier, with some elevation loss, to the East Buttress crossing notch. Scramble through the notch and down to the Pocket Glacier or slabs. The obvious 3rd-class bypass ledges leading onto the buttress begin from under the east wall. Follow the ledges all the way to the ridge crest near a small gendarme before starting up.

## SELECTED HISTORY

**1927 AUGUST**  Southwest Route. II, 5.0. Stan Henderson, Mills Winram, Fred Parkes.

**1952 AUGUST**  South Peak (7700 feet). II, 5.4. Fred Beckey, John Dudra, Herb Staley.

**1955 FEBRUARY**  FWA. Fips Broda, John Dudra.

**1963 AUGUST**  Northeast Buttress. V, 5.10, A2. Fred Beckey, Eric Bjornstad, Steve Marts.

**1972 JULY**  North Rib. IV+, 5.8. Rob Kiesel, Jeff Lowe.

**1977 JUNE**  South Peak, Southeast Buttress. V, 5.10+. Scott Flavelle, Keith Nannery.

**1977 JULY**  Northeast Buttress FFA. Bob Plumb, Dave Stutzman.

**1977 AUGUST**  East Buttress. V, 5.9 A2. Dennis Mullen, John Stoddard.

**1980 JANUARY**  North Face Couloir (to north notch). IV. Perry Beckham, Don Serl, John Wittmayer.

**1982 AUGUST**  *Fraser Ribber* (to north shoulder). III+, 5.8. Hamish Fraser, Peder Ourom.

**1986 MARCH**  Northeast Buttress, FWA. Kit Lewis, Jim Nelson.

**1987 SEPTEMBER**  South Peak, *Navigator Wall*. V, 5.10+. Bryan Burdo, Pete Doorish.

**1989 JANUARY**  *Arctic Wing* (to north shoulder). IV. Maxim de Jong, Adam Gibbs, Bob McGregor.

**1993 AUGUST**  East Buttress Direct. V, 5.10+. Greg Child, Perry Beckham.

**1997 JULY**  East Face. V+. Sean Easton, Dave Edgar.

**2015 MARCH**  *Heart of Darkness*. V. Colin Haley, Dylan Johnson.

**2015 MARCH**  Northeast Buttress, first free solo winter. Marc-André Leclerc.

**2017 SEPTEMBER**  East Face, *Welcome to the Wack*, FFA. V+, 5.11+. Jacob Cook, Tony McLane.

**2018 JANUARY**  East Face, *Navigator Wall*, FWA. Marc-André Leclerc, Tom Livingstone.

Brushy 4th class and a short 5.7 corner start the belayed climbing on the east side of the crest. A 5.8 corner leads to more 4th class as well as the ledges used on the first ascent that lead to the right, one full pitch to the north-face bypass corners (5.7). Avoiding the bypass, and keeping near the crest, is recommended where the rock is solid and clean. Two pitches of mid-5th class continue near the crest, followed by a steeper pitch with a short 5.9+ crux. Two more pitches with 5.8 cruxes lead to the four-person bivy sites overlooking the east face.

Several hundred feet of 3rd and 4th class lead to the upper buttress. Climb a couple of mid-5th-class pitches to a grassy ledge where the buttress steepens. A 5.8 pitch a bit right of the crest has some loose rock. A corner continues up before exiting a bit left past a bolt and small roof (5.9 crux), where the rock is solid and protection plentiful. Two more nice pitches lead to a large ledge, followed by two final pitches.

## DESCENT

From the true summit, walk south along the crest several hundred feet, turning slightly west of the crest until able to rappel toward a gully identified by a slender gendarme. It is possible to avoid the rappel by continuing south and following 3rd- and 4th-class ledges until able to move back west into the main southwest gully. When the gully steepens, find ledges traversing north until outflanking steeper terrain below. Once off the mountain, continue traversing northwest toward a wooded ridge.

**SLESSE MOUNTAIN TRAIL DESCENT:** From the wooded ridge, descend southwest to the end of the Slesse Mountain Trail at 6500 feet. Follow its many steep switchbacks down 2 miles, then descend an easier mile on an abandoned roadbed to the trailhead parking at Slesse Creek Road's end.

**CROSSOVER PASS DESCENT TO SLESSE MEMORIAL TRAIL AND CLIMB'S START:** Just before the wooded ridge leading to the Slesse Mountain Trail, climb up a couple hundred feet to a crossing of the ridge at about 7000 feet. Cross the ridge to the north and traverse to the right across the main gully, over to a second gully leading into the adjacent basin. Easy travel runs the ridge north across heather benches for about 1 mile to Mount Parkes (6942 feet). Scramble up nearly to the summit of Mount Parkes, then down-climb a short bit of the northeast shoulder (4th class) to a 100-foot (30m) rappel. Rappel past a gully and into a second gully just beyond. This gully leads down the northwest side of the peak until it is possible to easily traverse to the right to Crossover Pass at 6500 feet. From the pass, continue north up the ridge several hundred feet until it is possible to traverse across the east slope of the ridge, to where it is possible to descend a couple hundred feet to an orange scree slope. Cross the scree slope to the north, then descend by keeping left and eventually picking up the Crossover Trail. The trail reaches the forest at about 5000 feet and joins the Slesse Memorial Trail at the memorial at 3900 feet. Follow the trail back down 2 miles to the trailhead parking on Nesakwatch Road.

*Jens Holsten on Colchuck Balanced Rock, with Dragontail Peak behind* (Photo by Max Hasson)

# EASTSIDE CASCADES

# STUART RANGE

## INGALLS PEAK, NORTH PEAK  7662'

**PROMINENCE: 1222'**

### SOUTH RIDGE; EAST RIDGE

The three Ingalls Peaks anchor the north end of the Teanaway Mountains at the headwaters of Ingalls Creek. The Ingalls Creek valley not only defines the southern border of the Stuart Range, it also separates the Stuart Range granites from the Teanaway's Ingalls peridiorite or serpentine stones. Lower in elevation and less rugged, the Teanaway peaks are much appreciated for their nontechnical summits and endless scrambling options. The area is a real gem with abundant wildflowers, pleasant off-trail travel, and dramatic views of the nearby Stuart Range. For added inspiration, check out the view from Interstate 90 between Ellensburg and Cle Elum.

Ingalls is one of the few Teanaway peaks with rock climbing. The north (middle) peak of Ingalls is the tallest of the Teanaway peaks and an ideal perch from which to

*Carl Skoog on Ingalls Peaks, South Ridge* (Photo by Lowell Skoog)

plot Mount Stuart adventures. Its location east of the Cascade crest means that summer comes early and makes the Teanaway a good early-season destination. Expect a short but fierce mosquito season, typically about early July, and beware of the hot midsummer conditions. The approach is fully exposed to the summer sun.

## LAND MANAGER

Alpine Lakes Wilderness, Okanogan-Wenatchee National Forest, Cle Elum Ranger District. Northwest Forest Pass or interagency recreation pass required for parking. Free self-registered wilderness permit required for day or overnight trips.

# 57. SOUTH RIDGE: GRADE II, 5.5

**TIME:** 1 day. **GEAR:** minimal rack to 3 inches; crampons may be helpful on the approach in early season. This is a short climb on mostly solid rock, popular with groups and clubs, which can clog the route, especially if they descend the same route. **NOTE:** Water is scarce on the approach trail.

## APPROACH, GRADE II

Drive Interstate 90 to exit 85 and follow State Route 970 north 6 miles, then drive west on Teanaway Road for about 7 miles, where it becomes North Fork Teanaway Road (Forest Road 9737), and follow it for another 10 miles or so to its end and the Esmeralda Trailhead at 4243 feet. This trailhead melts out sometime around Memorial Day. There is 3200 feet of elevation gain to the start of the climb, 70 percent on trail, 30 percent off trail; much of the approach is snow covered early in the season.

Hike the Esmeralda Basin Trail No. 1394 for 0.4 mile to a junction; take the right fork onto the Ingalls Way Trail No. 1390 for 1.6 miles to a second trail junction at 5600 feet with the Longs Pass Trail No. 1229. Stay on the Ingalls Way Trail No. 1390, traversing north before climbing to Ingalls Pass at 6500 feet. From the pass, follow the trail down and across Headlight Basin toward Ingalls Lake. At the far end of the basin (6450 feet), leave the trail.

Head up, traversing north below a shoulder of Ingalls South Peak. Talus and a faint climbers path lead to the saddle between Ingalls South and North Peaks at 7350 feet.

*Ingalls Peak from the west* (Photo by John Scurlock)

## ROUTE

From the saddle, the route can start from either the east or west side of the ridge. **PITCH 1 EAST:** Begin just below the ridge crest and climb the central gully-crack (5.0). **PITCH 1 WEST (RECOMMENDED):** Start from the notch beyond the small dark crag, where a short slab leads around the corner to a short, narrow ridge crest connecting to the main face.

Both pitch 1 options lead to the low-angle, boulder-strewn area below the main face; scramble or move the belay up as necessary. **PITCH 2:** Climb the left crack (5.5) or a central crack (5.6), ending with a two-bolt belay at 100+ feet (with the amount of traffic, this could be a good place for a third bolt placed high). **PITCH 3:** Make a couple of face moves, followed by a right-facing corner a bit left, and you're up.

## DESCENT

The easiest route for descent is the west face; it involves a combination of down-climbing and one or two very short rappels. Rappelling the South Ridge route can work well too, but beware that double-rope rappels are not ideal due to snag and pull issues, particularly the second rappel, which is the bolted belay at the top of pitch 2.

# 58. EAST RIDGE: GRADE II, 5.7⁺

**TIME:** 1 day. **GEAR:** minimal rack to 3 inches. This route is longer than the South Ridge, but much less sustained—a nice climb with good exposure and solid rock.

*Ingalls Peak from the east* (Photo by John Scurlock)

## APPROACH, GRADE II

Follow the same approach as for the preceding climb, but don't ascend all the way to the saddle between Ingalls South and North Peaks.

## ROUTE

From below Ingalls North Peak, ascend the gully (snow in early season) leading toward the notch between Ingalls North and East Peaks. Ascend the gully on its left side until it steepens. **PITCH 1:** Climb to the ridge notch in one long or two short pitches and belay; on the ridge, the route wanders on or just right (north) of the crest. **PITCH 2:** Continue above the notch, passing two small gendarmes on the right (low 5th class); belay just before dropping down again into a small notch or just beyond this notch on the ridge crest. **PITCH 3:** Scramble to the right of the ridge on 4th-class rock and then back to the crest. **PITCH 4:** Begin with a short exposed knife-edge (low-5th-class) section, then continue on or just right of the crest. **PITCH 5:** The short crux pitch (about 5.7+) comes just below the summit; the route, which appears improbable, lies directly above.

## DESCENT

Follow either descent described in the preceding climb.

# MOUNT STUART                    9415'

### PROMINENCE: 5335' [10]

### NORTH RIDGE; STUART GLACIER COULOIR

The Wenatchee Mountains, or Stuart Range, is a major subrange of the Cascade Mountains, separating the drainage basins of the Yakima and Wenatchee Rivers. The range encompasses some of the Cascades' most-loved backcountry areas. Great spots to view the range and Mount Stuart's geographic significance include Elk Heights along Interstate 90 and Manashtash Ridge on I-82.

*Colin Haley leads the Great Gendarme on Mount Stuart's North Ridge.* (Photo by Andy Wyatt)

*Dylan Johnson on Mount Stuart's Northeast Face,* Lara Kellogg Memorial Route (Photo by Colin Haley)

Stuart, located in about the middle of the range, is a rugged quartz diorite, granodiorite, and granite peak with a pleasing architecture and three small glaciers. The primary attraction for climbers is alpine rock climbing, but seasonal mixed climbing also may occur in winter and spring. It's hard to do better than Stuart for outstanding alpine rock climbing. With the right conditions, Mount Stuart holds some of the finest technical alpine climbs in the Northwest.

Stuart has numerous climbs to recommend. For early season or winter, we love the Ice Cliff Glacier for its moderate climbing and dramatic location. The Northeast Face can be climbed winter or early spring as a mixed route, and it is also a great rock climb when the face is dry. Finishing the Northeast Face (1959 route) with the Great Gendarme is a stellar climb on good rock. Halfway between the Northeast Face and the Ice Cliff Couloir, the Girth Pillar climbs splitter cracks to the false summit. Likewise, the Northwest Face of the mountain has rock climbs with quality pitches and a very classic seasonal snow and ice climb. On the steep West Face of the mountain, *Gorillas in the Mist* (and variations) rivals the North Ridge for sustained climbing on good rock. Other routes of interest include the West Ridge, a much-loved fast route to the summit and the Cascadian Couloir, which is not only a superb descent route but also a fine summit route.

Climbs of Stuart are typically approached by one of two routes, seasonal conditions often being the primary consideration. North-side descents become more technical as conditions transition from spring to summer. Generally, winter and spring work well when approaching from the north, while the southern approach is often chosen for summer and fall. A vehicle shuttle arrangement can combine the slightly shorter northern approach with the less-technical southern descent via the Cascadian Couloir.

## LAND MANAGER

Alpine Lakes Wilderness, Okanogan-Wenatchee National Forest, Cle Elum or Wenatchee River Ranger District. Northwest Forest Pass or interagency recreation pass required for parking. Free self-issued wilderness permit required for day and overnight trips outside Enchantment Permit Area; camping prohibited within 0.5 mile of Ingalls Lake, but permit-zone boundary excludes climber bivouac sites immediately below Mount Stuart's north side.

# 59. NORTH RIDGE: UPPER, GRADE III⁺, 5.9; COMPLETE, GRADE IV⁺, 5.9

**TIME:** 1–3 days. **GEAR:** medium rack to 3½ inches; ice axe and crampons recommended for glacier crossing and false-summit snowfield on the descent. The North Ridge rises nearly 3000 feet, splitting the mountain's north face right down the middle. Much of the best climbing lies on the upper portion of the ridge, where low-5th-class climbing on clean rock combines with views and rumbles of the chaotic Ice Cliff Glacier Cirque.

Climbing the full ridge is a Cascades test piece presenting a classic dilemma: carry over with bivy gear, or pack light with plans that greater speed will see you off the peak by dark. One-day roundtrip ascents started happening in the late '70s, usually taking about 12–15 hours. While the one-day round-trip is still considered strong work, the endurance bar was raised substantially in 1986 when a visiting crag climber decided to check out the Leavenworth backcountry. With a predawn start from Icicle Creek and beginning with the complete North Ridge, Peter Croft was able to summit not only Stuart but also Sherpa, Argonaut, Colchuck, Dragontail, and Prusik Peaks before returning to Icicle Creek later the same day.

## APPROACHES

**SOUTHERN APPROACH, GRADE II:** Follow the approach for South Ridge (Climb 57) on Ingalls Peak, to Ingalls Lake. There is 5600 feet of elevation gain to Goat Pass, 50 percent on trail, 50 percent off-trail, and minimal snow or talus.

From the north end of Ingalls Lake, ascend to Stuart Pass (6400 feet) at the west end of the Ingalls Creek valley. A well-worn path climbs to a shoulder below Stuart's West Ridge (7100 feet). Make a short descent east and cross the rock glacier below Stuart's West Wall (*Gorillas in the Mist, King Kong*), then climb to Goat Pass at 7920 feet, where there are bivy sites.

For the complete North Ridge route described below, from Goat Pass make a traversing descent of 1500 feet to reach the base of the ridge at about 6600 feet.

**OPTION:** For the upper ridge route, from Goat Pass descend 100–200 feet and begin traversing steep snow slopes east across the Stuart Glacier. A short but exposed snow traverse gains entry to the midridge notch gully. Bivy sites exist at the 8200-foot notch. There may be water down the gully east from the notch.

**NORTHERN APPROACH, GRADE II:** This is a good approach route for most any route on the north side of the

*Mount Stuart from the north* (Photo by John Scurlock)

*Mount Stuart from the southeast* (Photo by John Scurlock)

mountain, especially if planning to descend via the Sherpa Glacier; approach difficulty depends greatly on snow conditions and season. From the west end of Leavenworth on the Stevens Pass Highway (US Highway 2), drive Icicle Creek Road (Forest Road 76) west 8.5 miles to Bridge Creek Campground (the road is gated here in winter, reopening about mid-April). Turn left (south) onto Mountaineer Creek Road (FR 7601) as it crosses Icicle Creek and follow it for 3.5 miles to the Stuart Lake Trailhead (3400 feet). The trailhead and lower valley begin to melt out in May; plan to walk, ski, or snowshoe FR 7601 before then. There is about 2100 feet of elevation gain from the trailhead to campsites in upper Mountaineer Creek.

Hike the Stuart Lake Trail No. 1599 and at about 3 miles pass the junction with the Colchuck Lake Trail No. 1599A to the left. Stay to the right to continue on the Stuart Lake Trail another 2 miles to where switchbacks begin at 4750 feet.

Leave the trail and cross the Mountaineer Creek branch from Lake Stuart. The next mile has several confusing paths; eventually a well-used path follows Mountaineer Creek to where the valley steepens abruptly at about 5000 feet. Keeping north of the creek, continue up along talus and open forest to enter the upper valley. Running

water is available for winter climbs in the forest just below the wetlands at the end of the valley (5400 feet); nice summer campsites lie among boulders just beyond. Continue up talus and moraine to the base of the ridge at about 6600 feet.

## ROUTE

The lower North Ridge rises from near the terminus of Ice Cliff and Stuart Glaciers and begins with three to five 100-foot (30m) solid pitches: two pitches of 5.8 followed by one of 5.9. Much easier 4th- and low-5th-class climbing follows for 1500 feet, then joins the upper North Ridge at the midridge notch. Climbing on or near the ridge crest is recommended. From the midridge notch, ten or more pitches lead to the Great Gendarme. Nearing the summit, the ridge steepens dramatically. While the gendarme can be bypassed, the pitches up it should not be missed.

**BYPASS OPTION:** Rappel 75 feet (25m) off the right (west) side of the ridge. Traverse into and across the gully behind the gendarme (can be wet or even icy). Ledges traverse right (west) to loose scrambling, interspersed with 5th-class steps to the summit.

**GREAT GENDARME OPTION:** The modern option is to climb the gendarme directly (see topo). **PITCH 1:** A short crux (5.9) leads to a perfect belay ledge. **PITCH 2:** Start is very exposed with a traverse to the right (5.7) to the wide splitter crack, 4 inches at the end (5.9); 100 feet (30m). **PITCH 3:** Continue up and right 130 feet (40m; low 5th) to a notch beyond the gendarme. **PITCH 4:** Climb a short 5.8 wall. **PITCHES 5-6:** Finish with blocky 4th- and 5th-class climbing.

## DESCENT

**SOUTHERN DESCENT:** The Cascadian Couloir is the recommended descent route for both routes when approaching from the south. From the summit, scramble east and down to paths that traverse east below the false summit at about 9200 feet. Make a few moves (5.0) to ledges traversing east to near the top of a steep snow slope with a long history of accidents. This snowfield can disappear in a hot summer, requiring several hundred feet of 3rd-class scrambling on loose rock. Continue descending below the snowfield toward a bench at about 8500 feet. Veer right (west) toward Cascadian Couloir. Scree and sandy boot tracks lead down and eventually to the Ingalls Way Trail No. 1390. Follow it down and find the Longs Pass Trail No. 1229 among forested campsites at about 4900 feet. Cross Ingalls Creek and climb the steep trail to Longs Pass (6200 feet) then descend to Teanaway Road (Forest Road 97) at 4240 feet. Drive the road 23 miles to State Route 970 and drive it south 6 miles to Interstate 90 at exit 85.

**NORTHERN DESCENT:** The Sherpa Glacier is the recommended descent route when either route is approached from the north. From the summit, descend the East Ridge and southeast slopes beyond the false summit. A descending traverse east leads past the top

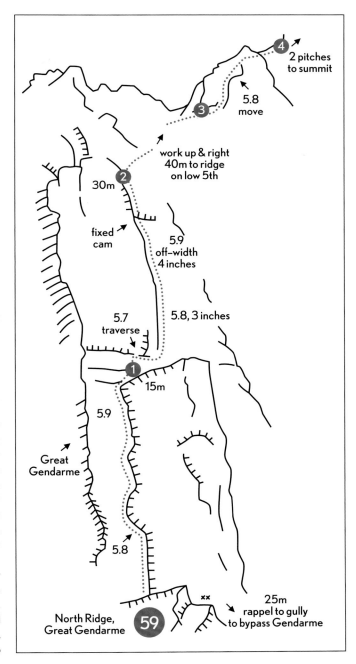

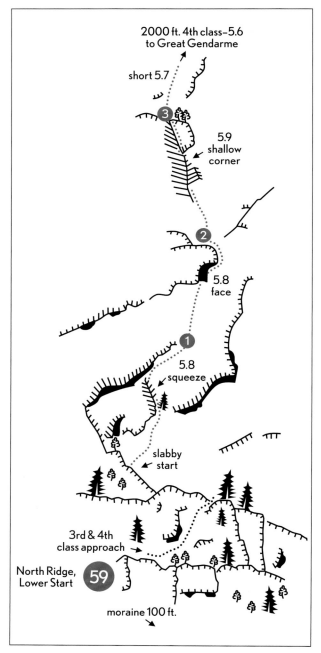

2000 ft. 4th class–5.6
to Great Gendarme

short 5.7

③

5.9
shallow
corner

②

5.8
face

①

5.8
↙ squeeze

slabby
↙ start

3rd & 4th
class approach →

North Ridge,
Lower Start  ⑤⑨

moraine 100 ft.
↙

of the Ice Cliff Glacier Couloir and, a bit farther, the top of the Sherpa Glacier Couloir at about 8400 feet. A steep snow descent of the 40-degree couloir leads to a bergschrund negotiation and the Sherpa Glacier at approximately 7800 feet. Lower on the glacier (6800 feet)—and depending on the season—it may be wise to avoid the gully, which is exposed to icefall; this requires one rappel from the far west edge of the slabs. Retrace the northern approach to the Stuart Lake Trailhead on Mountaineer Creek Road.

**OPTION:** The Northwest Buttress also has merit as a descent route when approaching from the north. It is a route that cleverly avoids snow climbing.

## 60. STUART GLACIER COULOIR: III, 5.7

**TIME:** 1–3 days. **GEAR:** small rack to 2½ inches. Because this route follows a major gully, we don't recommend it for summer; our recommendation is to do it as a snow climb—the earlier in the year, the better, for the simple reason they are the colder months. Spring can be hit or miss, cold one night, warm the next; wait for a cool-weather forecast and hope for clear night skies. Be wary when the snow does not freeze overnight.

We love the pleasing direct line, as well as the mixed nature of this climb. Frost- and snow-covered rock is a bonus, adding to the alpine ambiance. Considering the unexplored nature of the mountain in 1944, this was a very bold climb for a team of only two climbers. For Helmy Beckey, not yet twenty, this climb probably felt like child's play compared to Mount Waddington, which he had climbed two years prior with his older brother, Fred.

### APPROACH
Follow either approach for the preceding climb.

### ROUTE
From the Stuart Glacier, cross the bergschrund at about 7800 feet and climb the couloir to the crest of

*Ideal conditions for John Cooper on Mount Stuart's Northwest Face* (Photo by Jim Nelson)

**false summit**

**Mount Stuart**

**Girth Pillar**

**Northeast Face**

**Ice Cliff Glacier**

**Stuart Glacier**

**to Goat Pass**

*Mount Stuart from the northeast* (Photo by Steph Abegg)

the West Ridge at 9000 feet. A short traverse on the south side of the ridge leads to the West Ridge notch. The upper West Ridge can be tackled either directly above the notch (5.7) or by traversing onto the North Face for two pitches (5.0); both routes lead to a tiny notch on the ridge crest. From this notch, a short drop leads to a ledge traversing across the South Face. A final pitch of 5.7 finishes right at the summit.

### DESCENT
Follow the descent options for the preceding climb.

## SELECTED HISTORY

**1895** First ascents in 1873 and 1890 likely.

**1933 JULY** South Face, Ulrichs Couloir. II. Louis Ulrich, Lex Maxwell, Joe Werner.

**1935 AUGUST** West Ridge. II, 5.6. Fred Llewellyn, Lex Maxwell, John Vertrees.

**1937 AUGUST** Northwest Buttress. II, 4th class. Ed Rankin, John Riley, Louis Ulrich.

**1944 JUNE** Stuart Glacier Couloir. III, 5.6. Helmy Beckey, Larry Strathdee.

**1955 FEBRUARY** FWA. Everett Lasher, Dave Mahre, Bill Prater, Gene Prater, Don Torrey.

**1956 JUNE** Sherpa Glacier. II. Bill Prater, Gene Prater, Don Torrey, Nelson Torrey.

**1956 SEPTEMBER** Upper North Ridge. III. John Rupley, Don Gordon.

**1957 AUGUST** Ice Cliff Glacier. II–III. Dave Mahre, Bill Prater, Gene Prater.

**1959 AUGUST** Northeast Face. IV, 5.9. Don Anderson, Richard Hebble, Dave Mahre, Gene Prater.

**1960 AUGUST** Northeast Face, false summit. IV, 5.7. Fred Beckey, Ron Niccoli.

**1963 JULY** Complete North Ridge, west start. IV, 5.8. Fred Beckey, Steve Marts.

**1964 JULY** Great Gendarme. Jim Wickwire, Fred Stanley.

**1967 AUGUST** *Razorback Ridge*. III, 5.8. Scott Davis, Al Givler, Doug McGowan.

**1968 AUGUST** West Wall, West Ridge. IV, 5.9. Ron Burgner, Don McPherson.

**1970 JULY** Northwest Face, *Valhalla Buttress*. III, 5.8 A1. Dave Beckstead, Paul Myhre.

**1970 JULY** Complete North Ridge, east start. IV+, 5.9. Mead Hargis, Jay Ossiander.

**1975 MARCH** Ice Cliff Glacier, FWA. Reilly Moss.

**1975 MARCH** Upper North Ridge, FWA. Craig McKibben, Jay Ossiander.

**1976 FEBRUARY** Stuart Glacier Couloir, FWA. Paul Ekman, Joe Weiss.

**1978 JULY** North Ridge with Great Gendarme, FFA complete. 5.9. Bob Plumb, Dave Stutzman.

**1983 JULY** *Girth Pillar*. IV, 5.11. Kit Lewis, Jim Nelson.

**1985 FEBRUARY** *Girth Pillar*, FWA. Kit Lewis, Jim Nelson.

**1986 OCTOBER** *Girth Pillar East*. IV, 5.9 A2. Mark Bebie, Charlie Hampson.

**1987 JUNE** *Blue Moon in June*. IV. Bob Cotter, Jim Ruch.

**1987 JULY** Direct Northwest Face. IV, 5.10+. Alan Kearney.

**1990 DECEMBER** Full North Ridge 1963 start, *Surrogate Panama*. Jack Davis, George Sharrett.

**1991 JULY** Ice Cliff Arête. IV, 5.9. Matt Coleman, Paul Myhre.

**1993 SEPTEMBER** Northwest Face, FFA. IV, 5.10. Alan Kearney.

**2005 MARCH** Full North Ridge with Great Gendarme, FWA complete. Mark Bunker, Colin Haley.

**2005 MARCH** Northwest Face, FWA. John Cooper, Jim Nelson.

**2007 APRIL** Northeast Face, *Lara Kellogg Memorial Route*. III+. Colin Haley, Dylan Johnson.

**2009 JULY** *Gorillas in the Mist*. IV, 5.10. Blake Herrington, Jens Holsten, Sol Wertkin.

**2011 AUGUST** *Joe Puryear Memorial Route*. IV, 5.10+. Jens Holsten, Sol Wertkin, Mark Westman.

**2016 SEPTEMBER** *King Kong*. IV, 5.11+. Jon Gleason, Tyree Johnson, Sol Wertkin.

# COLCHUCK PEAK 8705'

## PROMINENCE: 665' [36]

### COLCHUCK GLACIER

A very high quartz diorite and granodiorite peak overshadowed by a couple of nearby giants, Colchuck Peak provides opportunities for year-round adventures. Routes on either rock or snow, a simple approach, and rain-shadow weather combine to make Colchuck one of the more popular Cascade climbs. It is also a high peak with reasonable winter access. Colchuck can be climbed from a base camp at spectacular Colchuck Lake (5570 feet) or as a day trip from the trailhead at 3400 feet.

### LAND MANAGER

Alpine Lakes Wilderness, Okanogan-Wenatchee National Forest, Wenatchee River Ranger District. Northwest Forest Pass or interagency recreation pass required for parking. Free self-registered wilderness permit required for day trips; limited permits, issued by lottery (see Resources), required for overnight trips in Enchantment Permit Area May 15–October 31.

## 61. COLCHUCK GLACIER: GRADE II

**TIME:** 1–2 days. This snow climb changes dramatically through the season, from powder snow in March to ideal crampon conditions in June and hard ice in late season. Expect everything from breakable crust to sticky glop before about mid-June. By midsummer, hazards increase as the glacier breaks open. The Colchuck Glacier descends below the slabs of Dragontail Peak's northwest face and provides an impressive backdrop for such an easy summit as Colchuck Peak.

*Colchuck and Dragontail Peaks from the north: (A) Backbone Ridge route, (B) Triple Couloirs route, (C) Colchuck Glacier route* (Photo by John Scurlock)

## SELECTED HISTORY

**1948 AUGUST** Colchuck Glacier. II. Elvin Johnson, Norma Johnson, William Long, Kathy Long.
**1960 FEBRUARY** Colchuck Peak, FWA. Gene Prater party.
**1962 JULY** North Buttress Couloir. II. Ray Lilleby, Jim Wickwire.
**1969 SEPTEMBER** East Face. III, 5.8 A1. Manuel Gonzales, Don Williamson.
**1970 JULY** Northeast Buttress. III+. Julie Brugger, Mark Weigelt.
**1975 JANUARY** Northeast Couloir, FA. Skip Edmonds, Clark Gerhardt, Paula Kregel, Greg Markov.
**1976 JANUARY** North Buttress Couloir, FWA. Dave Seman, Mark Thornton.
**1993 AUGUST** East Face. III, 5.10+ AO. Keith Hertel, Steve Risse.
**2011 JANUARY** Northeast Face. IV, mixed. Jens Holsten, Dan Hilden.
**2013 MARCH** Northeast Buttress, FWA. Jens Holsten, Shaun Johnson.

## APPROACH, GRADE II

Follow the northern approach for Climb 59, North Ridge of Mount Stuart, to the Stuart Lake Trailhead. There is 2900 feet of elevation gain to the bottom of the moraine, 80 percent on trail, 700 feet on snow or talus.

Follow the Stuart Lake Trail No. 1599 for 3 miles to where it forks. Take the left fork, the Colchuck Lake Trail No. 1599A, south; it crosses to the east side of Mountaineer Creek at about 4500 feet. At 5 miles reach the north shore of Colchuck Lake (5570 feet).

Continue around the southwest side of the lake on the Aasgard Pass trail, past a small lakelet, eventually reaching a large talus field below the Colchuck Glacier moraine. Climb talus and scree to the low point in the moraine, where a small stream runs at about 6100 feet.

## ROUTE

Head for the eastern segment of the glacier below Dragontail Peak. White scars high on Dragontail's face mark locations of recent rockfalls. Climb the glacier to the Dragontail-Colchuck col at 8100 feet. Scramble 3rd-class ledges followed by a snow slope (early season) to the summit plateau at about 8500 feet. The summit lies at the far northwest end of the plateau; expect some slogging on the summit plateau before midseason.

## DESCENT

Descend the climbing route, resisting the temptation to glissade unless snow conditions allow for full and total control.

# DRAGONTAIL PEAK 8840'

## PROMINENCE: 1760' [29]

### BACKBONE RIDGE; TRIPLE COULOIRS

The enormous north face of Dragontail Peak is a striking sight when viewed from Colchuck Lake: a mile wide and

*Gordy Skoog nears the summit of Dragontail's north face.* (Photo by Lowell Skoog)

*Ryan Lurie on the off-width pitch on Dragontail Peak's Backbone Ridge* (Photo by Sky Sjue)

2500 feet high from its low point only 700 feet above Colchuck Lake. From its lowest point, the face curves both west and east. Dragontail's northwest face shares a glacier with neighbor Colchuck Peak, while the northeast face borders the long climb to Aasgard Pass. The north face features a half dozen major ridges, interspersed with ledges, deep couloirs, slabs, walls, and endless corner systems. While lacking the classic lines of Stuart or Prusik, this complex face has a seemingly limitless amount of quartz diorite and granodiorite rock to be climbed.

**NOTE:** Anyone climbing Dragontail's north face should be aware of the potential for rockfall from parties above.

This is an accessible and popular mountain; scan the face and the proposed route from the base of the climb. If the location of other climbing parties is problematic, consider a change of plans.

### LAND MANAGER
Alpine Lakes Wilderness, Okanogan-Wenatchee National Forest, Wenatchee River Ranger District. Northwest Forest Pass or interagency recreation pass required for parking. Free self-issued wilderness permit required for day trips; limited permits, issued by lottery (see Resources), required for overnight trips in Enchantment Permit Area May 15–October 31.

## 62. BACKBONE RIDGE: GRADE IV, 5.9

**TIME:** 1-2 days. **GEAR:** crampons are often helpful to reach the rock and for the descent. Backbone Ridge is one of the more easily accessible of the long alpine rock climbs in the Stuart Range. Competent routefinding and the ability to move quickly are necessary to avoid a bivy on this climb.

### APPROACH, GRADE II

Follow the approach for Climb 61, Colchuck Glacier. There is about 3400 feet of elevation gain to the top of the moraine.

From the low point in the moraine, where a small stream runs at about 6100 feet, ascend to the top of the eastern moraine at about 6800 feet, where a steep snow patch guards access to Dragontail's northwest face.

### ROUTE

Find a moat crossing, aiming for the broad gully and slabs that divide Backbone Ridge from Serpentine Ridge. Traverse east on ledges past the base of the ridge and beyond until able to work back up and right (west) on ledges to the base of a corner below the crest. **PITCH 1:** Climb the corner (5.6) to the crest of the ridge and the start of the real difficulties. **PITCH 2:** Climb the 6-inch crack right (west) of the crest (5.9; protectable only with large pro). **PITCHES 3-4:** Continue near the crest (5.8; cracks and steps) to a belay on the narrow crest. **PITCH 5:** Move down and left (exposed 5.8) to gain a crack system left (east) of the crest. **PITCHES 6-7:** Follow the crack system (5.7), bypassing a 5.9 off-width crack, up to the crest of the ridge.

**PITCHES 8-11:** Continue up big blocks and short steps on or near the crest to the end of Backbone Ridge at the base of The Fin, the large white slab. Low-5th-class climbing leads up and across The Fin on the main ledge system. Face climbing followed by twin cracks (5.8-5.9) ends at a belay on the left end of a large ledge in the middle of The Fin. **PITCH 12:** Climb a flake with undercling moves (5.9) up, then back left to a belay. **PITCH 13:** Face climbing and small ledges lead right and up to the crest beyond a blocky gendarme (5.7). **PITCH 14:** From the crest, the final pitch leads to easier climbing, which leads to the top of the route just east of the summit.

### DESCENT

Descend 30-degree snow southeast, then east to Aasgard Pass. From the pass, go north down the Aasgard Pass trail to Colchuck Lake. Use caution below Aasgard Pass, where snow conditions can easily be underestimated. Several tragedies and many near misses have occurred on these friendly-looking slopes.

## 63. TRIPLE COULOIRS: GRADE III, 5.7

**TIME:** 1-2 days. The Triple Couloirs route is an appealing climb that provides the challenges of variable mixed climbing high in the alpine zone where conditions can change quickly. While the broad north face of Dragontail has many mixed-route possibilities, changeable conditions demand a savvy alpinist. The Triple Couloirs route has two crux sections: the first comes at the exit of the First, or "Hidden," Couloir and the second connects the Second and Third Couloirs. A two-pitch direct connection between the First and Second Couloirs is condition dependent, as are the other routes on the face. (One popular option beginning a bit west of Triple Couloirs takes one of the longest direct lines on the face.)

### APPROACH

Follow the approach for Colchuck Glacier (Climb 61) to Colchuck Lake, and continue around the southwest side of the lake on the Aasgard Pass trail. It's much faster to cross the lake when it's frozen than to follow the summer route around the lake; trips before May should have a good chance of being able to cross the frozen lake. On the far side of the lake, head up the Aasgard Pass trail to below the north face.

### ROUTE

The route begins a short distance uphill (east) of the lowest point of the north face. Straightforward snow climbing in the First (Hidden) Couloir leads up around 800 feet until just below a steep wall where ice runnels lead to the Second Couloir. From this point, there are three options:

**OPTION 1 (LEFT ON THE ROUTE PHOTO):** Climb the steep ice runnels (70-80 degrees) directly for three pitches into the Second Couloir. The difficulty of these pitches varies

*Priti Wright on the direct connection to the Second Couloir, on Dragontail's Triple Couloirs (Photo by Jeffry Wright)*

## SELECTED HISTORY

**1937 JUNE** Dragontail Peak. I. Dudley Kelly, William Long.

**1957 MARCH** Dragontail Peak, FWA. Barry Carlson, Gene Prater, Ralph Uber.

**1962 JUNE** Northwest Face. III, 5.6. Fred Beckey, Dan Davis.

**1963 AUGUST** Rooster Finch Tower. I, 5.5. Fred Stanley, Jim Wickwire.

**1970 JULY** Northeast Couloir. III, 5.7. Dave Beckstead, Paul Myhre.

**1970 AUGUST** Backbone Ridge. IV, 5.9. John Bonneville, Mark Weigelt.

**1971 JUNE** North Face, Hidden Couloir. III+, 5.7. Fred Stanley, Jim Wickwire.

**1971 AUGUST** North Face, Direct Route. III, 5.7. Eric Gerber, Charles Sink.

**1971 SEPTEMBER** Northeast Buttress. III+, 5.8. Fred Beckey, Ron Burgner, Thom Nephew.

**1972 JUNE** Northeast Arête. III, 5.7. Dave Anderson, Bruce Carson, Donn Heller, Steve Barnett.

**1973 JULY** Northwest Face, *Serpentine Ridge*. III+, 5.8. Tom Hargis, Jay Ossiander.

**1974 MAY** *Triple Couloir*. III, 5.7. Bill Joiner, Leslie Nelson, Dave Seman.

**1975 FEBRUARY** Northeast Couloir, FWA. Cal Folsom, Donn Heller.

**1975 FEBRUARY** North Face, *Stanley-Wickwire*, FWA. Skip Edmonds, Dick Heffernan.

**1977 AUGUST** Northwest Face, *Boving-Christensen*. III+, 5.10+. Paul Boving, Matt Christensen.

**1978 APRIL** North Face. IV, 5.9. Michael Croswaite, Thomas Stanton.

**1984 JULY** Northeast Buttress, *Cauthorn-Stoddard*. IV, 5.9. Dan Cauthorn, John Stoddard.

**1985 JULY** Northeast Buttress, *Dragonfly*. IV, 5.11. Bob McGowan, Jim Yoder.

**1987 OCTOBER** Northwest Face, *Kearney-Keleman*. III, 5.9. Alan Kearney, Peter Keleman.

**1988 AUGUST** Northeast Rib. IV, 5.8+. Tobin Kelly, Jim Yoder.

**1989 JULY** Northeast Buttress, *Dragons of Eden*. Bob McGowan, Wayne Wallace.

**2004 MARCH** *Serpentine Ridge*, FWA. Ade Miller, Alasdair Turner.

**2005 AUGUST** Northeast Buttress, *Hirst-Wehrly*. IV, 5.10 A0. Peter Hirst, Eric Wehrly.

**2009 JANUARY** *Backbone Ridge*, FWA. Ade Miller, John Plotz.

**2009 JULY** *Dragons of Eden*, FFA. IV, 5.12-. Jens Holsten, Sol Wertkin.

**2012 FEBRUARY** Northeast Buttress, FWA. Colin Bohannan, Nate Farr, Jens Holsten.

**2020 AUGUST** East Face, Northeast Towers, *This, My Friend*. III, 5.9+. Chris Potts, Andy Wyatt.

greatly depending on conditions and the amount of ice formed. This can be hard mixed climbing on thin ice with minimal protection (pitons useful).

**OPTION 2 (RIGHT ON THE ROUTE PHOTO):** This is the route that was used on the first ascent. Continue up the First Couloir another pitch or so until another small snow couloir leads up and then left to a good belay on rock very close to the Second Couloir. Gain entrance to the Second Couloir by climbing down and across or making a short rappel, depending on snow conditions.

**OPTION 3 (NOT SHOWN ON THE ROUTE PHOTO):** Continue up the First (Hidden) Couloir several more rope lengths to the very top of the Hidden Couloir where it is not feasible to reach the Second Couloir. This option bypasses the Second Couloir and climbs what in summer is 4th- and low-5th-class terrain (Direct Route used by Gerber-Sink).

Assuming the first or second option is taken, climbing the Second Couloir is straightforward snow climbing until it steepens below the Third Couloir. The difficulty of this pitch depends on snow and ice cover but often requires sketchy mixed climbing (pitons may be helpful). The Third Couloir is moderate snow with a final mixed bit onto the summit ridge, a bit east of the summit.

## DESCENT

Follow the descent for the preceding climb.

# COLCHUCK BALANCED ROCK    8200'

**PROMINENCE: 160'**

## WEST FACE; LET IT BURN

This magnificent alpine crag rivals Prusik Peak for high-standard rock climbs on great granodiorite rock. Colchuck Balanced Rock, or CBR as it's known, is located high above Colchuck Lake, where the presence of Dragontail, Colchuck, and Stuart present a stunning backdrop. Because of its altitude of more than 8000 feet and western exposure, plan for cool temperatures and sun only in the afternoon.

The first route on the west face was climbed in 1980 and became an instant classic. *Let It Burn*, climbed in 2010, features wild knobs that just barely connect incredible crack systems. With more than ten high-quality routes established since, CBR has earned a reputation as one of Washington's finest alpine crags.

*Jessica Campbell on the classic pitch 5 corner of Colchuck Balanced Rock's West Face* (**Photo by Max Hasson**)

## LAND MANAGER

Alpine Lakes Wilderness, Okanogan-Wenatchee National Forest, Wenatchee River Ranger District. Northwest Forest Pass or interagency recreation pass required for parking. Free self-issued wilderness permit required for day trips; limited permits, issued by lottery (see Resources), required for overnight trips in Enchantment Permit Area May 15-October 31.

# 64. WEST FACE: GRADE III, 5.11+

**TIME:** 1-2 days. **GEAR:** double rack to 2½ inches, plus one at 3½ inches. This was the first route on the face; along with the 1984 route, it remained one of the only two routes for thirty years. It is a classic line on a very steep wall, with several well-protected cruxes and one aid move that goes free at 5.12.

## APPROACH, GRADE II

Follow the approach for Climb 61, Colchuck Glacier, to Colchuck Lake. **NOTE:** In late season, water is scarce beyond the lake.

Leave the trail upon reaching Colchuck Lake and cross the outlet stream at the north end of the lake by the small dam. Follow the Aasgard Pass trail south a short way to a small clearing among boulders with talus on your

*Colchuck Balanced Rock from the west: (A) West Face, (B)* Let It Burn *(Photo by Steph Abegg)*

left. Head up the talus and slightly left into the woods above. The path leads to a scramble through a short rock step (3rd–4th class). The route continues up and south, following a cairned path through open forest until reaching a col (6800 feet) with nice campsites among boulders below. There won't be water here by late summer.

## ROUTE

The route begins a little left of center on the west face. Scramble up and left along the base to find the start. **PITCH 1:** Locate a few steep 5.8 moves out of the ramp and continue right, past trees to ledges below a short, thin crack. **PITCH 2:** Jam the thin crack for 40 feet (5.10+) and move up and left behind a block; belay behind the block/tower. **PITCH 3:** Move off to the right from the tower blocks and style up a slabby corner (5.9); continue up the 5.9 corner until you can work to the right to a ledge with trees. **PITCH 4:** The next short pitch either climbs a block (5.8) around to the left or takes the 5.10 finger crack to the right; belay in about 40 feet where the two variations join. **PITCH 5:** The steep crack (5.10+ sustained) up the corner is 1–3 inches and straightforward though strenuous; move out left on a flake and find the stance with pins and fixed trad gear. **PITCH 6:** Continue up the flake and move left (5.11) underneath the amazing roof; watch for a notorious rope-snagging pinch near the left end, and move up a short distance to the belay. **PITCH 7:** Follow a great 5.9 hand crack up to a well-protected small roof (5.11+), the crux. **PITCH 8:** Continue up flakes and edges to a difficult flaring chimney (5.10-); higher, work a second and easier chimney, then eventually a hand crack on a slab leads to blocky ground and the belay. **PITCH 9:** Go right for 30 feet, then simul-climb easier ground to the summit.

## DESCENT

Find slings on a horn down below Colchuck Balanced Rock; make a 100-foot (30m) rappel and scramble down (some 3rd class with snow till midseason) toward the Aasgard Pass trail and Colchuck Lake.

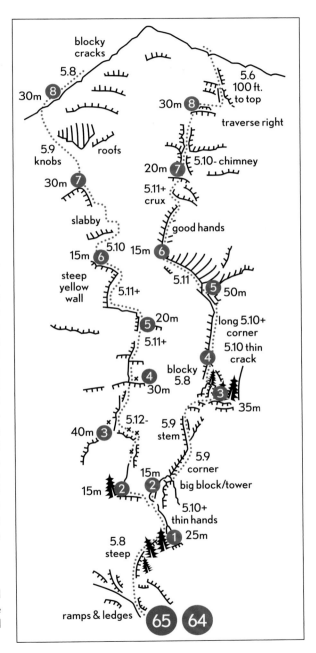

# 65. LET IT BURN: GRADE III, 5.12-

**TIME:** 1-2 days. **GEAR:** double rack to 2 inches, singles to 2½ inches; single set of wires. Blake Herrington calls this one of the top fifteen routes in the Cascades, and while that's quite a statement, this is undeniably an amazing climb for a team strong enough to pull it off. The supersteep, clean rock and dizzying exposure make for a line of great purity. The first-ascent team spent ten days working the route and placed only four bolts: a real statement about the quality of the cracks.

## APPROACH
Follow the approach for the preceding climb.

## ROUTE
**PITCH 1:** Same as the West Face route to the base of the 5.10+ thin-hands-splitter. **PITCH 2:** Climb the short 5.10+ thin-hands-splitter and move left on a ledge to belay with a tree. **PITCH 3:** Climb 5.10 finger cracks to a 5.11 V-slot, clip a bolt, and move left on a flake and back right again; higher, move left past two bolts (5.12-) and up a short finger crack to a belay with a single bolt. **PITCH 4:** Climb a

*Jens Holsten on* Let It Burn *(Photo by Max Hasson)*

## SELECTED HISTORY

**1958 OCTOBER**  South route. I, 3rd class. Gene Prater, Thomas Quin.

**1975 JUNE**  Northwest Buttress. II, 5.8. Jerry Barnard, Carla Firey, Al Givler, Jim McCarthy.

**1980 JULY**  West Face. III, 5.11+. Tomas Boley, Jack Lewis.

**1983 APRIL**  North Face. II. Dan Cauthorn, Tobin Kelly.

**1984 JULY**  West Face, Northwest Buttress. III, 5.10. Lee Cunningham, Monte Westlund.

**2009 JUNE**  *The Scoop*. III, 5.11+. Evan Cabodi, Matt Clifton, Stewart Matthiesen.

**2009 AUGUST**  *Full Tilt*. III, 5.12. Seth Angivine, John Berry, Evelyn Cheng, Jared Otto, and friends.

**2010 JUNE**  *Leche la Vaca*. II, 5.10. Tom Ramier, Craig Rankin, Abe Traven.

**2010 SEPTEMBER**  *Let It Burn*. III, 5.12-. Max Hasson, Jens Holsten.

**2010**  *Milk 'n' Honey*. III, 5.11-. Tom Ramier, Craig Rankin, Abe Traven.

**2010**  *Rikki Tikki Tavi*. III, 5.11. Tom Ramier, Abe Traven.

**2012 SEPTEMBER**  *Accendo Lunae*. II, 5.12-. Scott Bennett, Blake Herrington, Graham Zimmerman.

**2017**  *Tipping Point*. III, 5.12. Kerwin Loukusa, Luke Stefurak.

5.11 hand and finger crack to knobs and a double crack; belay at a stance with a bolt and a pin. **PITCH 5:** Climb the right-leaning slot-flare (5.11+); an athletic layback works up to a belay beside a huge golden flake. **PITCH 6:** Move up and left, across the flake, to an arching right-facing corner (5.11+); pass a reachy move and belay at a ledge. **PITCH 7:** Traverse to the right across the ledge and up, then move left across a slab (5.10), followed by easier climbing left and up to a belay below a large roof. **PITCH 8:** This long pitch climbs knobs and cracks left of the roof (5.9), followed by easier climbing. **PITCH 9:** Another long pitch of 5.8 reaches the top.

### DESCENT

Follow the descent for the preceding climb.

# AASGARD SENTINEL 8000'

**PROMINENCE: <50'**

## THE VALKYRIE; ACID BABY

Aasgard Sentinel is one of the many towers of steep quartz diorite, granodiorite, and granite on the left on the hike up toward Aasgard Pass and the Enchantments. Much of the nomenclature up here is somewhat nebulous despite having been explored by generations of local climbers. Julie Brugger, Dave Anderson, Bruce Carson, and others all made numerous trips up to these formations, and some parts of the more recent ascents were almost certainly climbed back in the day.

In recent years, much new climbing has occurred in this vicinity, and attempts to sort out the nomenclature for these features are reflected here. Whatever they were called in the past, it seems likely that the popularity of these routes will now lock in the naming convention for at least this formation.

### LAND MANAGER

Alpine Lakes Wilderness, Okanogan-Wenatchee National Forest, Wenatchee River Ranger District. Northwest Forest Pass or interagency recreation pass required for parking. Free self-issued wilderness permit required for day trips; limited permits, issued by lottery (see Resources), required for overnight trips in Enchantment Permit Area May 15–October 31.

## 66. THE VALKYRIE: GRADE III, 5.10

**TIME:** 1 day. **GEAR:** wires, double rack to #2 Camalot, single #3; optional #5 for pitch 2. This is the left-hand of the two routes on the Sentinel and perhaps the easier of these two lines.

*Jaime Bohle traversing the summit ridge on Aasgard Sentinel (Photo by Doug Hutchinson)*

## APPROACH, GRADE II

Follow the approach for Climb 61, Colchuck Glacier, to Colchuck Lake. Continue around the southwest side of the lake on the Aasgard Pass trail. Ascend the trail almost two-thirds of the way to the pass, leaving the trail at about 7300 feet, then hike east another ten minutes toward a small stand of tamarack trees beneath Aasgard Sentinel. Look for a deep chimney-gully that forms the right side of this rock.

## ROUTE

This route starts about 50 feet left of *Acid Baby* on an obvious right-leaning slab that leads to the obvious big roof system. **PITCH 1:** Climb about 100 feet of runout slab up to 5.8 and look for a way over the right end of the roof (5.10); continue up the corner above, and belay at a patch of orange-colored rock. **PITCH 2:** Work right on a thin flake, which gains a 15-foot off-width crack, and keep going above with a left-facing hand crack (5.10); face climbing above the corner finishes at a small stance with a horn. **PITCH 3:**

*Aasgard Sentinel from the south near Aasgard Pass* (Photo by Steph Abegg)

Continue with cracks on the crest of the rock until a ramp diagonals off left to reach a reasonable belay ledge. **PITCH 4:** Traverse right on slabs and flakes to move sideways (5.10) around a small pillar; work up a hand crack in a right-facing corner, and end on a slab with cracks and small ledges. **PITCH 5:** Small cracks and welcome knobs (5.10-) lead up and right across the steep face above; pass a short crack with good placements and aim for the prow up and right (this is the same belay used by *Acid Baby*). **PITCH 6:** Gain the main crest of the ridge and hand-traverse to the summit across fins and flakes, staying mostly on the lake side of the crest.

*Janet Arendall leading pitch 5 of* **The Valkyrie** *on the* **Aasgard Sentinel** (Photo by Steph Abegg)

## DESCENT

From behind the summit tower, twenty minutes of sometimes steep and sandy hiking to the northwest leads to the open terrain and meadows of the upper Enchantments. Eventually aim back down the scree and talus to the south and pick up the Aasgard Pass trail not far below the actual pass.

Another, shorter option is to descend by way of a more direct gully. From the summit, make a 20-foot 5.6 down-climb into a gully on the east side of the formation This is followed by some scrambling and routefinding among blocky ledges and slabs, until you attain the pass trail.

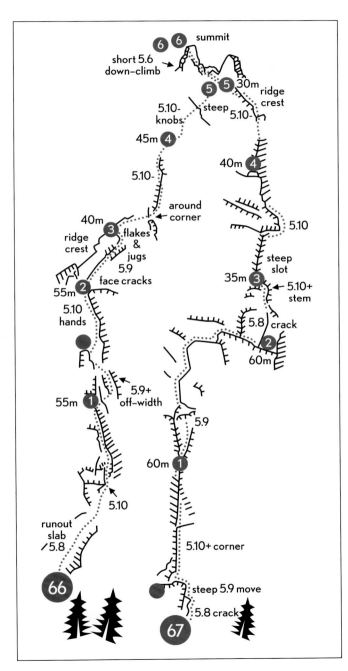

## 67. ACID BABY: GRADE III, 5.10+

**TIME:** 1 day. **GEAR:** wires, double rack to #3 Camalot, single #4 Camalot. *Acid Baby* is becoming something of a trade route for the location, and the good cracks and traditional climbing make for many different options on how to break up the pitches. Regardless of how you slice it, it's a fun climb in a spectacular location.

### APPROACH

Follow the approach for the preceding climb, to the deep chimney-gully that forms the right side of this rock.

### ROUTE

**PITCH 1:** Take an obvious left-leaning hand and finger crack (5.9), where there is an optional belay, followed by a steep corner crack (5.10+) to an alcove belay at 200 feet (60m). **PITCH 2:** Climb cracks to under the large roof, then traverse and down-climb steppy blocks a short distance out to the prow on the right and belay below an obvious crack; 200 feet (60m). **PITCH 3:** Hand and fist climbing (5.8) lead up into the crux stemming section (5.10+) and more hard moves left to the belay. **PITCH 4:** Climb into a continuously steep slot, then sneak beneath a roof to the right and reach a good crack around the corner, which continues steeply with fingers and hands; there are some loose blocks in this section. **PITCH 5:** Work up with short cracks and flakes just left of the ridge crest (5.10-) and locate a belay under a steep step, which sets you up for the unique summit ridge traverse. **PITCH 6:** Follow the last pitch of *The Valkyrie*.

### DESCENT

Follow one of the descent options for the preceding climb.

# PRUSIK PEAK                    8000'

## PROMINENCE: 160'

### SOUTH FACE, BURGNER-STANLEY; SOUTH FACE, LADY GODIVA AND DER SPORTSMAN; WEST RIDGE

One of the Cascades' most recognized rocks, iconic Prusik Peak is admired for its striking form and beautiful clean quartz diorite and granodiorite rock. Located at the west end of Temple Ridge high above a fairyland of lakes, streams, and rock outcrops, it is an unmistakable project. Prusik's wide south face holds more than a half dozen high-quality routes on great stone. On the first ascent of the peak, Fred Beckey described the eponymous final section: "From a lesser block Holben whipped a loop over the horn on the fourth try. Soon I reached the top on prusik slings, finding the last few overhanging feet very awkward."

Because Prusik receives most of the rock-climbing interest, the surrounding peaks and spires hold hundreds of neglected rock climbs, most with beautiful campsites away from the heavily traveled Enchantment Basin through-trail. On a weeklong expedition here in 1977, Chris Greyell and David Whitelaw climbed six new routes on the ridgeline west of Prusik Pass and added still another to the south face of the west ridge on Prusik itself.

At the Cashmere Crags' southern boundary above Ingalls Creek, you have the southern faces of Little Annapurna, and high above Crystal Creek are the barely known Nightmare Needles. On the northern border above Icicle Creek, find two other major summits, including the Mole

and the Blockhouse, surrounded by smaller crags. Located roughly in the middle of the Enchantments, Temple Ridge comprises more than a dozen high summits just begging to be traversed. Three Musketeer Ridge and D'Artagnan Tower, immediately north of Mount Temple, hold several other gems also climbed by Greyell and Whitelaw back in the day.

### LAND MANAGER

Alpine Lakes Wilderness, Okanogan-Wenatchee National Forest, Wenatchee River Ranger District. Northwest Forest Pass or interagency recreation pass required for parking. Free self-issued wilderness permit required for day trips; limited permits, issued by lottery (see Resources), required for overnight trips in Enchantment Permit Area May 15–October 31.

*Alan Kearney belaying Bobby Knight on their 1993 free variation of the original* Lady Godiva *route (Photo by Paul Sloan)*

*Prusik Peak through the trees* (Photo by Carl Skoog)

## 68. SOUTH FACE, BURGNER-STANLEY: GRADE III, 5.9+

**TIME:** 1–3 days. **GEAR:** medium rack to 4 inches, with doubles from ¾ inch to 2½ inches. Rock on the south face of Prusik is of such quality that it has become the standard by which other Cascade climbs boasting good rock are compared. Pitch after pitch of sustained crack climbing on solid granite puts this route in a select class.

### APPROACH, GRADE III

Two approach routes are possible, and debate continues as to the relative merits of each. Both approaches are approximately 10 miles.

**VIA SNOW CREEK:** From the west end of Leavenworth on the Stevens Pass Highway (US Highway 2), drive Icicle Creek Road (Forest Road 76) west 4.3 miles to the Snow Lakes Trailhead at 1360 feet. The unmistakable roomy Snow Lakes parking lot, located on the left near the mouth

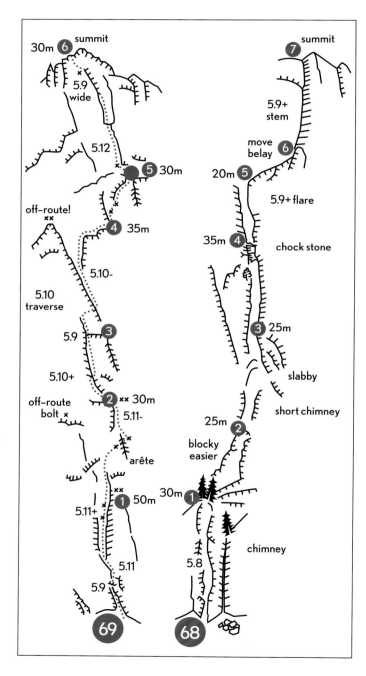

of the canyon, is heavily patrolled: in the truly olden days, thefts and break-ins at the trailhead were not uncommon. There is 6100 feet of elevation gain, 90 percent on trail, 10 percent off trail.

Hike the Snow Lakes Trail No. 1553 as it ascends the first set of many switchbacks. At about 2 miles, pass the Snow Creek Wall. Continue slogging 3 miles to Nada Lake at 5000 feet, and at 7 miles reach the Snow Lakes at 5415 feet. From Snow Lakes, cross the dam and proceed around the east side of upper Snow Lake, then cross the creek. In 2 more steep miles, reach Lake Vivian at 6785 feet. Find a faint path up to the ridge east of Vivian and west of Temple Lake. A route up through talus and small trees leads to the base of the south face.

**VIA AASGARD PASS:** Follow the approach for Climb 61, Colchuck Glacier, to Colchuck Lake. There is a total of 4800 feet of elevation gain, 90 percent on trail, 10 percent off trail.

Continue around the southwest side of Colchuck Lake on the Aasgard Pass trail. Hike up the long, steep slope to Aasgard Pass (7800 feet). Follow the trail east past several lakes for about 3 miles to the north end of Perfection Lake at 7000 feet. For the south face routes, find a trail east from Perfection Lake up to picturesque Gnome Tarn at 7400 feet, a short way from Prusik's south face.

## ROUTE

Start at the left of two deep chimneys. **PITCH 1:** Climb the awkward chimney (5.7) or the crack (5.8) immediately left of the chimney; both options end at a belay below larch trees. **PITCH 2:** Continue up through a second patch of larch trees. **PITCH 3:** Climb corner systems (5.8) up and slightly right toward a shallow chimney. **PITCH 4:** Climb the chimney (5.8) to a point below the chock stone; squeeze under the large chock stone (5.8), watching for loose blocks, and belay a short bit above. **PITCH 5:** Jam up to an awkward flaring chimney (5.9+; protectable with 2- to 3-inch gear) ending at the west end of the large ledge about 150 feet below the summit. **PITCH 6:** Move the belay to the right (east) end of the ledge. **PITCH 7:** Jam a strenuous (5.9+) crack to the top.

## DESCENT

It is possible to make four or five 75-foot (25m) rappels to the north and then comfortably scramble back to just north of Prusik Pass.

## 69. SOUTH FACE, LADY GODIVA AND DER SPORTSMAN: GRADE III, 5.12

**TIME:** 1–2 days. **GEAR:** medium rack with double set of cams to 3½ inches and small nuts. This is another climb that pushed the free-climbing ethos forward and went unrepeated for several years, though it was rediscovered by Leavenworth locals in 2008 and recognized for both its quality and vision.

Portions of the route were climbed using aid in 1974. Alan Kearney returned with Bobby Knight in 1993, finding a free variation but avoiding the squeeze/off-width at the top by finishing with the last pitch of the *Burgner-Stanley* route. In 2005 *Der Sportsman* was established all free, including the upper pitches avoided on the 1993 ascent.

The three routes certainly share pitches, including the first 40 feet and the last 150 feet, but where they differ in

*Jessica Campbell on the first pitch of* Der Sportsman *(Photo by Max Hasson)*

*Prusik Peak from the south:* (A) Lady Godiva *and* Der Sportsman, *(B)* Burgner-Stanley, *(C)* West ridge **(Photo by John Scurlock)**

the middle section is not clear. Brooke Sandahl provided the following comments: "In 2005 Doug [Ingersoll] and I climbed it top to bottom (no falls for me). I did the first pitch without bolts originally, but decided it had a lot better flow with the two at the top of the pitch. So I added those. I'd originally hoped to do the stunning overhanging headwall crack (one of the three), but opted out for the crack far right (easier) on the summit tower to just finish the dang thing!"

## APPROACH

Follow either approach for the preceding climb.

## ROUTE

Start the route on the west side of the main arête and fire away! **PITCH 1:** Begin in a left-angling crack system (5.9) and continue as the crack thins to 5.11 and leads into a wide stemming feature; stem the box and work up the right side with strenuous 5.11+ to reach the exposed bolted anchor on the right. **PITCH 2:** This complicated 5.11- pitch moves up and right, crossing corners and arêtes. There is enough fixed gear to stay oriented; however, avoid an off-route bolt above a seam about midway up the pitch. Finally, a thin crack-corner on the arête with a fixed pin leads up to the bolted belay. **PITCH 3:** Climb the obvious flake to the left and continue with great flakes, cracks (5.10+), and a corner to reach a big ledge and set up a gear belay. **PITCH 4:** Climb a 5.9 corner for about 20 feet, then make a sharp right traverse (5.10) to reach a right-facing system; higher, another tricky move right (5.10-) reaches a pillar and up to a fixed pin and gear belay. **PITCH 5:** Climb the brief corner above and left, then move back right to find a slab with belay bolts on it; however, continue past the bolts, passing a corner on the left, and reach a ledge to build a gear anchor. **PITCH 6:** Step left on the ledge and pass a bolt; work up to a clean off-hands-sized crack (5.12), which opens a bit and leads to a chimney with an unstable block inside. Find a bolt on the left that exits the difficulties, and continue a short distance to the top.

## DESCENT

Follow the descent for the preceding climb.

## 70. WEST RIDGE: GRADE II, 5.7

**TIME:** 1–2 days. **GEAR:** medium rack to 3 inches. The West Ridge is a not-as-hard-as-it-looks fun route to the top of this famous peak. A short, exposed slab midway provides the crux, where unprotected moves demand care and confidence. A bigger challenge may be obtaining a permit into this popular area.

### APPROACH
Follow either approach for Climb 68, South Face, *Burgner-Stanley*. From the base of the south face, follow a trail north to Prusik Pass at 7500 feet.

### ROUTE
The climb begins just above Prusik Pass; locating sections of worn lichen may help find the start. **PITCHES 1–2:** Begin with two short pitches of 5.0; blocky, solid rock leads to the crest of the ridge a short way below a short slab. **PITCH 3:** Climb the poorly protected short slab (5.7) and continue; easier climbing traverses below a small horn on the south side of the ridge. **PITCH 4:** When possible, drop a bit to the north and walk ledges until under the summit area. **PITCH 5:** Climb a left-facing corner (5.7) to a ledge, move to the right to a flake, and continue up a short chimney to the top.

### DESCENT
Follow the descent for Climb 68, South Face, *Burgner-Stanley*.

## SNOW CREEK WALL          4000'

### OUTER SPACE WITH REMORSE START: HYPERSPACE

Long considered the culmination of the Leavenworth experience, Snow Creek Wall presents an obvious challenge to all who drive up Icicle Creek Road. While the approach is fairly casual, it does take a bit over an hour and includes a creek crossing followed by a short scramble up to the base of the wall. The striking 800-foot shield formed by the left-central part of the wall, obvious even from town, is home to one of the most incredible hand cracks in creation.

The legendary crack up the middle of the shield is part of the *Outer Space* route and has been a rite-of-passage sort of climb for decades. Indeed, Ken Wilson, the long-ago editor of *Mountain Magazine*, thought it one of the greatest cracks in the world, and that may even be true for climbs of that standard. Certainly, a two-pitch 5.8 hand crack at the top of an exposed wall is something of a wonder!

Located to the left is the *Hyperspace* route, which offers a more modern grade and an interesting, well-protected path up a big, steep, and intimidating portion of the cliff. Still farther left, *Orbit* is another quality route from back in the day, featuring an old-school 5.8 pitch about halfway up that is a bit of a sandbag. Both *Outer Space* and *Orbit* can get a bit crowded on sunny spring days; midweek adventures may be the answer to that.

### LAND MANAGER
Alpine Lakes Wilderness, Okanogan-Wenatchee National Forest, Wenatchee River Ranger District. Northwest Forest

*Ed Cooper approaches Snow Creek Wall in the spring of 1959; it was the first attempt and climb of the main wall. Their route* Remorse *included a night out sitting on a small ledge. (Photo by Don Gordon)*

Pass or interagency recreation pass required for parking. Free self-issued wilderness permit required for day trips; limited permits, issued by lottery (see Resources), required for overnight trips in Enchantment Permit Area May 15–October 31.

**NOTE:** The only real issue with climbing at Snow Creek Wall these days is the mountain goats. These large, pointy-horned creatures were born here, and they are not afraid of people. They are desperate for salt and know exactly what's coming if a climber stands by a tree and reaches for their zipper! Beware!

# 71. OUTER SPACE WITH REMORSE
## START: GRADE III, 5.9

**TIME:** 1 day. **GEAR:** depending on abilities, take enough gear and doubles to 3½ inches for long crack pitches. Snow Creek Wall is located directly on the Snow Lakes Trail, and anyone who has hiked up into the Enchantments will have walked right past it. The original route started off to the right of the main shield and climbed an easy right-facing system before traversing left onto a big ledge, where this and several other routes get started. These days it is more common to use the first pitches of the *Remorse* route to reach the big ledge.

## APPROACH, GRADE II
Follow the approach via Snow Creek for Climb 68, South Face, *Burgner-Stanley*. At about 2 miles on the Snow Lakes Trail No. 1553, the wall is in plain sight. Leave the trail where a well-used climbers path descends a few feet to the creek and crosses it on logs before gaining about 500 feet to the base of the wall.

## ROUTE
Start almost directly beneath the upper crack pitches and work up past a tree to a small belay stance located under a big right-facing corner-roof feature. **PITCH 1:** Work up and left a bit on 5.4–5.6 rock and belay at a small stance beneath a big flake. **PITCH 2:** Move up to the flake and make some athletic 5.8 undercling moves directly left to easier climbing; continue a bit higher and belay. **PITCH 3:** Locate a right-trending but left-facing corner-ramp (5.7) and climb that to reach Two-Tree Ledge. **PITCH 4:** Climb a left-facing corner affair (5.8) beneath an obvious steep block-pillar until it is possible to move out to the right on a thin finger crack–edge. Continue to the right (5.9 crux) and a bit up for about 15–20 feet and belay at an exposed small stance. **PITCH 5:** Work out to the right a bit and then wander up (5.4) and back left until it's possible to gain a small pedestal (5.7 move) on the left. **PITCH 6:** The crack! Climb the amazing hand crack (5.8 move near the start) up the knobby wall for a full pitch to reach Library Ledge. **PITCH 7:** Step to the right from the ledge and make some reachy moves (5.9) to get into the crack again, or climb straight up

*Looking down the two-pitch headwall crack on* Outer Space, Snow Creek Wall; *the climber is Caleb Ng.* (Photo by Steph Abegg)

off the ledge on a flake feature and make a 5.8 move right to gain the crack. Either way, the crack continues at about 5.6-5.7 to reach a ledge with a tree about 50 feet below the top. **PITCH 8:** A very short bit of easier ground reaches the top and the extremely eager mountain goats.

## DESCENT

All the routes use the same descent to the left. When free of the goats, amble off to the southwest to pick up the trail to the bottom. Many have gotten into trouble by attempting to head down too soon, which leads to cliffy predicaments, so make sure to stay well back from the wall and on the main trail. Near the base of the wall, scramble back north, around

blocks, corners, and more goats, until able to reach the base near the start of the *Orbit* route.

## 72. HYPERSPACE: GRADE III, 5.11-

**TIME:** 1 day. **GEAR:** fairly deep rack with multiples in fingers to thin hands sizes. *Hyperspace* is a surprising and amazing line up the complicated corners and features that form the left edge of Snow Creek Wall's central shield area. It is a continuously strenuous and mostly well-protected trad route with sustained climbing on nearly every pitch. Like *Outer Space*, the *Hyperspace* route takes the first two pitches of the old *Remorse* route. It then climbs two and a half pitches of *Iconoclast* before finishing with three pitches up the *Hyperspace* corner.

### APPROACH

Follow the approach for the preceding climb.

### ROUTE

**PITCHES 1-2:** Follow the same two starting pitches for Climb 71, *Remorse* and *Outer Space*, to gain the ledge system. **PITCH 3:** Continue left on the ledge to find the *Psychopath* crack leading

Snow Creek Wall from the east: (A) Outer Space, 1960, (B) Remorse, 1959, (C) Iconoclast, 1971, (D) Hyperspace, 1983, (E) Psychopath (Photo by Steph Abegg)

### SELECTED HISTORY

**1959 AUGUST** *Remorse*. III, 5.9. Ed Cooper, Galen McBee.

**1960 MAY** *Easy Day*. III, 5.8. Ed Cooper, Don Gordon, Gordon Thompson.

**1960 MAY** *Outer Space*. III, 5.9. Fred Beckey, Ron Niccoli.

**1962** *Orbit*. III, 5.8. Fred Beckey, Dan Davis.

**1964** *Galaxy*. III, 5.8. Pat Callis, Bob Phelps.

**1971 JUNE** *Iconoclast*. III, 5.10+. Mead Hargis, Tom Hargis.

**1975** *RPM*. III, 5.10+. Pat Timson, Rick LeDuc, Steve Graupe.

**1983** *Hyperspace*. III, 5.11-. Kevin Buselmeier, Neil Cannon, Jim Yoder.

**1985** *Edge of Space*. 5.11. Pat McNerthney, David Rubine.

*Loren Foss on the fifth pitch of the* Remorse-Iconoclast-Hyperspace *connection of routes* (Photo by Steph Abegg)

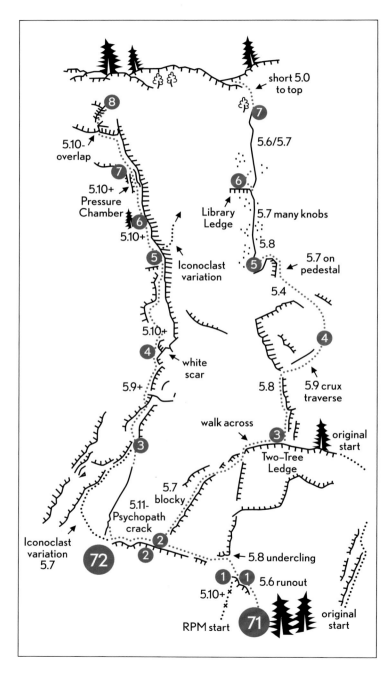

upward; climb the crux thin crack (5.11-), making use of thin face holds on the left as the crack gets thinner. Small cams and wired gear are great, but the pitch still probably deserves a PG rating since you're above your gear at the crux. Ultimately reach a belay ledge with slings on a rock horn. **PITCH 4:** Follow a shallow right-facing corner-crack system (5.9+) up and somewhat right until a move left pulls a small overlap and continues up to a belay near a recent white scar. **PITCH 5:** Work up toward the *Iconoclast* corner, reaching a lighter-colored steep wall and up to a steep (5.10+) right-facing corner-overlap feature. Work up and right, crossing a small arête to the *Iconoclast* corner. **PITCH 6:** This is where *Iconoclast* leaves the corner, moving to the right onto the face; for *Hyperspace*, continue up the impressive left-facing corner. Jam and stem your way up the corner (5.10+); higher, shuffle a few moves to the left and then work back into the corner and up to a belay past a small tree. **PITCH 7:** Continue to jam and stem above the anchors and move right to avoid some vegetation; a bit of easier terrain leads up to the infamous Pressure Chamber, an overhanging section of off-width and wild stemming (5.10+) above crazy exposure. Stem out to the right to exit the flare. There is a short left-facing corner above, then move out left on a small ledge and arrange a gear anchor. **PITCH 8:** Work left on easy but mildly unstable rock and then go up to pull a small roof (5.10-). From here, lower-angle rock leads easily up and to the right, to the top.

## DESCENT

Follow the descent for the preceding climb.

# LAKE WENATCHEE AREA/US 2

## TUMWATER CANYON WATERFALLS 4600'

### DRURY FALLS; THE PENCIL

Waterfall climbing came into vogue with the advent of modern ice tools in the early 1970s. Drury Falls and *The Pencil* are two classic multipitch ice climbs that have been attracting Washington ice climbers since the early '80s. Located in Tumwater Canyon high above the Wenatchee River, Drury is one of Washington's longest water-ice climbs.

Unfortunately, conditions for water-ice climbing can be fickle, usually with a short season and not within every year. Climbers must watch conditions closely and make haste when favorable conditions arrive, most likely in December, January, and hopefully February. *The Pencil* forms less frequently than Drury, but is reported to be equally classic when in condition. Both *The Pencil* and the Drury Falls climbs follow the Falls Creek drainage, a spectacular setting with opportunities for shorter climbs if Drury or *The Pencil* don't feel right.

### LAND MANAGER

Okanogan-Wenatchee National Forest, Wenatchee River Ranger District. No permit required.

### NOTES

A boat or inflatable raft is usually required to cross the Wenatchee River. Beware of recent snowfall, and always consider avalanche risk. The aspect of these climbs is mostly east; the slopes above the approach–Falls Creek drainage–face south and north.

*Jens Holsten descends from* **The Pencil** *with the bottom of Tumwater Canyon peeking through the clouds below.* (Photo by Doug Hutchinson)

*Justin Busch on Drury Fall's main upper tier, Tumwater Canyon* (Photo by Doug Hutchinson)

# 73. DRURY FALLS: GRADE III, WI 3-4

**TIME:** 1-2 days. The falls face east-southeast and get mid-morning sun. Once many of the smaller and more accessible Washington waterfalls were climbed, Drury Falls could not be ignored. Several early attempts were thwarted by warm conditions, and the falls was not climbed in full until 1978. While moderate by current standards, Drury is considered a classic.

## APPROACH, GRADE II-III
Drive the Stevens Pass Highway (US Highway 2) to about 4 miles west of Leavenworth at Falls Creek (1550 feet).

While the Wenatchee River has been known to freeze directly across from Falls Creek, unless you get very lucky, a boat or raft is necessary: continue 1 mile downstream from Falls Creek to Lake Jolanda (1550 feet), the recommended launch point for boat crossings. The river crossing is followed by winter snow travel with 2200 feet of elevation gain.

Once across to the west side of the river, head upstream about 1 mile to Falls Creek, then directly up the Falls Creek drainage, a major avalanche terrain trap. At about 3400 feet, the gully narrows and a short bit of ice leads to a basin with a couple of small campsites at about 3750 feet, not far from the lower falls.

*Jens Holstein on* **The Pencil,** *Tumwater Canyon* **(Photo by Doug Hutchinson)**

## ROUTE

Lower Drury Falls is approximately 200 feet high; it is usually climbed in two pitches, the ice approaching 80 degrees near the top. The upper or main falls is several hundred feet above the lower, reached by a pitch of 30-degree snow. The main falls is climbed in a series of vertical steps of three or four pitches, depending on belays, totaling approximately 400 feet. The climb finishes on a vertical pillar on the left (south) side of the falls.

## DESCENT

Walk south below the falls until able to rappel from tree anchors to the base of both falls, then retrace the approach.

## 74. THE PENCIL: GRADE III, WI 4–5

**TIME:** 1-2 days. **GEAR:** 60m rope to surmount pitch 1. Without a significant stream flow, the formation of *The Pencil* is a bit more fickle than its neighbor, Drury Falls. When formed, the narrow shaft of ice is visible from the highway. Beware of avalanches both on the approach and while on the route. "You are a real sitting duck if something were to let go," remembers Kjell Swedin of the first ascent. "But Bob [McDougall] and I were psyched to do the climb because it was such an inspiring line and harder than anything either of us had done." This is a beautiful climb to watch for anytime cold arctic air makes a visit.

## APPROACH

Follow the approach for the preceding climb. *The Pencil* is the thin ribbon of ice snaking up the rocks just west of Drury Falls.

## ROUTE

*The Pencil* is a three-pitch route, but some climbers break it up into four pitches. **PITCH 1:** Classic and most difficult—

### SELECTED HISTORY

**1978 FEBRUARY** Drury Falls, FA. III, WI 3–4. Bob McDougall, Steve Pollack.
**1983 FEBRUARY** *The Pencil*, FA. III, WI 4–5. Bob McDougall, Kjell Swedin.

a good portion of this pitch is vertical, giving climbers a good pump by the end of it. **PITCH 2:** Trend up and then left; depending on conditions, this pitch may be mixed. **PITCH 3:** Climb a broad curtain of ice averaging 80 degrees.

## DESCENT

Descend by rappelling the route.

## TENPEAK MOUNTAIN　　　8200'

**PROMINENCE: 400'**

### SOUTHEAST FACE

Glacier Peak is the northwestern-most mountain in a subset of the Cascade Mountains dubbed Dakobed by the Puget Sound Salish natives. Considerably glaciated by east-of-the-crest standards, the quartz diorite Dakobed Range includes the area surrounding the headwaters of the White, Napeequa, and Suiattle Rivers and comprises Glacier Peak, Kololo Peaks, Kopeetah Divide, the Hive, Luahna Peak, Clark Mountain, and the Tenpeak massif. Although visitors to either end of the Dakobed Range are relatively frequent, the middle portion of the Dakobed—including Tenpeak Mountain—is seldom visited.

Without any formal trails within one day's travel of Tenpeak's summit, access to it is arduous no matter which way it is approached; it includes 6 miles of typically overgrown White River Trail and a cross-country brush bash up Thunder Creek that provide access to lonely Thunder Basin, a logical camping location for climbs of Tenpeak or its prominent west summit. A way trail is unofficially maintained by local hunters and horse riders, but how easy it is to follow is directly related to how long it's been since it has seen a pair of clippers. Avalanches also wreak havoc on the upper Thunder Basin trail, as it travels directly up a slide path. Scenic high-alpine camping can be found at the low point between Tenpeak and West Tenpeak, with unique, commanding views over to Glacier Peak and the Suiattle River headwaters. Here, a foundation of soft pumice provides for a serene, low-impact high camp (expect snow until mid-August).

*Tenpeak Mountain (foreground) and Glacier Peak from the southeast* **(Photo by John Scurlock)**

Several traverses that involve a visit to Tenpeak Mountain are possible. From White River Trail, a route via Boulder Pass, connecting the Clark, Pilz, Richardson, and Butterfly Glaciers, has been done (3rd class). Finding a crucial talus and heather ramp from the Butterfly Glacier down into upper Thunder Basin is key. The exit via lower Thunder Basin and White River makes a lollipop loop, or there's the option of continuing on to make a high traverse over to the Honeycomb Glacier and Kololo and Glacier Peaks. A route traversing the southwest slopes of Clark Mountain and Luahna Peak has been done as well,

but despite its abundance of scenic views and alpine splendor, it isn't recommended due to loose rock and tedious travel.

From the Sauk River and White Pass, a cross-country approach can be taken over Kololo Peaks and the Honeycomb Glacier to access Tenpeak. This would be best done as part of a grand high traverse from the Sauk River to the White River. Unfortunately, logistics of a car drop on each end are difficult. Parking on the west end of the traverse would be at the North Fork Sauk River Trailhead parking area (16 miles south of Darrington off

*Tenpeak Mountain from the east; Sloan Peak is in the distance.* (Photo by John Scurlock)

the Mountain Loop Highway). On the east side of the traverse, parking would be at the White River Trailhead (22 miles up Chiwawa River Road off US Highway 2). Although Trinity and the North Fork Sauk River parking area are less than 15 miles apart as the bird flies, the road between the two travels 170 miles—about four hours, forty-three minutes of drive time.

## LAND MANAGER
Glacier Peak Wilderness, Okanogan-Wenatchee National Forest, Wenatchee River Ranger District. Northwest Forest Pass or interagency recreation pass required for parking. Free self-issued wilderness permit required for day and overnight trips.

## 75. SOUTHEAST FACE: GRADE II, 5.0

**TIME:** 3 hours round-trip from upper Thunder Basin. Several routes on the southern aspect of Tenpeak Mountain have been done, and all involve two to several pitches of easy to moderate rock. The easiest route is from the notch northeast of the summit. We consider the west summit of Tenpeak Mountain to be one of our favorite scramble routes in the Cascades. A trip to this summit is highly recommended for those in the area.

### APPROACH, GRADE III
From the Stevens Pass Highway (US 2) at Coles Corner, 15 miles west of Leavenworth, take State Route 207 north

to a junction near the east end of Lake Wenatchee. Turn left (west) onto North Shore Drive, which past the west end of the lake becomes White River Road (Forest Road 64). Drive to its end past White River Falls at the White River Trailhead (2300 feet).

Hike the White River Trail No. 1507 for about 6 miles to Thunder Creek at 2759 feet. About 0.5 mile after crossing Thunder Creek, look for a faint way trail west of Thunder Creek.

After this path flattens out at around 3600 feet, it continues through a broad, dense slide alder thicket. It is worth finding the trail here, the start (and middle and end) of which may be obfuscated by slide debris. **HINT:** the trail goes right through the slide alder. Beyond the slide path, keep above the west side of Thunder Creek to a meadow area at 4200 feet before climbing steeply to Thunder Basin at 5200 feet.

### ROUTE

From Thunder Basin, the route climbs the south ridge with surprising exposure and unique position but easy climbing on blocky rock (4th class, with one move of 5.6). From the notch northeast of the summit of Tenpeak, make a leftward-ascending traverse across a ledge and easy face moves (5.0) to a south-facing gully. From here, an easy scramble leads directly to the summit.

### DESCENT

Down-climb from the summit to an established rappel station. Rappel directly back to the notch with a 60m rope, then descend the ascent route back to Thunder Basin.

### SELECTED HISTORY

**1940 SEPTEMBER** Southeast Face, FA. II, 4th class. Lloyd Anderson, Tom Campbell.

**1957** North Couloir. II. George Carter, Art Ford.

**1960 JUNE** West Ridge. II, 5.0. Dwight Crowder, Lesley Tabor, Rowland Tabor.

**1971 SEPTEMBER** Northwest Face. II, 5.0. Fred Beckey, William Nicolai, Peter Williamson.

**1973 AUGUST** North Buttress. III, 5.7. Philip Leatherman, Greg Markov.

# BUCK MOUNTAIN  8528'

### PROMINENCE: 1888' [52]

### WEST FACE

This is a high, somewhat solitary black schist peak just east of the Dakobed Range and the Napeequa River. The west side of the mountain features beautiful high country above the Napeequa, while the north side of the mountain is as rugged as anywhere in the Cascades. The route begins from the small mining settlement of Trinity at the base of Buck Mountain's south peak, also known as Brahma Peak (8078 feet). Fall is a great time for this trip, as it offers the ideal combination of abundant color, few bugs, and easier stream crossing.

### LAND MANAGER

Glacier Peak Wilderness, Okanogan-Wenatchee National Forest, Wenatchee River Ranger District. Northwest Forest Pass or interagency recreation pass required for parking. Free self-issued wilderness permit required for day and overnight trips.

## 76. WEST FACE: GRADE I

**TIME:** 1–2 days. Our route described here is an off-trail "shortcut" via Mounts Cleator and Berge to the classic high traverse from the northeast via High Pass. Mount Berge is named for Richard Berge, who was killed descending from an early attempt on Mount Baring's north face. **NOTE:** this more direct approach to the mountain's west face does include bushwhacking; close-up views of Buck's north face should justify the difficulties.

### APPROACH, GRADE III+

From the Stevens Pass Highway (US Highway 2) at Coles Corner, 15 miles west of Leavenworth, turn north on State Route 207. Go 4.4 miles north on SR 207, then turn right on Chiwawa Loop Road, keeping right at the intersection. Then turn left at the second intersection, onto Chiwawa River Road (Forest Road 62), and follow it for about 23 miles. The road becomes gravel and dirt at 11 miles, with the final 12 miles very rough to Trinity Trailhead near the road end at 2800 feet. There is 4500 feet of elevation gain to the campsites at about 6600 feet.

Take the Buck Creek Trail No. 1513, passing the Chiwawa River Trail at 1.5 miles and crossing the Chiwawa River at 2.5 miles. Now following Buck Creek and directly under Buck's north face, continue on Trail No. 1513 maybe another mile to about 4200 feet, below the east ridge of Mount Cleator.

Ford Buck Creek and ascend Cleator's forested east ridge. At about 5800 feet, traverse below the steepening ridge and into the basin between Cleator and Mount Berge. Traverse the basin a bit higher, keeping above slide alder and then descending a bit to cross below Berge's east ridge as high as possible, at around 5900 feet. Beyond Berge's east ridge, pleasant alpine travel continues south to beautiful camping below Buck Mountain's west face at 6650 feet.

*Buck Mountain from the north* (Photo by John Scurlock)

### SELECTED HISTORY

**1976 SEPTEMBER**  North Face, North Ridge. IV, 5.8. Cal Folsom, Mark Moore.
**2008 DECEMBER**  North Face, *Buckshot*. IV, WI 4+. Dan Cappellini, Rolf Larson.
**2015 FEBRUARY**  North Face, *Wild Game*. IV. Braden Downey, Will Hinckley.

### ROUTE
The climb is a beautiful walk through alpine terrain with about 1900 feet of elevation gain and a year-round snowfield just below the top.

### DESCENT
Descend the ascent route.

# LAKE CHELAN AREA

## MOUNT FERNOW         9249'

**PROMINENCE: 2809' [11]**

### EAST RIDGE FROM HOLDEN

One of Washington State's highest mountains, Mount Fernow is also the high point on a massive ridgeline with Seven Fingered Jack (9105 feet) and Mount Maude (9040 feet) to the south and Copper Peak (8964 feet) to the north. The peak, of friable gneissic granite, has diminishing glacial remnants on three of its flanks: above the Entiat River on the southeast, Copper Creek to the east, and Big Creek on the northwest. Fernow is often combined with a climb of Copper Peak from Copper Basin by making a high traverse of Copper Peak's glacier, east face, and north ridge.

Washington's highest mountains that were climbed first were the volcanoes, between about 1854 (Mount Adams) and 1897 (Glacier Peak). Just behind the volcanoes in height are a dozen mountains collectively known as the elusive nine-thousanders; Fernow's first ascent in 1932 was part of the race to climb the four or five not yet climbed.

One of the more interesting climbers of the day was Hermann Ulrichs (1902-1988) who graduated from the University of California-Berkeley in 1925 as a chemical engineer. His climbs in the Sierras included the solo first ascent of Bear Creek Spire in 1923. He traveled frequently to climb in the Canadian Rockies and made a solo ascent of Mount Sir Donald while on his way east to attend Harvard.

In 1927, Ulrichs moved to Seattle and taught drama and music at the Cornish School. While working for the US Forest Service, he laid out the Pacific Crest Trail from Glacier Peak to Snoqualmie Pass. He served six years in the Navy and after World War II earned a master's degree in music to improve his concert work. He was able to make twenty-one first ascents of mountain peaks in the Northern Cascades, often as a weekend climber.

*Hermann Ulrichs in 1925, a couple of months before he set out on his journey east to Cambridge and Boston via the Cascades and Canadian Rockies* (Photo courtesy Harry Majors)

### SELECTED HISTORY

**1932 AUGUST** Southwest route. Oscar Pennington, Hermann Ulrichs.

**1961 SEPTEMBER** North Face. Fred Dunham, Bill Prater, Gene Prater, Jim Wickwire.

**1979 JULY** North Face, direct finish. Mark Hanson, Peter Hendrickson, Jim Smith.

**1983 SEPTEMBER** North Face, east finish. Fred Beckey, Dave Beckstead, Mark Hutson.

false summit 9040

East Ridge

to Copper Basin

*Mount Fernow from the east* (Photo by John Scurlock)

*Mount Fernow from the north* (Photo by John Scurlock)

Point 9040 East Ridge

Mount Fernow

Mount Maude

Seven Fingered Jack

Mount Fernow has two popular approaches: from the south via Phelps Creek-Leroy Creek, as used on the first ascent, or from the east via a passenger ferry on Lake Chelan and a shuttle bus to Holden Village, which is what this route uses. The village, located at the foot of Mount Fernow and Copper Peak, provides a comfortable base camp. Originally a mining town, Holden was closed down in 1957. The US Environmental Protection Agency declared the Holden Mine area as a Superfund site, with remediation efforts occurring from 2011 to 2016, followed by a five-year testing and analysis period. Holden is currently owned and operated as a year-round retreat center by the Lutheran Church.

### LAND MANAGERS
Glacier Peak Wilderness, Okanogan-Wenatchee National Forest, Chelan Ranger District; free self-issued wilderness permit required for day and overnight trips. Field's Point Landing, Holden Village (see Resources); parking fee required.

## 77. EAST RIDGE FROM HOLDEN:
### GRADE II, 3RD CLASS

**TIME:** 1–2 days. From Holden, the ascent can be made as a day trip or from a high camp at about halfway. The climb is mostly nontechnical, other than the seasonal snow slopes climbing out of Copper Basin.

### APPROACH, GRADE II
From US Highway 97 Alternate (97A) at Chelan, take South Lakeshore Road 17 miles to Field's Point Landing, the typical starting point. Board the *Lady of the Lake* passenger ferry (see Resources) up Lake Chelan to Lucerne Landing (1098 feet). Reserve space in advance for the Holden Village shuttle bus (see Resources) for the 11 miles from Lucerne Landing to Holden Village at 3226 feet (and back). There is 2400 feet of elevation gain to the Copper Basin campsites.

From just west of Holden Village, find the footbridge across Railroad Creek. The path leads to Bypass Road, which leads to the east side of Copper Creek. From there, hike the unmaintained Copper Basin Trail No. 1240.1 as it climbs steeply through a burn area (the 2015 Wolverine Creek Fire). At about 3 miles, a short drop reaches Copper Basin (5600 feet). There are campsites in the basin, but plan for bugs in July. There are nice bivy areas up on the east ridge of Fernow as well.

### ROUTE
Climb out of Copper Basin to the 7200-foot low point on Fernow's long east ridge. Careful routefinding around small cliffs leads to alpine slopes with some talus. Once on the ridge, follow it to about 8600 feet, where it makes sense to traverse southern slopes below the eastern false summit (9040 feet) and regain the ridge at about 9000 feet. Keep to the south side of the ridge crest near the top.

### DESCENT
Descend the ascent route.

## BONANZA PEAK                                   9511'

### PROMINENCE: 3711' [8]

### EAST FACE, MARY GREEN GLACIER
Bonanza is a major North Cascades peak with sprawling high ridges and four widely spaced summits spread over

*Ida Zacher Darr in May 1991; Ida was a member of early Mazama expeditions that explored Bonanza Peak.* (Photo by John Roper)

*Mark Bebie on the summit of Bonanza Peak: first winter ascent* (Photo by Lowell Skoog)

several miles. Looking at the numbers, Bonaza is the highest nonvolcanic peak (composed of hornblende, quartz diorite, and gneiss) in the Washington Cascads, the Chelan County high point, and the eighth-highest mountain in Washington State. Add a few glaciers, and the options for wilderness mountaineering on this peak are alluring.

Located a few miles east of the crest behind Glacier Peak and Dome Peak, Bonanza often receives more favorable climbing weather. The east face, or Mary Green headwall, is the most traveled route on the mountain, both up and down. For those seeking something more challenging, our recommendation is to traverse the mountain's summit by climbing one route and descending another. The Mary Green Glacier's adjoining northeast and southeast ridges are two classic traverse routes. More ambitious ridge traverses have incorporated either the Southwest or Northwest Peak along with the Main (highest) Summit. The ridgeline traverse from northern satellite Dark Peak looks exceptional. Expect sections of loose rock mixed with good rock for any of the less-traveled routes.

The shortest route to Bonanza begins with a passenger-ferry ride most of the way up 55-mile-long Lake Chelan and a shuttle-bus ride to Holden Village, located at the foot of Copper Peak and just down valley from Bonanza Peak.

### LAND MANAGERS

Glacier Peak Wilderness, Okanogan-Wenatchee National Forest, Chelan Ranger District; free self-issued wilderness permit required for day and overnight trips. Field's Point Landing, Holden Village (see Resources); parking fee required.

## 78. EAST FACE, MARY GREEN GLACIER: GRADE III, 5.0

**TIME:** 3 days. This, the original route climbed on the mountain, is often called the Holden Face. Climbers from the Mazamas club made several attempts before achieving success. The final rock face to the summit is straightforward scrambling on mostly good rock.

### APPROACH, GRADE II

Follow the approach for Climb 77, East Ridge from Holden, to Holden Village (3226 feet). There is about 3200 feet of elevation gain to Holden Pass, about 5 miles on trail plus a rough path beyond Holden Lake.

From Holden Village, walk west on the heavily traveled Hart and Lyman Lake Trail No. 1256. At less than 1 mile, take the Holden Lake Trail No. 1251 north. The trail climbs steeply for 4 miles to Holden Lake (5278 feet). There are

Above: *Bonanza Peak from the west* (Photo by Steph Abegg). Below: *Bonanza Peak from the northeast* (Photo by John Scurlock)

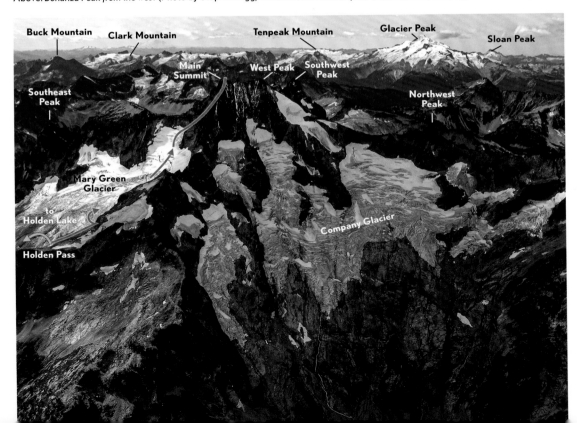

Southwest Peak

Main Summit

Southeast Ridge

East Face

Northeast Ridge

Mary Green Glacier

to Holden Pass

*Bonanza Peak from the east (Photo by John Scurlock)*

good campsites nearby, but no overnight camping or campfires within 200 feet of the lakeshore.

The wetlands area beyond the north end of Holden Lake is best circumvented on its north edge; the area is a tangle of boulders, bushes, and streams. Once past it, find a climbers path that climbs steeply northwest to Holden Pass at 6400 feet. There are small campsites near Holden Pass, but expect them to be dry later in the summer.

## ROUTE

From Holden Pass, a trail (if not snow covered) leads up the ridge to the west. After several hundred feet, talus slopes traverse south toward slabs and streams below the Mary Green Glacier (6900 feet). The slabs can be climbed directly (4th class) or crossed higher from the right (north). Look

## SELECTED HISTORY

**1937 JUNE**  West Peak. II. Everett Darr, Ida Darr, Curtis James, Barrie James, Joe Leuthold.

**1937 JUNE**  Bonanza Peak, East Face. III, 5.0. Curtis James, Barrie James, Joe Leuthold.

**1940 JULY**  Southwest Peak, Isella Glacier. II. Hans Altenfelder, Larry Penberthy.

**1956 AUGUST**  Southeast *(Holden)* Ridge. III, 5.8. Jim Burrows, David Isles.

**1970 MAY**  Southwest Peak, *Beowulf Couloir*. III. Alex Bertulis, Mark Fielding.

**1971 SEPTEMBER**  South Face, Isella Glacier. III, 5.5. Charles Raymond, Patricia Raymond.

**1975 SEPTEMBER**  Southwest Peak, Northwest Buttress. V, 5.9. Sergei Bershov, Alex Bertulis, Valentin Grakovich, Anotoly Nepomnyashchy, Vyacheslav Onishchenko.

**1978 FEBRUARY**  Southwest Peak, FWA. Ted Gannon, Mark Hutson.

**1978 JULY**  Northeast Ridge. III, 5.7. Dave Seman, Mark Thornton.

**1979 DECEMBER**  Bonanza Peak, East Face, FWA. Mark Bebie, Gordy Skoog, Lowell Skoog.

**2006 AUGUST**  Northwest Ridge traverse from Dark Peak. V, 5.8. Tim Halder, Blake Herrington.

**2011 FEBRUARY**  Northwest Peak, FWA. Jason Hummel, Forest McBrian.

**2013 SEPTEMBER**  Northwest Buttress, *Oregonian Route*. V, 5.9+. Erik Bonnett, Seth Keena.

for a rappel tree near the top of the high traverse for use on the descent. Once on top of the slabs (7200 feet), pick a route to the top of the glacier below the east (Holden) face. The upper portion of the glacier generally forms a long crevasse-'schrund, followed higher by a moat crossing to reach the rock (8700 feet). The rock climbing consists of ledges interspersed with more-exposed sections of 4th- to low-5th-class climbing trending left (south) to begin with, then straight up following a natural line to the ridgetop. Follow the ridge crest a short way to the main summit.

## DESCENT

Descend the route with a combination of down-climbing and short rappels. Find your way across the moat and onto the glacier with the final rappel.

# REYNOLDS PEAK 8512'

## PROMINENCE: 2032' [55]

### SOUTH PEAK, REYNOLDS CREEK

Reynolds sits at the northern end of the high and jagged Sawtooth Ridge located between Lake Chelan and the Methow Valley, a rain-shadow range of alpine lakes and beautiful high country. The Sawtooth is home to nearly a dozen of the state's highest mountains, peaks with friendly off-trail travel and mostly nontechnical summit routes in a vast wilderness.

These are the Top 100 highest peaks in Washington located in the Lake Chelan-Sawtooth Wilderness: North Gardner Mountain (8956 feet), Gardner Mountain (8898 feet), Oval Peak (8795 feet), Star Peak (8690 feet), Raven

*Reynolds Peak from the north* (Photo by John Roper)

Ridge (8580 feet), Reynolds Peak (8512 feet), Hoodoo Peak (8464 feet), Mount Bigelow (8440 feet), Courtney Peak (8392 feet), Martin Peak (8375 feet), Abernathy Peak (8321 feet), and Switchback or Cooney Mountain (8321 feet). How many of these can you see from the summit of Reynolds? This peak has the location.

Much of Sawtooth Ridge has steep northern cirques carved by glaciers, with only a few tiny remnants left. The high open ridges are home to rugged alpine plants and dotted with sturdy whitebark pines, often sitting above acres of alpine larch. Go early to see the alpine plants in bloom (June–July) and late for the fall color (October).

While we describe the Reynolds Creek approaches here, several other approaches are also popular. Both War Creek-Tony Basin and Williams Lake-Williams Butte are excellent approach routes leading to high on War Creek Ridge, just east of Sawtooth Ridge near Camels Hump Peak (8015 feet). Reynolds's southwest and southeast aspects lie a short distance north. Reynolds's southwest slopes (Boulder Basin) can also be approached from the west near the town of Stehekin, at the far end of Lake Chelan.

## LAND MANAGER

Lake Chelan-Sawtooth Wilderness, Okanogan-Wenatchee National Forest, Methow Valley Ranger District. Northwest Forest Pass or interagency recreation pass may be required for parking. Free self-issued wilderness permit required for day or overnight trips.

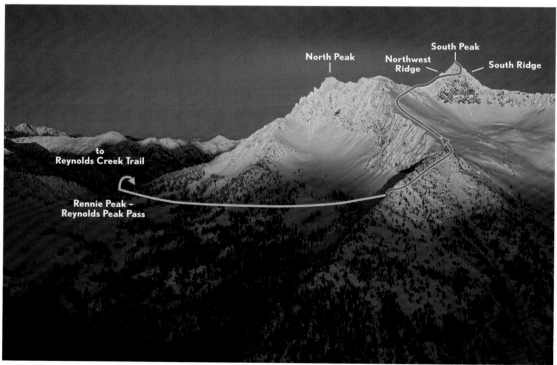

*Reynolds Peak from the west* (Photo by John Scurlock)

# 79. SOUTH PEAK, REYNOLDS CREEK:
## GRADE II

**TIME:** 1–2 days. The mountain has two primary summits: the North Peak and the slightly higher South Peak. The 300-foot summit pyramid of the South Peak can be scrambled from the northeast, southeast, and southwest.

## APPROACH, GRADE II

From the North Cascades Highway (State Route 20) at Twisp, turn west onto Twisp River Road, which becomes Forest Road 44 at 12 miles and reaches Mystery Campground at 18 miles. At Mystery Campground, turn left over the bridge across the Twisp River, then turn right onto FR 4435. In 1 mile, take the spur road to the left for 1 mile up to the Reynolds Creek Trailhead at 3150 feet.

Follow the Reynolds Creek Trail No. 402, which is no longer maintained and can be a bit brushy in the middle section. The impressive north face of Reynolds's North Peak dominates the upper valley. The trail stays on the north side of Reynolds Creek and crosses Sawtooth Ridge between Reynolds and Rennie Peaks at 6874 feet.

**MORE DIRECT OPTION:** A more direct approach leaves the Reynolds Creek Trail after several miles, at about 4700 feet. Cross Reynolds Creek and follow the west side of the south fork of Reynolds Creek. Expect some brush before reaching the high country below the southeast aspect of Reynolds's South Peak.

**MOST DIRECT OPTION:** Even more direct is the smaller branch of Reynolds Creek which leads to the eastern basin between Reynolds's two summits. Leave the Reynolds Creek Trail beyond the southern branch (mentioned in the "more direct option" description), at about 5100 feet. Cross the creek and ascend the steep forested slope, keeping west of the small tributary stream. The eastern basin holds remnants of the rapidly diminishing Reynolds Glacier, helpful for identifying the peak as viewed from Twisp River Road.

## ROUTE

From the south side of the Rennie Peak–Reynolds Peak Pass (6874 feet) traverse alp slopes south, reaching the southwest ridge of Reynolds Peak at about 6600 feet. This southwest ridge is easily followed to the ridge connecting the North Peak to the South Peaks. From the north side of the South (main) Summit at 8200 feet, a 4th-class slab leads to easier climbing. Keep left of a gendarme, then follow a ledge traversing across the south face to a gully. Ascend the gully to the ridge and scramble to the summit.

**MORE DIRECT OPTION:** To climb the summit pyramid from the southeast, look for a gully onto the east ridge not far from the top.

## DESCENT

Descend the climbing route.

## SELECTED HISTORY

**1882 AUGUST** South (main) Peak. Lieutenant Henry Pierce.
**1898** South (main) Peak. Albert H. Sylvester survey party.
**LATE 1970S** South (main) Peak, Northwest Face, *Horsefly Couloir*. II. Northwest Outward Bound.
**1980 JUNE** North Peak, Northeast Face, North Rib. III, 5.0. Rick LaBelle, Bob Loomis.
**1989 JULY** North Peak, Northeast Ridge. III, 5.0. Howard Armstrong, Dallas Kloke, Mark Desvoigne.
**1990 JUNE** North Peak, Northwest Ridge. II+, 5.4. Bill Centenari, Rick LaBelle.
**1993 AUGUST** South (main) Peak, East Ridge. II+, 5.4. Bill Centenari, Rick LaBelle.

# NORTHERN CASCADES

## GOODE MOUNTAIN — 9200'

### PROMINENCE: 3800' [12]

#### NORTHEAST BUTTRESS

Tall and strikingly solitary as viewed from throughout the North Cascades, Skagit gneiss Goode Mountain is completely hidden from roads or civilization. It is a classic wilderness objective by any route, with the north face rising a full 6000 feet above Bridge Creek's North Fork valley. (Note: The name of the mountain is pronounced "good.")

The mountain withstood first-ascent attempts by the most experienced climbers of the 1930s and was considered a great prize. O'Brien-Ulrichs and Blair-Grigg-Winder parties made attempts in 1934. A couple years later, George McGowan reached the summit and reported that "Wolf [Bauer's] sense of humor got the best of him at this juncture, and quickly building a small cairn, informed me as I came over the top that the Mazama boys had made the ascent before us."

#### LAND MANAGER

North Cascades Scenic Byway, Okanogan-Wenatchee National Forest, Methow Valley Ranger District. Northwest Forest Pass or interagency recreation pass required for parking. North Cascades National Park, Marblemount Wilderness Information Center; permit required year-round for all overnight trips within the park.

*Goode Mountain from the north: (A) Northeast Buttress, 1966, (B) Northeast Face, 1954* **(Photo by John Scurlock)**

*Jennie Minier negotiating the bergschrund crossing to reach Goode Mountain's Northeast Buttress* (Photo by Pete Erickson)

# 80. NORTHEAST BUTTRESS: GRADE IV, 5.5

**TIME:** 2–3 days. Most everyone approaches the mountain from the North Cascades Highway and the Pacific Crest Trail. The classic approach from Stehekin was popular until 2003, when the road up the valley washed out, significantly reducing backcountry use. Like many climbs where the quickest descent route is on the opposite side of the mountain, ascending Goode's north face presents the classic dilemma: whether to carry over or not.

## APPROACH, GRADE III+

Drive the North Cascades Highway (State Route 20) to 1 mile east of Rainy Pass and the Bridge Creek Trailhead (4400 feet) on the north side of the highway. There is 3800 feet of elevation gain to bivy sites at about 5400 feet, with 12 miles of trail followed by a stream crossing and steep off-trail travel.

Follow the Pacific Crest Trail No. 2000 south as it follows Bridge Creek for about 7 miles to North Fork Bridge Creek (2550 feet). Follow the North Fork Trail for 5 miles, to about 1 mile past Grizzly Creek, looking for a place to cross Bridge Creek at about 3300 feet. Hope for a logjam, but be prepared to wade the creek. This has been a pretty good place to begin the climb toward the Goode Glacier. **NOTE:** A similar route out of the valley begins farther up the valley at about 3800 feet.

Head for a steep slabby area between 3800 and 4000 feet, and continue up with some alder and brush travel. Small bivy sites can be found below the glacier between 5200 and 5400 feet.

*Goode Mountain from the east: (A) Northeast Buttress, 1966, (B) Northeast Face, 1954* (Photo by John Scurlock)

## SELECTED HISTORY

**1936 JULY**  Southwest Couloir. II, 5.0. Wolf Bauer, Philip Dickert, Joe Halwax, Jack Hossack, George McGowan.

**1937 JULY**  South Face, Bedayn Couloir. II, 5.0. Kenneth Adams, Raffi Bedayn, Kenneth Davis.

**1953 AUGUST**  West Tower. II, 5.5. Fred Beckey, Don Gordon.

**1953 SEPTEMBER**  Northwest Buttress. II+. Fred Beckey, Bill Fix, Don Gordon, Jim Henry, John Parrott.

**1954 JULY**  Northeast Face. III, 5.0. Fred Beckey, John Parrott.

**1966 AUGUST**  Northeast Buttress. III, 5.5. Fred Beckey, Tom Stewart.

**1977 JULY**  East Face/Couloir. II+. Bill Fryberger, David Hambley.

**1978 AUGUST**  North Couloir. III. Rick Ferrens, Kurt Mendenhall.

**1984 MARCH**  Northeast Buttress, FWA. Steve Mascioli, Bill Pilling.

**2007 SEPTEMBER**  East Ridge, *Megalodon Ridge*. IV+, 5.10. Blake Herrington, Sol Wertkin.

## ROUTE

Navigating the small glacier and finding a way onto the northeast buttress will depend on conditions that change throughout the season, as well as from year to year; the buttress toe has been accessed from both sides. Once across the moat and onto the rock, find a route near the crest of the ridge. The route has room to wander, but the rock tends to be best near the crest. The climbing is not steep and with very little 5th class. Keeping near the ridge crest, there is a large ledge at about three-quarter height. Above the ledge, the buttress becomes two ridges that meet again after a pitch or two. Climbing up to low 5th class reaches the east ridge not far from the summit.

## DESCENT

This is the shortest route back to the trailhead on SR 20: Down-climb east to a rappel on the north side of the east ridge. A second rappel to a ledge leads to the distinctive Black Tooth Notch. From just below the notch, two rappels lead into the Southwest Couloir. Descend slabs and scree until able to begin traversing a series of ledges west above cliff bands. A return to camp on the north side of the mountain can be made through the Goode-Storm King Col and usually requires a rappel.

Descending southwest to the Park Creek Trail and Stehekin River adds several trail miles to the return hike.

# SOUTH EARLY WINTER SPIRE 7807'

## PROMINENCE: 647'

### SOUTH ARÊTE; THE PASSENGER; THE HITCHHIKER; NOTHING

South Early Winter Spire, also known as SEWS, is the highest peak of the granodiorite Liberty Bell group, and when viewed from the hairpin turn on the North Cascades Highway, it and the North Spire are two huge, jagged peaks of light, buff-colored granite. Some would argue that the eastern aspect of these two fangs rivals even Liberty Bell itself for grandeur. That the South Spire also features an easy route on the other side from the highway is a big plus. The downside is that on sunny summer weekends, good and easy mountain routes with casual approaches may look like the crowd at a Pearl Jam concert.

The view of the spires from the east is simply jaw-dropping; the entire massif consistently offers popular Grade II-III routes on the western aspect and Grade IV-V routes from the east. The broad, continuously steep southeast face of the South Spire has been a magnet for climbers since the earliest days. Numerous folks have explored all over this face, but the promise of the wall wasn't truly realized until modern skills and ideas arrived with Pete Doorish and Bryan Burdo around the turn of the twenty-first century.

While the spire is mostly loved for summer rock climbing, mixed climbing can be enjoyed in both early spring and late fall, conditions permitting. When the cross-state North Cascades Highway is open, it provides quick access to the high granite.

### LAND MANAGER

North Cascades Scenic Byway, Okanogan-Wenatchee National Forest, Methow Valley Ranger District. Northwest Forest Pass or interagency recreation pass required for Blue Lake Trailhead parking.

*Wayne Wallace on the Early Winters Couloir, the classic east facing mixed climb between the two spires* (Photo by Doug Hutchinson)

## NOTES

Beyond the trailhead, the mountain goats loitering near the bottom of the climbs are only slightly less bold than their Leavenworth kin. Goats on gravel slopes above climbers regularly kick stones. Mosquitoes in midseason can be nearly lethal at the parking lot but usually get blown away at the higher elevations.

# 81. SOUTH ARÊTE: GRADE II, 5.6

**TIME:** 1 day. In 1942 this was the second route on the spire, which at that time was still undefined and referred to simply as "Liberty Bell Mountain." The route is largely a scramble, with only two spots of minimal 5th-class climbing. Still, it is a fun route up an incredible spire and remains very popular.

## APPROACH, GRADE II

All of these SEWS routes may be approached from either the east or the west. Most climbers pay the fee to use the Blue Lake Trail to reach the western aspect of everything from Liberty Bell to South Early Winter Spire.

**FROM THE WEST:** Drive the North Cascades Highway (State Route 20) to about 1 mile west of Washington Pass and park at the Blue Lake Trailhead (5230 feet); pay a fee if you don't have a pass, and apply bug repellent. Some live-free-or-die types will want to skip the fee and park out on the main highway; make sure vehicles are entirely off the pavement. Hike the gradual, switchbacked Blue Lake Trail No. 314 about 1.5 miles to an open area at 5800 feet, where the trail swerves to the right to reach Blue Lake. There is a small stream here early in the summer. Leave the main trail, following an obvious boot track that branches off to the left.

*South Early Winter Spire from the southeast* (Photo by Steph Abegg)

Wander across a small meadow area, then work up through small trees and slabs in the general direction of the Liberty Bell–Concord Tower gully. Find the climbers path and ascend into the gully between the two peaks, passing cairns, and cross the open meadow slopes beneath the west side of the whole massif. Continue hiking toward the South Spire; cross beneath the Southwest Couloir and finally make a short, sandy scramble up to the ridge crest at the start of the South Arête.

**FROM THE EAST:** Drive the North Cascades Highway (SR 20) to the huge hairpin turn east of Washington Pass—about 2 miles east of the Blue Lake Trailhead—and park (5151 feet). Hiking up to the face from the highway hairpin turn requires some routefinding and creative scrambling. In early season, this can make a great ski descent when paired with climbing one of the SEWS routes; later in the season, it becomes a huge gravel field (when the Blue Lake Trail described above is recommended).

From the highway, hike straight up the basin snowfield for 1600 feet to the col-ridge at the base of the South Arête.

## ROUTE

**PITCH 1:** This is the crux of the route; from the highest point where the ridge hits the actual spire, move about 15 feet right and climb a smooth slab up a short left-arching corner. A tricky move left (5.6) reaches easier ground and continues up to a good stance with a bolted anchor. **PITCHES 2–3:** 3rd- and 4th-class climbing continues 100 feet or so up a gully-chimney affair until it is blocked by a big chock stone; climb around the chock stone on the left (5.4) with some hidden buckets, and belay from slings on trees not far above. Various paths continue; some are almost walking, but staying to the right as much as possible can make it a little more exposed and fun. Ultimately, make an exposed hand traverse (4th class) across the Whale's Back and continue up and then left to reach the top.

## DESCENT

All the routes on the spire use the South Arête as a descent route. While much of the route can be comfortably down-climbed, it is common to make a couple of short rappels along the way, then a final 100-foot (30m) rappel from the bolts at the top of the first pitch. Expect to encounter people moving in both directions, some roped and some not.

## 82. THE PASSENGER: GRADE IV, 5.12- OR 5.12- OR 5.11 AO5.11 AO

**TIME:** 1 day. *The Passenger* is perhaps the first "successful" route on the southeast face, and for those climbing at this standard, it's thought to be among the very best in the area. The climbing is varied and sustained; all the pitches are 5.10 or 5.11, with one move rated 5.12-.

### APPROACH

Follow the approach for the preceding climb. From the start of the South Arête, scramble down slabs and a gully several hundred feet until able to traverse back to the base of the wall. Look for a ledge with a couple of small trees on it, and continue out to the right on the ledge.

### ROUTE

Start near a left-facing corner that turns into a roof. **PITCH 1:** Climb interesting parallel cracks up the corner and look for a bolt that lets you underclimb a roof (5.10+) out to the left; solid face climbing then works up and slightly right to a small ledge with a tree and bolts. **PITCH 2:** Climb the intimidating slab above the belay, then move up and right again to find a bolt that protects a strenuous (5.11) section. Reach a right-facing fingers-in-a-corner thing (5.10) and sail up that past another roof. Find a small stance out to the left and set up an anchor. **PITCH 3:** This shorter pitch climbs a great 5.11 thin crack until it works through a steep, awkward roof feature and, above that, reaches an exposed bolted belay to the left. **PITCH 4:** Start by moving slightly down and traversing out left on less-than-vertical but slabby (5.11-) rock. Reach a shallow, rounded corner and work up that past several more bolts and a short runout. Higher, find a bolt on the steep bulge (5.12-, or 5.11 AO) that is the crux of the entire route. Rope drag may become an issue, and directly above that, it is possible to belay on a stance with some gear and one of the pro bolts. If not using this alternate belay, continue up and right, past a bolt, aiming for the unique A-shaped roof feature. Step out to the right on a narrow edge-crack to exit the A-slot and find the belay stance on a ledge with

*Pitch 5 of* **The Passenger** *on South Early Winter Spire* **(Photo by Steph Abegg)**

a dead snag and good cracks. **PITCH 5:** Work out to the right on some mildly runout 5.9 and reach a thin crack. Follow the thin crack up to a roof-slot and work through that to reach a left-trending corner (5.10-) and splitter cracks. Belay on the left at a ledge with a tree. **PITCH 6:** From the belay, work the crack (5.10+) in the leaning corner, passing a ledge on the left, then work up to a belay from a single bolt and gear. (The original route belayed on the ledge below,

then continued left and up 5.7 corners to reach the South Arête.) **PITCH 7:** Continue up the face past a bolt (5.10-) and reach a thin crack in a small right-facing corner, then climb up to the ridge crest. Several hundred feet of 3rd and 4th class complete the route to the summit.

## DESCENT
Follow the descent for Climb 81, South Arête.

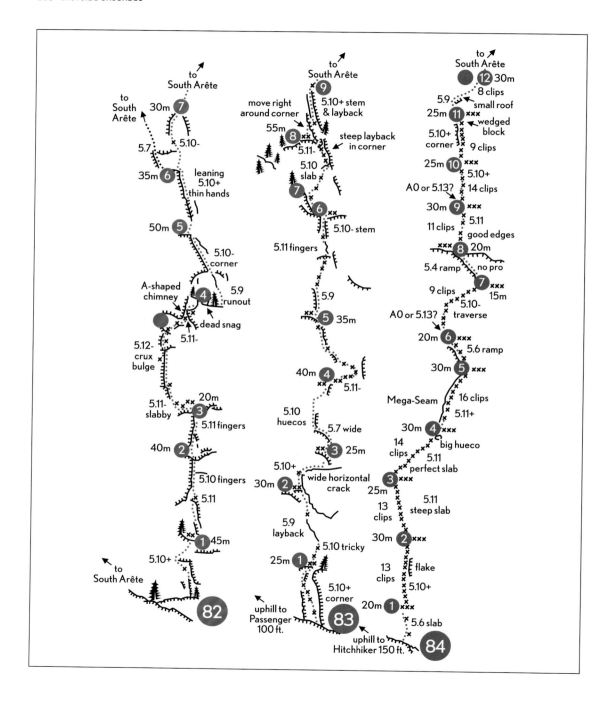

to South Arête

to South Arête

to South Arête

30m **7**

5.10-

5.7

35m **6** leaning 5.10+ thin hands

50m **5**

5.10- corner

A-shaped chimney

**4** 5.9 runout

dead snag

5.12- crux bulge

5.11-

5.11- slabby 20m **3**

5.11 fingers

40m **2**

5.10 fingers

5.11

**1** 45m

5.10+ to South Arête

move right around corner

**9** 5.10+ stem & layback

55m **8** 5.11- steep layback in corner

5.10 slab

**7**

**6** 5.10- stem

5.11 fingers

5.9

**5** 35m

40m **4** 5.11-

5.10 huecos

5.7 wide

**3** 25m

5.10+

30m **2** wide horizontal crack

5.9 layback

5.10 tricky

25m **1**

5.10+ corner

uphill to Passenger 100 ft.

**82**

**83**

to South Arête

**12** 30m

8 clips

5.9 small roof

25m **11** ××× wedged block

5.10+ corner 9 clips

25m **10** 5.10+

A0 or 5.13? 14 clips

30m **9** ××× 5.11

11 clips good edges

**8** 20m

5.4 ramp no pro

9 clips **7** ××× 15m

5.10- traverse

A0 or 5.13?

20m **6** ×××

5.6 ramp

30m **5** ×××

Mega-Seam 16 clips 5.11+

30m **4** ××× big hueco

14 clips 5.11 perfect slab

**3** ××× 25m 5.11 steep slab

13 clips

30m **2** ×××

13 clips flake

5.10+

20m **1** ×××

5.6 slab

uphill to Hitchhiker 150 ft.

**84**

*South Early Winter Spire from the southeast: (A) The Passenger, 1991, (B) The Hitchhiker, 2007, (C) Nothing, 2001, (D) Direct East Buttress, 1968 (Photo by Steph Abegg)*

# 83. THE HITCHHIKER: GRADE IV, 5.11– OR 5.10 A1

**TIME:** 1 day. This is the second Burdo route on the southeast face and is probably a full standard less difficult than *The Passenger* (Climb 82). Of course, its position directly up the middle of the wall is incomparable. Overall, the climbing remains varied and challenging but perhaps a bit more friendly and less sustained. It does reach 5.11 in a few places, but those cruxy sections can be mitigated with a little bit of pulling on protection or standing in a sling.

## APPROACH

Follow the approach for Climb 81, South Arête. From the start of the South Arête route, hike down and right, along the base of the wall, and descend about 100 feet beyond *The Passenger* (Climb 82). Look for a bolted left-facing corner that is the first pitch.

## ROUTE

**PITCH 1:** Climb the corner crack (5.10+) using the bolts on the left and find a small crack-corner, also on the left, then cut back right and continue up past a couple of ledges and small trees to find a bolted anchor to the left. **PITCH 2:** Techy face moves (5.10) work up from the belay to pass a bolted flake and more interesting rock, which leads up to the big corner-roof feature above; a 5.9 layback up and left reaches the vicinity of the bolted belay station. **PITCH 3:** Continue a short distance up the corner and pass a bolt (5.10+) to reach the unique horizontal offset crack-edge;

*Janet Arendall finishing pitch 6 of* **The Hitchhiker,** *on South Early Winter Spire* (Photo by Steph Abegg)

shuffle easily to the right and then climb flakes and edges past a short corner and up to the bolted anchor. **PITCH 4:** Climb out to the right from the anchor and up to a wide crack-ramp feature (5.7), which trends back left and up into a corner system with nice large-crystal face holds. Find a spike or horn above that and traverse up and right to find small corners and flakes that lead to a ledge with two separate bolted anchors. **PITCH 5:** This pitch is basically a big traverse (5.11-) out to the right and then up and back, passing five or six bolts but not gaining much elevation. An optional belay opportunity is better skipped by continuing 30 feet farther left and then working up a rounded left-facing corner (5.10-) to a bolt; from here, step left to a ledge and bolt anchor. **PITCH 6:** Climb the corner system (5.9) above the belay to a fixed pin; work up and to the right, past bolts and gear on very steep face holds, to a short but difficult (5.11) finger crack. From the crack, continue up and left, past a bolt, and finish with a 5.10- stemming problem. Exit right and reach a big ledge with a

bolted anchor. **PITCH 7:** Climb the left-trending low-angle corner to the first of three bolts on the slab. While this pitch can be combined, it is recommended to make this a short pitch by belaying at a tree about 20 feet left of and slightly above the first of the three slab bolts. **PITCH 8:** Climb past the two higher bolts on the short slab (5.10), trending up and right. Continue up cracks and corners, and work up a thin crack into a corner with three more bolts heading out left (5.11-) and over a roof. There are bolted anchors in the alcove above. **PITCH 9:** Climb out to the right from the belay past two bolts, then traverse left, across a left-facing corner and past a hidden bolt, into another steep (5.10+) corner–hand crack. Continue up and a bit left with a wide crack, then finish up moving back to the right to a one-bolt and gear anchor on the edge of the South Arête. Scrambling reaches the summit.

## DESCENT

Follow the descent for Climb 81, South Arête.

*Brian Robinson catches a rest on the eighth pitch of* The Hitchhiker *after exiting the steep 5.11 corner.* (Photo by Doug Hutchinson)

# 84. NOTHING: GRADE IV, 5.11⁺

**TIME:** 1 day. This route climbs a section of the wall with very few cracks. There are many pitches of both slab and face climbing. After a short warm-up pitch, the climb gets down to business quickly with several pitches of very sustained climbing on the perfect slab. The wall steepens for the upper pitches before finishing with a spectacular pitch of 5.9 to join the South Arête.

## APPROACH

Follow the approach for Climb 81, South Arête. From the start of the South Arête route, hike down and right, along the base of the wall, to about 150 feet right of *The Hitchhiker* (Climb 83).

## ROUTE

**PITCH 1:** Climb the slab (5.6) with 2 bolts to a bolted belay anchor. **PITCH 2:** Head straight up (5.10+) with 13 bolts to the left of a flake and belay at the bolted anchor. **PITCH 3:** Ascend the steep left-trending slab (5.11) with 13 bolts and belay at the bolted anchor. **PITCH 4:** Angle up and right on a perfect slab (5.11) with 14 bolts to belay above a giant hueco. **PITCH 5:** Climb the right-leaning "Mega-Seam" (5.11+) with 16 bolts to a bolted anchor. **PITCH 6:** Follow a ramp (5.6) up and left with 3 bolts to the belay anchor. **PITCH 7:** This 9-bolt pitch includes a short A0 section straight up, then traverses right (5.10-) to the bolted anchor. **PITCH 8:** Follow the runout ramp (5.4) up and left to belay on a big ledge (where *Nothing* crosses the *Inferno* route). **PITCH 9:** Climb straight up (5.11) with great edges and 11 bolts to a bolted anchor. **PITCH 10:** Ascend straight up 5.10+ with an A0 overhang and 14 bolts. **PITCH 11:** Climb the very exposed corner (5.10+) past a wedged block on 9 bolts to the belay anchor. **PITCH 12:** Climb over the small airy roof (5.9) and trend to the right on 8 bolts to a gear anchor on the edge of the South Arête. Scrambling reaches the summit.

## DESCENT

Follow the descent for Climb 81, South Arête.

## SELECTED HISTORY

**1937 JULY** Southwest Couloir. II. Kenneth Adams, Raffi Bedayn, Kenneth Davis.

**1942 JUNE** South Arête. II, 5.6. Fred Beckey, Helmy Beckey.

**1964 AUGUST** Southwest Rib. II+, 5.8. Donald Anderson, Larry Scott.

**1965 JUNE** Southeast Face. IV, 5.8 A2. Donald Anderson, Paul Myhre, Jim Richardson, Margaret Young.

**1965 JULY** Northeast Corner. III, 5.8 A1. Steve Marts, Don McPherson, Fred Stanley.

**1966 AUGUST** Southeast Face, *Inferno*. III+, 5.10. Steve Marts, Don McPherson.

**1967 JULY** West Face. III, 5.10. Fred Beckey, Jim Madsen.

**1968 JULY** *Direct East Buttress*. III+, 5.11. Fred Beckey, Doug Leen.

**1976 OCTOBER** Northwest Face. III, 5.11. Paul Boving, Steve Pollack.

**1977 JULY** Southeast Face, *Icarus*. Duane Constantino, David Whitelaw.

**1977 OCTOBER** Southeast Face, *Midnight Ride*. IV, 5.9 A3. Henry Coultrip, Eric Sanford.

**1978 MAY** Early Winters Couloir. III, 5.8. Gary Brill, Lowell Skoog.

**1984** Southeast Face, *Inferno*, direct finish. IV, 5.10+. Gordon Briody, Jim Yoder.

**1988 JULY** North Face. III, 5.11 A1 or 5.12. Doug Ingersoll, Andy Selters.

**1991 OCTOBER** Southeast Face, *The Passenger*. IV, 5.11 A0 or 5.12. Bryan Burdo, Pete Doorish, Greg White.

**2001 JULY** Southeast Face, *Nothing*. IV, 5.11+ A0. Ron Cotman, Leland Windham.

**2007** Southeast Face, *The Hitchhiker*. IV, 5.11. Bryan Burdo, Scott Johnston.

**2008 AUGUST** Southeast Face, *Southern Man*. IV, 5.11+. Mark Allen, Leighan Falley, Joel Kauffman.

*The Liberty Bell group from the northeast: (A) Cornice Peak, (B) South Early Winter Spire, (C) North Early Winter Spire, (D) Lexington Tower, (E) Concord Tower, (F) Liberty Bell* (**Photo by John Scurlock**)

# LIBERTY BELL MOUNTAIN    7720'

**PROMINENCE: 200'**

### SOUTHWEST FACE, BECKEY ROUTE; LIBERTY CRACK; THIN RED LINE

The spectacular eastern escarpment of the Liberty Bell massif may be as familiar to nonclimbers as Shuksan or Rainier. The iconic view from the Washington Pass overlook on the North Cascades Highway seems to find its way onto a great many posters, menus, and insurance-company calendars. Though Liberty Bell is modest in altitude, its dramatic vertical relief is arguably the poster child for the North Cascades as a whole.

Liberty Bell is the northernmost of five summits closely spaced and aligned north–south. It is a remarkable collection of sheer granodiorite peaks seemingly out of place for the Cascades, home to one of the highest concentrations of quality multipitch rock climbs in the range.

In a part of the Cascades known for challenging approaches and mondo hikes, the curbside ambiance of *this* group is a unique gift. With the opening of the North Cascades Highway in 1972, the 15-mile approach happily became a historical footnote. It is worth remembering that all the Liberty Bell routes featured here were originally pioneered after a big walk with a lot of gear.

### LAND MANAGER

North Cascades Scenic Byway, Okanogan-Wenatchee National Forest, Methow Valley Ranger District. Northwest Forest Pass or interagency recreation pass required for Blue Lake Trailhead parking.

### NOTES

Beyond the trailhead, the mountain goats loitering near the bottom of the climbs are only slightly less bold than their Leavenworth kin. Goats on gravel slopes above you regularly kick stones. Mosquitoes in midseason can be nearly lethal at the parking lot but usually get blown away at the higher elevations.

# 85. SOUTHWEST FACE, BECKEY ROUTE: GRADE II, 5.6

**TIME:** 1 day. **GEAR:** earlier in the season, you may want crampons and a trekking pole or light ice axe. This was the first-ascent route for the peak and is perhaps second only to South Early Winter Spire's South Arête (Climb 81) as the most popular route on the entire massif. This climb is commonly done in three or four pitches on good rock and can be descended with one 50m rope.

## APPROACH, GRADE II

Follow the approach from the west for Climb 81, South Arête, in the general direction of the Liberty Bell-Concord Tower gully. Find the climbers path and ascend into the gully between the two peaks. The gully is often snow-filled until

Wine Spires

Liberty Bell

Silver Star Mountain

Concord Tower

Lexington Tower

to Blue Lake climbers trail

*Liberty Bell Mountain from the southwest:* Beckey Route (Photo by John Scurlock)

late June; later in the season, the gully is loose, sandy gravel and rocks. Mountain goats will almost surely be hanging around and occasionally kicking stones. Ascend almost all the way to the notch between the two peaks, and find a narrow ledge on the left that leads out to the start of the climb.

## ROUTE

**PITCH 1:** From a gear belay on the narrow ledge mentioned above, step left and up onto a rounded arête (5.3); climb about a half rope length to reach a large ledge with numerous trees (look for a steep chimney with chock stones above). **PITCH 2:** From the belay on the forested ledge, climb the chimney (5.6) and corner system above to reach an open ledge. **PITCH 3:** Climb low-angle rock to a crack leading to a small roof, where the rock steepens and there may still be old fixed steel. A difficult move left (5.6) leads past the roof, then up and right, followed by friction climbing below a good crack. This leads around the corner to ledges at the southwest shoulder. **PITCH 4:** A bit higher, a 12-foot 5.7 friction slab is followed by another 100 feet of 4th-class scrambling to the summit.

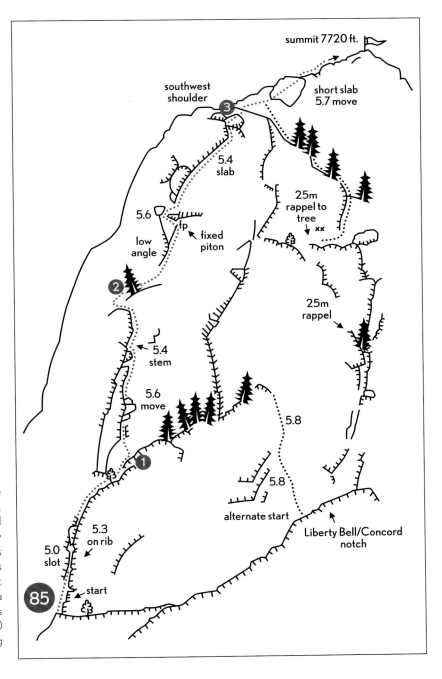

## DESCENT

Down-climb to the shoulder below the friction slab about 200 feet from the top. Climb down left (east) through trees (3rd class) 100 feet until able to walk back right (west) to the end of an exposed ledge below a steep wall, where there is a bolted rappel anchor. Two 80-foot (25m) rappels lead to the Liberty-Concord notch. Beware of loose rock and exposure to other parties when descending the approach gully to the trail.

## 86. LIBERTY CRACK: GRADE V, 5.10 A2

**TIME:** 1–2 days. **GEAR:** single set of small cams to ½ inch, single set of wires, double set of cams ½–3 inches, one cam to 3½ inches; pair of light aiders for each climber, ascenders. This was the first Washington Pass climb to tackle one of the big east faces. It is a very famous route, with tremendous position and a big-wall personality. The climbing is surprisingly friendly considering what it is, and most climbers use some aid on the early pitches. The Lithuanian Lip and the face above it are the technical cruxes, and numerous people have worked at making clean ascents of this portion. With the free version, rated at 5.13, the discussion is, for most of us, purely academic. For climbers comfortable with 5.9–5.10 free climbing, there will likely be only three or four short aid sections.

It is a popular outing and there may be several parties strung out along the route. If climbers above are doing much aiding, then the entire conga line will slow down. Still, experienced climbers with basic aiding skills commonly do the route in a day. Others will fix the first couple of pitches and go for it the following day.

## APPROACH

Drive the North Cascades Highway (State Route 20) to just east of Washington Pass and park on the shoulder across the highway from a small pond at about 5400 feet. From the south side of the pond, follow a climbers trail up about 1 mile through trees to reach open snow or talus leading to the east-face climbs.

*Liberty Bell Mountain from the northeast. (Photo by John Scurlock)*

*Brooke Sandahl working out the moves to make the first free ascent of* Liberty Crack. *Rated 5.13 and likely unrepeated free following the original bolted line above the roof.* Liberty Crack *was one of the very first Grade V rock climbs at the 5.13 rating.* (Photo by Kurt Schmeirer)

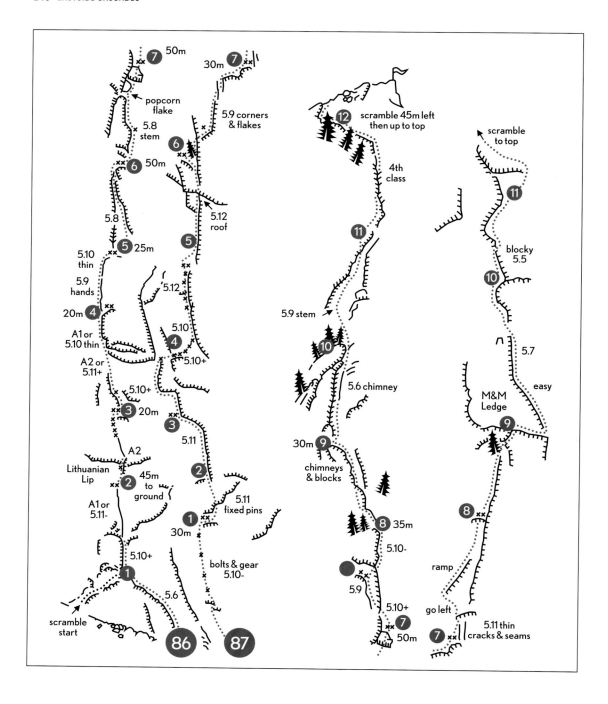

50m

7

30m

7

popcorn
flake

5.9 corners
& flakes

5.8
stem

6

6

50m

6

scramble 45m left
then up to top

12

scramble
to top

4th
class

5.8

11

5

25m

5

5.12
roof

blocky
5.5

11

5.10
thin

5.9
hands

5.12

10

20m

4

4

5.10

5.7

A1 or
5.10 thin

5.10+

5.9 stem

A2 or
5.11+

10

5.6 chimney

easy

5.10+

M&M
Ledge

3

20m

3

5.11

9

A2

chimneys
& blocks

8

Lithuanian
Lip

2

45m
to
ground

2

30m

9

A1 or
5.11-

1

30m

5.11
fixed pins

8

35m

5.10-

ramp

5.10+

1

bolts & gear
5.10-

5.9

go left

7

5.10+

5.6

scramble
start

86

87

7

50m

7

5.11 thin
cracks & seams

## ROUTE

**PITCH 1:** Climb a small 30 foot slab at the bottom of the wall, 5.6 on the right side, or scramble in from the left. **PITCH 2:** Climb a right-facing shallow corner (5.11- or A1) up about 100 feet to a belay about 20 feet below the roof known as the Lithuanian Lip. **PITCH 3:** Move up and over the roof where a splitter thin crack is followed by a bolt ladder (A2 or 5.11+) to a belay. **PITCH 4:** Continue with small cracks and some sketchy fixed pieces to the left edge of a roof, where the crack improves; very steep climbing continues (5.11+ or A2) to a nice belay ledge. **PITCH 5:** Climb a straight-in face crack that starts with a few 5.9 moves, then ramps up to solid 5.10 and reaches a ledge below a chimney. **PITCH 6:** Climb the chimney, which turns into a left-facing corner (5.8) and climbs to a small ledge on the right. **PITCH 7:** Climb a right-facing corner (5.8) with some possible loose blocks. Layback a "popcorn flake" that leads to a rotten-"appearing" block-roof. The block, which probably still retains some old fixed angle pitons, leads to a comfortable belay on top of the block.

**PITCH 8:** Start with difficult moves right (5.10+ or A1), which lead to a nice left-facing corner (5.9); continue up the steep finger crack (5.10-) or left across a slab and up to the belay stance. From here a 120-foot (40m) rappel can be made down and left to a very good bivy ledge. **PITCH 9:** Start with a tricky traverse left (5.7) to reach easier, tree-covered ledges and a short, easy chimney. **PITCH 10:** This mid-5th-class pitch follows a chimney system to a good ledge. **PITCH 11:** This long pitch climbs the left-facing corner (5.9) until it is possible to move left into another system (5.8+) leading to a sandy ledge in a gully. **PITCH 12:** Climb the gully, leading to 4th-class ground until it is possible to traverse left toward the standard descent route near the rappel bolts. Scramble to the right through trees and up to reach the summit.

## DESCENT

Follow the descent for the preceding climb.

# 87. THIN RED LINE: GRADE V, 5.9 A2 OR 5.12

**TIME:** 1-2 days. Originally climbed with a good amount of aid, the route was free-climbed in 2008 by Mikey Schaefer and quickly gained a reputation as a high-quality free climb. Bolts were added for both protection and belays as necessary for difficult free climbing. The pendulum on pitch 5 was eliminated with 5.10+ face climbing across a steep slab protected with three bolts. The climbing is varied and sustained to the top of pitch 9 (M&M Ledge); 330 feet of mid-5th class continues to the summit.

## APPROACH

Follow the approach for *Liberty Crack* (Climb 86).

## ROUTE

**PITCH 1:** Face-climb on gear about 100 feet (5.10-) with 4 bolts to finish at a station with chains. Clip the chains and move down and right 12 feet to another 2-bolt station and belay there. **PITCH 2:** Move to the right to a small corner, then over a small roof (5.11); finish a short way up the large left-facing corner. **PITCH 3:** Climb the corner (5.11) to a small bolted stance. **PITCH 4:** Traverse under the roof (5.10+); at the lip, move left onto the face. Head left past a pin, then a bolt on the *Freedom or Death* route, before climbing to the right across a flake to a bolted belay ledge. **PITCH 5:** The original route climbed the arching crack, followed by a pendulum (5.12) right to the left-facing corner; follow the free variation as it climbs rightward (5.10+) with 3 bolts to the corner. The corner takes gear to start before finishing with 4 bolts (5.12). End at a small bolted stance or a better stance 20 feet higher with gear. **PITCH 6:** Climb the corner past fixed gear and a small tree below the double roof. Move to the right at the first roof, where a finger crack leads to the larger second roof and 5.12 crux. Above the roofs, a finger crack leads to a bolted belay stance with a better belay spot a little higher. **PITCH 7:** Continue up until able to step to the

## SELECTED HISTORY

**1946 SEPTEMBER** Southwest Face. III, 5.5. Fred Beckey, Jerry O'Neil, Charles Welsh.

**1956 AUGUST** Northwest Face. III, 5.9. Hans Kraus, John Rupley.

**1958 JUNE** West Face. III, 5.8 Fred Beckey, John Rupley.

**1965 JULY** *Liberty Crack.* V, 5.9 A3. Steve Marts, Don McPherson.

**1966 MAY** *Independence.* V, 5.9 A3. Alex Bertulis, Don McPherson.

**1966 JUNE** *Liberty Crack* direct finish. V, 5.8 A1. Hans Baer, Alex Bertulis, Mark Fielding, Jim Madsen.

**1967 JULY** *Thin Red Line.* V, 5.9 A3. Jim Madsen, Kim Schmitz.

**1968 JULY** East Couloir. III, 5.7 A1. Cary Kopczynski, Chris Kopczynski, John Roskelley.

**1975** *Liberty Loop.* V, 5.9 A3 (26 bolts). Chris Chandler, Pete Doorish, Jim Langdon.

**1977 FEBRUARY** *Liberty Crack,* FWA. Jamie Christensen, Matt Christensen, Dale Farnham, John Znamierowski.

**1988 AUGUST** *Freedom Rider.* V, 5.11. Bryan Burdo, Steve Risse.

**1991 AUGUST** *Liberty Crack,* FFA. V, 5.13. Brooke Sandahl, Adam Growski, Kurt Schierer.

**1991 AUGUST** *Independence,* FFA. V, 5.12. Keith Hertel, Steve Risse.

**1997 AUGUST** *Freedom or Death.* III, 5.12. Eli Helmuth.

**2008** *Thin Red Line,* FFA. V, 5.12. Mikey Schaefer.

**2014 SEPTEMBER** *Liberty and Injustice for All.* IV, 5.12-. Mikey Schaefer.

**2016 AUGUST** *A Slave to Liberty.* V, 5.13-. Mikey Schaefer.

**2017 AUGUST** *Live Free or Die!* V, 5.12. Nathan Hadley, Blake Herrington, Seth Keena-Levin.

**2019 AUGUST** *The Dark Side of Liberty.* V, 5.13+. Shanjean Lee, Mikey Schaefer.

right to a better crack (5.9) leading to a good ledge with a bolted belay on the right side of the ledge.

**PITCH 8:** Continue up the crack system with small gear and some fixed (5.11). After the difficulty eases, move left to a clean ramp to avoid a grassy section. Once back in the main corner, belay at a small stance with gear. **PITCH 9:** Near the top of the left-facing corner, turn a small roof on the right (5.10) above a small tree via a right-facing corner. Belay at the large M&M Ledge. **PITCH 10:** From the right

side of the ledge, climb the left-leaning ramp system (5.7), followed by a blocky corner system and short chimney to a good ledge. **PITCH 11:** Climb a blocky corner system (5.5) to an optional belay ledge. Head to the right across a slab, and over the arête, then scramble to the top.

### DESCENT

The route rappels well with two ropes and is a reasonable alternative to descending the west side of the mountain if continuing to the top. See Southwest Face, *Beckey Route* (Climb 85), for the standard descent route.

# MOUNT LOGAN 9087'

## PROMINENCE: 1487' [15]

### FREMONT GLACIER

Mount Logan is a high and strategically situated summit of Skagit gneiss, centrally located but closely east of the main Cascade crest, with drainages both west (Fisher, Logan, and Thunder Creeks) and east (Bridge Creek). Satellite summits top four sprawling, lengthy ridgelines, supporting a half dozen pristine alpine valleys. Logan was a must-survey point for mapmaker Lage Wernstedt, who used it and many other previously unclimbed peaks to make the first accurate map of the North Cascades.

A 360-degree panorama from its summit includes Mount Buckner, Sahale Peak, Snowking Mountain, Boston Peak, Forbidden Peak, Eldorado Peak, Klawatti Peak, Austera Peak, Mount Baker, Primus Peak, Tricouni Peak, Mount Triumph, Mount Shuksan, Snowfield Peak, the Pickets, Mount Spickard, Jack Mountain, Ragged Ridge, Golden Horn, Black Peak, Silver Star Mountain, Goode Mountain, McGregor Mountain, Copper Peak, Mount Fernow, Bonanza Peak, Agnes Mountain, Luana Peak, Gunsight Peaks, Sinister Peak, Dome Peak, Elephant Head, Glacier Peak, Spider Mountain, Sloan Peak, Mount Formidable, and more—plus Diablo Lake. Mount Logan is an awesome viewpoint, and going for a look around is reason enough to climb it.

Other routes on the mountain include the Banded and Douglas Glaciers. The first-ascent history of the Douglas Glacier is unknown, although an ascent in the 1920s is

*Cascades mountain explorer extraordinaire John Roper on Mount Logan, July 1972. Since 1966, Dr. Roper has reached 242 summits in the Washington Cascades where no evidence of previous ascent was found. (Photo by Gary Mellom, JR Collection)*

suggested in the *Cascade Alpine Guide*. These two climbs are of moderate difficulty, off the beaten path, and typically approached from the east via Easy Pass.

## LAND MANAGER

Ross Lake National Recreation Area; North Cascades National Park, Marblemount Wilderness Information Center. Permit required year-round for overnight trips within the park.

## 88. FREMONT GLACIER: GRADE II, 4TH CLASS

**TIME:** 2–4 days–a very pleasant three days or a fast two days. This climb can be approached from the south via Lake Chelan and Stehekin, and while this southern approach is a few miles shorter, it also requires significantly more time to reach the trailhead–allow an extra day or more. The approach described below is from the north, up the Thunder Creek valley.

## APPROACH, GRADE III

Drive the North Cascades Highway (State Route 20) to 25 miles east of Marblemount or 60 miles west of Winthrop, to Colonial Creek Campground at milepost 130. Begin at the Thunder Creek Trailhead at the south end of the campground (1300 feet). There is 4300 feet of elevation gain to Thunder Basin Hiker Camp, over 19 miles of trail. **NOTE:** It is necessary to ford the stream a bit before the stock camp at about 4300 feet.

Follow the Thunder Creek Trail as it crosses to the east side of silt-laden Thunder Creek at 1.5 miles, continues past McAllister Camp at 6.7 miles, and reaches Tricouni Camp at 8 miles. At Tricouni Camp, the trail leaves the Thunder Creek valley to follow Fisher Creek to Junction Camp at 10.2 miles, near the junction with the Fisher Creek Trail. Beyond Junction Camp, the Thunder Creek Trail descends back to Thunder Creek, losing about 900 feet, then climbs back up to reach Skagit Queen Camp (3100 feet) at 14.8 miles. Reach Thunder Basin Stock Camp at 17.7 miles and Thunder Basin Hiker Camp (4640 feet) at 18.7 miles.

*Climbers high on Mount Logan's Douglas Glacier* (Photo by Doug Hutchinson)

## ROUTE

From Thunder Basin Hiker Camp, the trail climbs toward Park Creek Pass (6100 feet). Leave the trail before reaching the pass, at about 5800 feet, where a path begins an ascending traverse north.

Cross two rocky gullies and continue traversing below a spur ridge, followed by slabs and talus leading to the Fremont Glacier. Ascend the glacier northeasterly to its highest point, where a moat crossing leads up to ledges traversing left (north) to a low point on the ridge. Once on the ridge, a system of ledges traverses the east side of the ridge. The climbing here is mostly 3rd class with some 4th class leading to a false summit and the final pinnacle.

## DESCENT

Descend the climbing route. A short rappel may be helpful to reach the glacier.

## SELECTED HISTORY

**1926** Fremont Glacier. II+, 3rd class. Lage Wernstedt, possibly Alfred Shull.

**1932 JULY** Middle Peak (8960 feet). II. Forest Farr, Art Winder.

**1972 JULY** Banded Glacier. II, 3rd class. Gary Mellom, John Roper, Reed Tindall.

**1972 JULY** Thunder Peak (8800+ feet). II+, 4th class. Gary Mellom, John Roper, Reed Tindall.

**1972 AUGUST** Douglas Glacier. II, 3rd class. Bill Arundell, Marilyn Jensen, Stan Jensen, Frank King, Joanne Williams.

**1980 SEPTEMBER** Northwest Buttress. Alan Kearney, Robert Sweeney.

**1981 DECEMBER** FWA. Jerry Crofoot, Mike Hill, Troy Ness.

**1998 SEPTEMBER** Thunder Peak, East Ridge. III, 5.7. Lowell Skoog, Silas Wild.

**2003 OCTOBER** Northwest Ridge. V, 5.8. Wayne Wallace.

*Mount Logan from the northwest* (Photo by John Scurlock)

# SILVER STAR MOUNTAIN 8876'

## PROMINENCE: 2436' [27]

### EAST RIDGE; SILVER STAR GLACIER

Driving over the North Cascades Highway at Washington Pass from the west, Silver Star's north-to-south ridgeline fills the sky. This is truly one of the finest mountain scenes in the North Cascades. First-timers are encouraged to pull over and get oriented. The western wall of granodiorite Silver Star can be completely riveting; at 50 miles per hour it's easy to miss the Yosemite-like walls of the Early Winter Spires group.

Picture the culmination point of three high jagged ridgelines: the southern Snagtooth Ridge with ten named summits, the northern ridge including the phenomenal Wine Spires and Vasiliki Ridge, and the East Ridge—all converging

*Mark Allen on Silver Star Mountain's East Ridge. After warming up on the lengthy East Ridge, Mike Layton and Mark continued their ridge-line traverse finishing at the north end of Vasiliki Ridge, completing one of the longest technical routes in the range. (Photo by Mike Layton)*

*Silver Star Mountain from the south* (Photo by John Scurlock)

at Silver Star's West Summit (8840 feet), not far from the higher main summit.

### LAND MANAGER
North Cascades Scenic Byway, Okanogan-Wenatchee National Forest, Methow Valley Ranger District. Northwest Forest Pass or interagency recreation pass required for parking for Climb 89, East Ridge.

## 89. EAST RIDGE: GRADE IV⁺ –V, 5.9

**TIME:** 1–2 days. Expect the route to be dry and without water beyond early summer. The difficulty depends on whether climbers keep near the ridge crest over the top of Silver Horn Spire (8351 feet) or pass the spire on its south side. The first-ascent party, believing in a light and fast single-push style, was successful in fourteen hours car to car. Bypassing the spire enabled them to complete the traverse without a single piece of gear placed or a pitch belayed. The final portion of the climb joins a spectacular section of tower-hopping climbed in 1932 by Hermann Ulrichs and Oscar Pennington.

In August 2005, Mark Allen and Mike Layton followed the ridgetop as much as possible, including Silver Horn, to the main summit. The next day, the pair continued over the West Summit and four Wine Spires. The third day of their grand traverse finished with Vasiliki's summits and down.

The recommended descent route reaches State Route 20 about 11 miles west of Forest Road 5310-200. Arrange a car shuttle or hitchhike down the highway to finish the trip.

### APPROACH, GRADE II
Drive the North Cascades Highway (SR 20) west of Mazama for 4 miles to FR 5310-200 on the south side of the highway. Follow this road about 1 mile to the road end and the Cedar Creek Trailhead at 3230 feet.

After 200 yards on the Cedar Creek Trail No. 476, turn right on an unsigned trail. This trail gains elevation quickly, reaching Silver Star's East Ridge after 2 miles, at about 6000 feet. The trail continues near the ridgetop, passing a spur trail to Mudhole Lake on the right at about 6200 feet. Stay on the ridge toward Point 7054.

*Silver Star Mountain from the east* (Photo by John Scurlock)

## ROUTE

As the ridge narrows beyond Point 7332, solve-as-you-go routefinding may include a couple of short rappels. Continue over Silver Moon (Point 8252) and down to Varden Col at 7720 feet. A potential bivy site with late-season water is a tarn at 7141 feet, several hundred feet below the ridge and east of Silver Moon. The first-ascent party traversed the south side of Silver Horn Spire on a narrow ledge; climbing over the top of Silver Horn has short sections up to about 5.8. The climbing beyond Silver Horn keeps near the ridge crest, joining the 1932 route somewhere below the east summit. A final narrow section of ridge leads to the main summit.

## DESCENT

Descend via Climb 90, Silver Star Glacier, and Burgundy Col.

## 90. SILVER STAR GLACIER: GRADE II⁺

**TIME:** 1-2 days. The glacier becomes icy by late summer as the winter snowpack melts, exposing more consolidated snow or ice. While this is true throughout the Cascades, it is even more so for the drier eastside glaciers.

## APPROACHES, GRADE II

The glacier has two popular approach routes, both beginning from the North Cascades Highway (State Route 20).

The Silver Star Creek route starts 1000 feet lower but without the risks involved crossing Burgundy Col.

**VIA SILVER STAR CREEK:** On SR 20 where the highway crosses Silver Star Creek, park on the shoulder at 3440 feet; this is several miles east down the highway from the Burgundy Col approach's start.

There are climbers trails on both sides of the creek; the path on the east side of the creek eliminates the need to cross the creek at about 4500 feet. Near the end of the creek valley, at about 5000 feet, a talus field on the east side of the valley avoids brushier routes to the upper basin where there are nice campsites at around 6400 feet.

**VIA BURGUNDY COL:** On SR 20 at 3.7 miles east of Washington Pass, near milepost 166, park at the lower end of a broad pullout at about 4300 feet. Burgundy Spire and most of the approach path are visible from the car.

From the road, descend along the edge of the scree about 300 feet and cross Early Winter Creek. The climbers trail is just left (north) of Burgundy Creek, which drains the basin to the west of the spires. Finding Burgundy Creek is key, as it locates the start of the hike. The trail climbs steeply, staying well left (north) of the creek. At 6450 feet, reach a larch bench with good camping; July can be buggy, and late season here may be dry. The route crosses over 7800-foot Burgundy Col to reach the Silver Star Glacier.

## ROUTE

**FROM SILVER STAR CREEK:** Gaining access to the glacier is straightforward from the Silver Star Creek camping areas: use the wider eastern gully to reach the glacier, avoiding the steeper gullies below the Wine Spires.

**FROM BURGUNDY COL:** Reaching the glacier from the campsites west of Burgundy Col involves some loose 3rd class to reach the col, followed by a 200-foot descent on the north side, best when snow covered and becoming unpleasant in late summer once the snow retreats. The

*Silver Star Mountain from the northeast* (Photo by John Scurlock)

## SELECTED HISTORY

**CIRCA 1926**  Southwest Couloir. II. Frank Burge, Lage Wernstedt.

**1932 SEPTEMBER**  Southeast Face, East Ridge. III, 5.0. Oscar Pennington, Hermann Ulrichs.

**1952 MAY**  West Summit, Silver Star Glacier. II. Fred Beckey, Joe Hieb, Herb Staley, Don Wilde.

**1953 JUNE**  Silver Horn Spire. II, 5.0. Fred Beckey, Joe Hieb, Art Maki, John Parrott.

**1965 MARCH**  Silver Star Glacier, FWA. Fred Beckey, Mike Borghoff.

**1973 JULY**  West Summit, West Buttress. III, 5.8. Carla Firey, Brad Fowler, Jim McCarthy, Earl Hamilton.

**1986 SEPTEMBER**  East Ridge, Northeast Spur. III, 5.8. Fred Beckey, Dave Beckstead.

**1993 SEPTEMBER**  West Summit, Northeast Ridge. II, 5.8. Chris Dolejska, Fletcher Taylor.

**2000 SEPTEMBER**  East Ridge with Silver Horn bypass. IV, 5.0. Geoff Childs, Larry Goldie.

**2001 JUNE**  Wine Spires, *El Gato Negro*. IV, 5.10. Larry Goldie, Scott Johnston.

**2005 MARCH**  West Summit, West Face, Central Couloir. III. Mark Allen, Anne Keller.

**2005 JUNE**  Silver Horn, Southeast Face, *The Chalice*. III, 5.10-. Darin Berdinka, Justin Thibault.

**2005 AUGUST**  East Ridge with Silver Horn–Wine Spires–Vasiliki Traverse. VI, 5.9+. Mark Allen, Mike Layton.

**2007 JUNE**  Varden Creek Spire, North Arête. III, 5.9. Larry Goldie, Scott Johnston.

**2008 AUGUST**  Silver Horn, Southeast Face, *Playing Not Spraying*. III, 5.10. Blake Herrington, David Trippett.

**2010 AUGUST**  Silver Horn, Southeast Face. III, 5.10 A1. Mike Pond, Matt Van Biene.

**2019 OCTOBER**  West Summit, Northwest Face. IV, WI 4+ M6-. Seth Keena-Levin, Steph Williams.

**2020 JULY**  West Summit, West Rib. IV, 5.10. Seth Keena-Levin, Steph Williams.

west side of the col melts out by early summer, and great care should be taken to avoid the central gullies; keeping close under Burgundy Spire or north of the central gullies is strongly advised. Once on the north side of Burgundy Col, a traverse south below the Wine Spires leads to the central portion of the glacier.

**FROM EITHER APPROACH:** Follow the steepening glacier to the 8600-foot col between the West Summit and the main summit. Climbing to the summit is mostly 3rd class, with some very exposed 4th class near the top.

### DESCENT
Descend the climbing route.

## BURGUNDY SPIRE                    8400'

### PROMINENCE: 80'

### PAISANO PINNACLE WEST RIDGE TO NORTH FACE

The Wine Spires! These are the sharply serrated granodiorite peaks so visible to the east of the Liberty Bell group. Pick one: Chianti, Chablis, or Burgundy. They pair well with beef stroganoff or chili mac. While this route on Burgundy often gets done in a day, there is certainly something to be said for camping out beneath big granite and drinking fine wine from a plastic cup.

Burgundy Spire is pretty tall for a Cascades rock climb and has gained something of a reputation as one of the more difficult summits in the range, not because it is so hard but because its easiest route is so hard. Many peaks have an almost-scramble route somewhere on them, but the easiest way up Burgundy includes several pitches of 5.8. A grand traverse of the spires is also possible; it will surely test rope-handling and anchor-assessment abilities.

The rock is great and the scenery from up there is impressive! Expansive views as far away as Cascade Pass and Dome Peak are visible, as well as fresh angles on the Liberty Bell group. There are great bivy sites on a 6450-foot larch bench beneath the west faces of the winery, and Burgundy Col can sometimes offer a breezy respite from the bugs.

### LAND MANAGER
North Cascades Scenic Byway, Okanogan-Wenatchee National Forest, Methow Valley Ranger District.

# 91. PAISANO PINNACLE WEST RIDGE TO NORTH FACE: GRADE III+, 5.8

**TIME:** 1-2 days. The twelve-pitch linkup with the North Face route makes for one of the best climbs at this standard in the region. It is much more sustained than, for instance, the Southwest Rib of South Early Winter Spire. While Fred Beckey was, as usual, way ahead of the curve to realize the early potential of the place, later pioneers like Carla Firey and Jim McCarthy were impressed enough to establish several new routes. Don't be too surprised if there are several other parties here as well!

## APPROACH, GRADE II+

Follow the Burgundy Col approach for Climb 90, Silver Star Glacier. On the trail toward 7800-foot Burgundy Col, at about 7650 feet, traverse down and across a compact dirt slope-gully. Work back uphill a short way, through a few trees, and locate a sandy ledge that leads out to the right to the start of the climb.

## ROUTE

**PITCH 1:** At 5.8, this pitch has been called a bit of a sandbag; it gets better soon! Move up, then left a bit, then back right, all through a few trees, then straight up to a

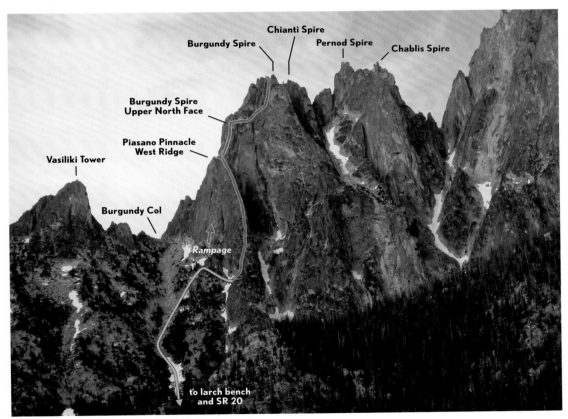

*The Wine Spires from the northeest* (Photo by Steph Abegg)

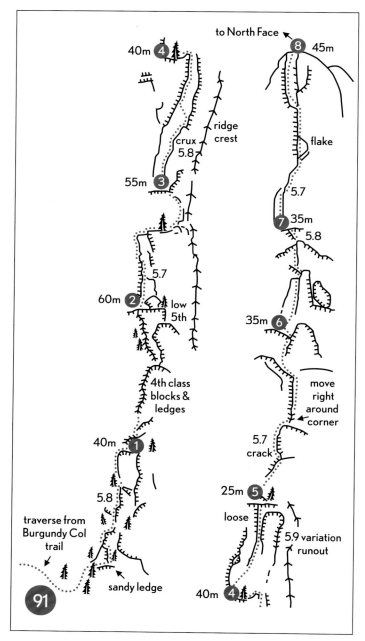

ledge with a tree. **PITCH 2:** Move up off the ledge and climb easy 4th-class blocks and ledges; the rest of the pitch is low 5th-class climbing, ending on a ledge with an obvious block. **PITCH 3:** Ascend high-quality, continuous 5.7-5.8 crack climbing; move to the right on a ledge with a tree and up to belay below the double cracks. **PITCH 4:** This is surprisingly steep with an awkward pair of cracks (5.8 crux); some call it pumpy, but there are a few good rests before the belay ledge with a tree. **PITCH 5:** There are several options; two are popular enough. **OPTION 1:** More fun climbing, but start with a funky short traverse to the right, then up (5.9); beware rope drag. **OPTION 2:** Perhaps more straightforward, it starts hard straight up but quickly backs off in a shallow chimney; the pro is a bit difficult to arrange, but there is enough. **PITCH 6:** Easier route-finding up a ridge reaches a step with a splitter 5.7 crack; above that, work around the right side of a gendarme and continue with low 5th to the belay. **PITCH 7:** Good climbing works up 5.8 cracks for 110 feet. **PITCH 8:** Climb a widening crack (5.7), then move out onto face climbing with some small cams possible; continue past some sketchy moves, then it's easier to the top of Paisano.

**PITCHES 9-10:** From ledges left of the top of Paisano, climb left and up into a crack system (5.8) for two pitches. **PITCH 11:** Traverse to the right on ledge systems and under a giant block down and around to a roomy ledge on the west side of the spire 150 feet below the summit. **PITCH 12:** From west-side ledges, climb crack and flake systems (5.8) directly to the summit, or take the right-hand crack system beside the steep slab (5.7) to the summit block.

*The Silver Star Wine Spires from the northeast.* (Photo by John Scurlock)

## DESCENT

Rappel with two ropes (or one 70m rope) from the summit block to a bolted anchor; a single 60m rope is a couple meters short here. From the anchor, several rappels arrive at a ledge. Move across the ledge and make a few more rappels to sandy ledges and more broken ground. Several more rappels eventually descend to Burgundy Col.

## SELECTED HISTORY

**1953 AUGUST**  North Face. Fred Beckey, Michael Hane, John Parrott.

**1958 JUNE**  Northwest Face. III, 5.8 A1. Donald Anderson, Jim Richardson.

**1971 SEPTEMBER**  Paisano Pinnacle, West Ridge. III+, 5.8. Carla Firey, Jim McCarthy.

**1973 JULY**  West Face, *Corkscrew*. III, 5.7. Jerry Barnard, Carla Firey, Brad Fowler, Jim McCarthy.

**1978 OCTOBER**  West Face, *Annie Greensprings*. III, 5.9. Chris Greyell, David Jay.

**1983 AUGUST**  Paisano Pinnacle, *Rampage*. III, 5.10 A1. Bob Koen, Arno Springer.

**1984 DECEMBER**  Burgundy Spire, FWA. Kevin Joiner, Kit Lewis, Jim Nelson.

**1984 JULY**  Paisano Pinnacle, *Rampage*, FFA. III, 5.10+. Bryan Burdo, Greg White.

**2004 JULY**  East Face, *Action Potential*. III, 5.10+. Mark Allen, Mike Layton.

**2004 JULY**  Northeast Buttress, *Ultramega OK*. III, 5.11. Mark Allen, Tom Smith.

# MAZAMA & PASAYTEN

## GOAT WALL             4000'

**PROMINENCE: 3800'**

### METHOW INSPIRATION; SISYPHUS

Driving east on the North Cascades Highway from Washington Pass, the magnificent Methow Valley comes into view, the dark rock of Goat Wall—Midnight Peak Formation, andesitic breccia and tuff or metamorphosed sedimentary rock—on full display above the valley floor near the town of Mazama. The 1500-foot-high central wall, adjoining buttresses, and numerous smaller crags offer a great contrast to the alpine trad climbing at Washington Pass.

The rock, while challenging for trad climbing, is well suited to modern sport-climbing methods. The first significant climb on the wall, *Promised Land*, was a bold affair that pushed the limits of traditional ground-up methods. Recognizing the potential of a methodical approach and the liberal use of thoughfully placed fixed anchors, locals and visitors from the coast got to work in the late '80s. Currently there are more than a half dozen established routes, with more in progress.

Two climbs popular for their length and moderate difficulty include eleven-pitch *Prime Rib*, established as an "entry-level" multipitch sport climb, one of Washington's great routes and the equally popular eighteen-pitch *Flyboys*, also fully equipped with fixed anchors and belay/rappel stations. The longest climbs are about Grade III if you arrange a car shuttle near top of the wall, Grade IV or more if you descend by rappel. Allow extra time and care if descending by rappel when the routes are crowded.

Raptors are known to nest in the Diamond Point Buttress area. During spring nesting season (May–July), check for raptor closures and give the birds plenty of space. The area around Goat Wall is known for rattlesnakes, so be aware and keep your eyes open.

### LAND MANAGER

Okanogan-Wenatchee National Forest, Methow Valley Ranger District. The Forest Service notes that roadside pullouts below Goat Wall and Gate Creek are *not* sustainable places to camp due to proximity to the Methow River and lack of toilets. In the greater Mazama area, there are private and Forest Service campgrounds, as well as low-impact free dispersed areas with toilets within a few miles, including Goat Creek and Yellowjacket Sno-Parks (April–October only), and dispersed sites west of Monument Creek Trailhead. The Methow Valley Climbers, a chapter of the Washington Climbers Coalition (see Resources), asks visiting climbers not to camp or sleep in vehicles anywhere along the paved section of Lost River Road or in the Fun Rock parking lot and to please use a blue bag when on route and take all trash home.

## 92. METHOW INSPIRATION: GRADE II, 5.10

**TIME:** 1 day. The *Methow Inspiration* route is the oldest multipitch bolt-protected route on Goat Wall. It offers five pitches of high-quality climbing in a lovely setting above the valley floor. The climbing is a bit harder than on *Prime Rib*, with most of the climbing in the 5.7–5.8 range and several sustained sections of 5.9.

### APPROACH

Drive the North Cascades Highway (State Route 20) to Mazama and turn north off the highway into town. Turn left on Lost River Road and continue 3 miles past the Mazama Store; park at the pullout on the west side of the road (2250 feet).

*Clare Ellis enjoys a beautiful fall day climbing* Sisyphus *on Goat Wall.* (Photo by Doug Hutchinson)

*Goat Wall from the southwest: (A)* Prime Rib, *2004, (B)* Flyboys, *2017, (C)* Restless Native, *1998, (D)* Sisyphus, *2002, (E)* Promised Land, *1989, (F)* Methow Inspiration, *1996, (G)* Rebuttal, *2018, (H)* Mazama Queen, *2019 (Photo by John Scurlock)*

Walk south down the road several hundred yards and find the trail near the yellow "curved road" sign. Head up to the start of the route at the toe of Buffalo Point Buttress, near a prominent fir tree on a huge ledge at the bottom of the route.

## ROUTE

Because the climb is fully equipped with fixed anchors, routefinding is very straightforward. However, while there are bolts to protect the hardest moves, there is plenty of space between most bolts to make it sporting. **PITCH 1:** Long pitch, 130 feet (40m); 5.8; 8 bolts. **PITCH 2:**. Long pitch, 130 feet (40m); 5.6; 8 bolts. **PITCH 3:** Climb 4 bolts to a ledge on this short (less than 80 feet–25m) pitch (5.7); belay above past a small tree. **PITCH 4:** The crux on this short pitch–80 feet (25m)–is halfway over a small roof (5.9); 4 bolts. **PITCH 5:** This long pitch–160 feet (50m)–is the killer money pitch, with two crux sections (5.10); 10 bolts.

## DESCENT

Rappel stations were thoughtfully established so the route could be descended easily in seven rappels with only one 60m rope. The rappel route uses the belay stations, plus intermediate rappel stations on the three longer pitches.

## 93. SISYPHUS: GRADE III, 5.11

**TIME:** 1 day. This climb has nine pitches of 5.8–5.10 climbing with one short 5.11 crux that can be aided by pulling on quickdraws. The route is variable, offering different types of climbing, and is fairly sustained. Being comfortable climbing 5.10 between bolts is necessary, as the spacing is farther than is typical on sport routes. The route finishes at a large ledge below Diamond Point Buttress, where several routes of 5.11 and harder have been established. Raptors nest on the Diamond Point Buttress above the top of the route from

May to July: during nesting season, do not continue higher from the top of the climb, talk, walk around, or walk off. Descend by rappel as quickly and quietly as possible.

## APPROACH

Follow the approach for the preceding climb, and find the trail near the yellow "curved road" sign. Once close to the wall, take the trail left from below the solitary pine tree around the toe of a buttress. The climb is located on the buttress to the right (south) of *Restless Natives* and right of the *Goat's Beard* water streak. A fixed rope leads up slabs, then back right across a ramp to a ledge below pitch 1.

## ROUTE

**PITCH 1:** Begin with a bolt at chest height and climb 5 bolts past a bush to a ledge; 100 feet (30m); 5.7; belay left on a higher ledge. **PITCH 2:** 100 feet (30m); 5.9; 7

bolts—end on a ledge with bushes. **PITCH 3:** 150 feet (45m); 5.10; 10 bolts. **PITCH 4:** Pass a rappel station with chains on the left before continuing higher on 2 bolts to the belay; 130 feet (40m); low 5th. **PITCH 5:** Climb 5.5 to a ledge, then 5.8 to a small belay stance; 100 feet (30m); 7 bolts. **PITCH 6:** The crux pitch (5.11; 8 bolts) ends at a hanging belay; 80 feet (25m). **PITCH 7:** This long pitch—165 feet (50m)—passes a rap station before reaching the belay; 5.10; 12 bolts. **PITCH 8:** This is a move-the-belay pitch on 3rd-class ledges; 80 feet (25m). **PITCH 9:** 100 feet (30m); 5.9; 10 bolts. **PITCH 10:** 100 feet (30m); 5.6; 7 bolts.

## DESCENT

Rappel the route, which is rigged for one 60m rope. During raptor nesting season May–July, descend by rappel as quickly and quietly as possible.

# JACK MOUNTAIN     9066'

### PROMINENCE: 4186' [17]

### SOUTH FACE, JERRY LAKES

Jack is the solitary peak east of Ross Lake and north of the North Cascades Highway with no easy summit route. The greenstone or metamorphosed basalt mountain dominates the entire North Cascades west of Shuksan and north of Logan in terms of size. Visible from virtually any high point in the North Cascades, Jack is a large massif with great relief on all sides. The western aspect rises 7500 feet from Ross Lake, the full south face is about 5500 feet above Crater Creek, and the northeastern slopes rise 5500 feet from the depths of Devils Creek.

While the south face sees the most traffic, there are several routes worth considering. With good snow conditions, both the Northeast and Nohokomeen Glaciers are classic big-mountain snow climbs when climbed by early summer. The great northern cirque holds the large Nohokomeen Glacier, sitting under the high ridgeline cresting Jack's western, southern, and eastern faces. An alternative to the south face is the east ridge, also using the Jerry Lakes approach.

*Eric Wehrly utilizes late spring snow conditions for a ski descent of Jack Mountain's South Face. (Photo by Sky Sjue)*

**LAND MANAGER**

Pasayten Wilderness, Okanogan-Wenatchee National Forest, Methow Valley Ranger District. Northwest Forest Pass or inter-agency recreation pass required for parking. Free self-issued wilderness permit required for day or overnight trips.

## 94. SOUTH FACE, JERRY LAKES: GRADE III, 4TH CLASS

**TIME:** 2–3 days. This is the most popular route on the mountain and probably the easiest. It likely has a longer climbing season (when conditions are favorable) than the northern routes, and the approach is well traveled. The face is about 1600 feet high, with loose gullies and 3rd-class scrambling when snow-free. With good snow conditions, late spring–early summer can work well, although the route seems to be more popular once snow-free. While the majority of the climbing is class 3, the length both up and down can be intimidating. Small party size is recommended to limit exposure to climber-caused rockfall.

### APPROACH, GRADE III+

Drive the North Cascades Highway (State Route 20) to 33 miles east of Marblemount or 55 miles west of Winthrop, to the Canyon Creek Trailhead (1950 feet). There is 5700 feet of elevation gain and 1200 feet of loss to campsites in the upper Crater Creek basin.

Follow the Jackita Ridge Trail No. 738 as it crosses first Granite Creek and then Canyon Creek before climbing steadily to the junction (5460 feet) at 3.7 miles with the unsigned Crater Mountain Trail No. 746. Take Trail No. 746 northwest to the meadow just east of Crater Lake at 5800 feet. From Crater Lake there are two routes to access the Crater Glacier, located on the north side of Crater Mountain's east ridge. **OPTION 1:** Continue on the Crater Mountain Trail No. 746 until able to make a traverse to the 7160-foot pass on Crater Mountain's east ridge. **OPTION 2:** Find Trail No. 746A and follow it east to the 7000-foot pass on Crater's east ridge, near the abandoned Lookout No. 2 site.

From Crater's east ridge, make a descent of several hundred feet and traverse to the north end of the Crater Glacier at about 6500 feet, followed by a short traverse to the 6600-foot pass just east of Crater's north ridge and above Jerry Lakes. Once over the 6600-foot pass, either continue down to the lakes (5900 feet) or traverse around to Crater's long north ridge near Point 6761. From just north of Point 6629 on the divide between Crater Lake (east) and Crater Creek (west), make a descent west into the Crater Creek basin where there are nice campsites at about 6100 feet.

*Jack Mountain from the southeast* (Photo by John Scurlock)

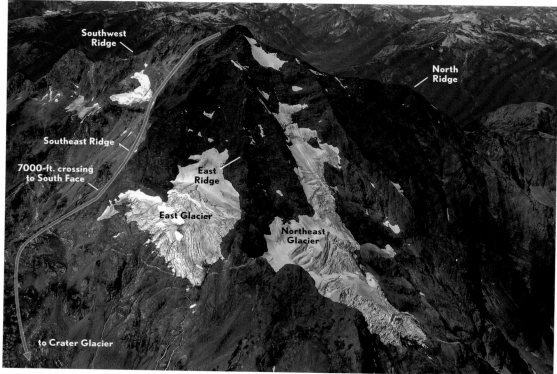

*Jack Mountain from the east* (Photo by John Scurlock)

## ROUTE

From the Crater Creek basin, find your way west to about 7000 feet on Jack's southeast shoulder. Make a traverse toward the center of the south face, where a rock island-buttress divides an early-season snowfield below the face. The south face holds snow until about midsummer, with a short cliff band near the bottom of the face. There is plenty of loose rock once the snow is gone, but except for a short section of 4th class through the initial rock band, the climbing is 3rd class or less all the way to the summit. Pass a higher cliff band to the west, aiming for the top of the face west of the summit pyramid.

## DESCENT

Descend the climbing route.

## SELECTED HISTORY

**1904 SEPTEMBER** South Face via Little Jack. Sledge Tatum, George Loudon Jr.

**1971 AUGUST** North Ridge via Devils Creek. III, 4th class. Joe Vance, Bill Weitkamp.

**1976 MAY** North Ridge via Nohokomeen Glacier. III. Mike Bialos, Bette Felton, Dick Kegel, Russ Kroeker.

**1977 AUGUST** Southeast Ridge. III, 5.6. John Anderson, Alan Kearney.

**1978 JULY** Northeast Glacier. III. Fred Beckey, Dallas Kloke, Reed Tindall.

**1981 JANUARY** FWA via May Creek. Greg Anderson, Ansel Wald.

**1984 JULY** East Ridge. III, 5.0. Carl Skoog, Gordy Skoog.

# MOUNT LAGO 8745'

## PROMINENCE: 3265' [34]

### SOUTH FACE

Lago sits roughly in the center of the Pasayten Wilderness, a vast area of the North Cascades that contains seventeen of Washington's 100 highest mountains. Seven of them are generally connected to Lago: Osceola Peak (8587 feet) and Mount Carru (8595 feet) comprise a high east–west ridgeline with Lago. Ptarmigan Peak (8614 feet) sits on the ridgeline north of Lago; Blackcap Mountain (8397 feet), Monument Peak (8592 feet), and Lake Mountain (8371 feet) are on the ridgeline south. Lonely Lost Peak (8464 feet) is to the east. While the whole Pasayten area was once heavily glaciated, with the exception of Jack Mountain and Castle Peak, only Carru, Lago, and Ptarmigan still have remnants of year-round ice; Lago is composed of Tonalite plutons in Methow block (Late Cretaceous).

Swedish-born Lage Wernstedt (correctly pronounced "Loggy," mispronounced "Lago" by his friends) was a mechanical engineer and Yale-trained forester who pioneered advancements in mapmaking using photogrammetry and stereoscopy techniques. Carrying a heavy plate camera and survey equipment to mountain summits, Wernstedt mapped about 700 square miles of the Cascade Mountains in the 1920s. At the time, most peaks were unclimbed, and Wernstedt is credited with seventy-seven first ascents of major North Cascades peaks. In 1925 or '26 Wernstedt was in the Mount Lago area surveying from ridgetops and mountaintops; however, it is undetermined exactly which peaks Wernstedt climbed in the central Pasayten region.

### LAND MANAGER

Pasayten Wilderness, Okanogan-Wenatchee National Forest, Methow Valley Ranger District. Northwest Forest Pass or interagency recreation pass required for parking. Free self-issued wilderness permit required for day or overnight trips.

*The Mount Lago group from the north* (Photo by John Scurlock)

# 95. SOUTH FACE: GRADE I

**TIME:** 3 days. The two lakes, Freds Lake and Lake Doris, were named by Lage Wernstedt for two of his children, and the 8220-foot peak on the ridge between Lago and Ptarmigan for his wife, Dot. While there are tempting campsites in the Eureka Creek Meadows below the west side of Shellrock Pass, water will be scarce in the second half of summer. With careful planning, high tarns and lingering snow patches can sometimes be utilized for multipeak excursions.

## APPROACH, GRADE II+

Drive the North Cascades Highway (State Route 20) to Mazama and turn north off the highway into the small town. Turn left on Lost River Road, which at 7.5 miles turns to gravel, becoming Forest Road 5400. Continue for 13 miles to Harts Pass (6198 feet). Go right on spur FR 600 for about a mile on the final steep and narrow climb to the Slate Pass Trailhead at 6880 feet. There is 2500 feet of elevation gain, 2400 feet of loss, and 14 trail miles to camping at Lake Doris.

Take the Buckskin Ridge Trail 498, reaching Slate Pass about five minutes from the trailhead. Continue on Trail No. 498 down the north side of the pass. After about 1 mile, leave Trail No. 498 and take the right branch onto the Whistler Cutoff Trail No. 575. The trail continues down valley, crossing the Middle Fork Pasayten River at 5950 feet and then passing the junction with the Ferguson Lake Trail No. 474A (to Eureka Creek) a bit farther. At 9 miles from the trailhead (4950 feet), turn right on Trail No. 474. Leave the valley, climbing steeply to Freds Lake at 6507 feet. In another mile and shortly after the 7200-foot high point, the trail passes near Lake Doris at 6975 feet, about 14 miles from the Slate Peak Trailhead. From Lake Doris, the trail loses 400 feet before traversing the headwaters of Eureka Creek toward Shellrock Pass (7500 feet) south of Mount Lago.

## ROUTE

The climb can be done as a steep hike from Shellrock Pass at 7500 feet, but a more direct climb of the south face starts from about 6000 feet before the trail crosses Eureka Creek.

*The Mount Lago group of peaks from the west* (Photo by John Scurlock)

**1925 OR 1926**  FA unknown. Lage Wernstedt may have climbed Lago when he surveyed the area.

**1933 JULY**  First recorded ascent. Dick Alt, Hermann Ulrichs.

Good routes on the south face of Lago either follow the seasonal streambed up to the Mount Carru–Mount Lago Col (7600 feet) or head east of the streambed, joining the east ridge at about 8400 feet. With either route, try to avoid the loose scree on the way up and enjoy it on the way down.

## DESCENT
Descend the south face or southeast ridge.

# HOZOMEEN MOUNTAIN    8066'

**PROMINENCE: 3966'**

### NORTH PEAK, NORTH ROUTE

Hozomeen is a large massif composed of two entirely separate peaks, both of which have huge relief to the valley floor. While the North Peak is a pleasant 3rd-class scramble, the South Peak has considerable 4th-class climbing with serious exposure. Many consider the South Peak among the most difficult in the range. Traversing and climbing both peaks has the distinction of combining two of the Cascades' steepest mountains, which is determined by measuring the average slope angle in every downward direction over a fixed distance from the mountain summit. Using the average compilation of three distance criteria combined—100m,

*The gnarly northern faces of Hozomeen Mountain's South Peak from the summit of the mountain's North Peak* (Photo by Tom Sjolseth)

*Hozomeen Mountain from the north (Photo by John Scurlock)*

800m, and 1600m—ranks Hozomeen's South Peak Number 1 and the North Peak Number 4.

The cliffs on Hozomeen are some of the most impressive in the range. Irresistible to climbers, the spectacularly beautiful walls were considered too difficult and committing until very recently. The rock is metamorphosed basalt—also called greenstone or Hozomeen chert—and was valued by the native Salish for making knives and arrowheads: Hozomeen is Salish for "sharp." While the rock generally has abundant holds for climbing, it is also known to be brittle, loose, and hard to protect. All technical routes on Hozomeen should be considered extremely serious.

## LAND MANAGERS

Ross Lake National Recreation Area, North Cascades National Park, Marblemount Wilderness Information Cen-

ter. Northwest Forest Pass or interagency recreation pass required for parking. Free self-registered wilderness permit required for day or overnight trips. Skagit Valley Provincial Park, British Columbia, Canada; no permit required.

## 96. NORTH PEAK, NORTH ROUTE: GRADE II, 4TH CLASS

**TIME:** 1–3 days. This is essentially the route used by the boundary survey party on the first ascent. The earliest ascents finished the climb by both the northeast ridge and the north face. This climb finishes with an exposed scramble on the north ridge, preceded by moderate snow climbing in early season. Plan for more snow climbing until about midsummer and more rock climbing later.

## APPROACHES, GRADE III

The Skyline II Trail near the north end of Ross Lake is the recommended route to access the Hozomeen Ridge Trail. It's more expensive to approach via Ross Lake than through British Columbia, but it's a shorter drive if coming from the US. There is about 5000 feet of elevation gain, depending on campsite location, which often depends on season and availability of water.

**VIA ROSS LAKE WATER TAXI:** Drive the North Cascades Highway (State Route 20) to 38 miles east of Marblemount or 59 miles west of Winthrop, to mile marker 134 and the Ross Dam Trailhead. Take the Ross Lake Resort water taxi (see Resources) by prior arrangement to the north end of the lake at Hozomeen North End Dock. From the north end of Ross Lake, walk the Silver Skagit Road north about 3 miles to the Skyline II Trailhead (about 1650 feet).

**VIA SILVER SKAGIT SILVER ROAD:** From Interstate 5 north of Bellingham, take exit 256A and follow SR 539 north about 13 miles to Lynden, then turn right onto Badger Road (SR 546) and drive east about 8 miles to SR 9. Turn left onto SR 9 north and drive 5 miles to Sumas and the border crossing into British Columbia, Canada. Continue north on Sumas Highway (BC Highway 11) for 2 miles to the Trans-Canada Hwy. 1 (Canadian Hwy. 1). Drive east on it for 47 miles to exit 168 for Silverhope Creek, just before the town of Hope. Drive east on Flood Hope Road about 1 mile, then south on Silver Skagit Road for 34.8 miles of mostly gravel. About 2 miles before the road ends at Ross Lake, reach the Skyline II Trailhead (about 1650 feet).

From either approach, follow the Skyline II Trail east as it climbs 6.6 miles to the Hozomeen Ridge Trail near 5800 feet. Take the Hozomeen Ridge Trail as it follows the ridge south, up and down over several high points, including a 700-foot gain over the highest point, where keeping on the ridge is recommended. Another descent reaches Monument 74 near Point 6000. From Monument 74, the route to the mountain's north basin is visible and straightforward; a 200-foot descent southwest provides a good access point to the north basin.

## ROUTE

The north face holds a couple of snow patches, with the largest currently lasting through the summer. Late-summer climbs typically avoid the central snowfield by climbing

*Hozomeen Mountain from the northwest* (Photo by John Scurlock)

## SELECTED HISTORY

### NORTH PEAK

**1904 SEPTEMBER** Northeast Ridge. II+, 4th class. Sledge Tatum, George Loudon Jr.

**1968 AUGUST** Southwest Buttress. IV, 5.6 A2. Dick Culbert, Alice Purdy.

**1988 FEBRUARY** North Face, FWA. Bruce Fairley, Harold Redekop.

**2013 AUGUST** West/Zorro Face. V, 5.9. Rolf Larson, Eric Wehrly.

### SOUTH PEAK (8003')

**1947 MAY** Southwest Route. III, 5.6. Fred Beckey, Melvin Marcus, Jerry O'Neil, Ken Prestrud, Herb Staley, Charles Welsh.

**1974 SEPTEMBER** North-Northeast Ridge. IV, 5.5. Fred Douglas, Paul Starr.

**1988 JUNE** Southeast Buttress. III+, 5.6. Dave Adams, Don Goodman, Ken Johnson, John Petroske.

**2016 AUGUST** North Face. V, 5.9. Rolf Larson, Eric Wehrly.

slabs where the rock is driest. From the upper west side of the central snowfield, exposed 3rd-class climbing gains the north ridge. Some 4th-class climbing on do-not-fall terrain is necessary before the grade eases back with a marvelous walk to the summit. Enjoy distant vistas of everything, including rare views west into Silver and Perry Creeks.

### DESCENT

Descend the climbing route, often including a couple of short rappels.

# CASTLE PEAK                              8306'

## PROMINENCE: 3226' [100]

## SCRAMBLE ROUTES

Way up in a forgotten corner of the Pasayten Wilderness sit three high peaks: Hozomeen Mountain, Castle Peak, and Mount Winthrop. With great regional prominence, the

*Castle Peak from the north: (A) Northeast Buttress, 1986, (B) Middle Buttress, 2008, (C) Middle Buttress, 1993, (D)* The Drawbridge, *2017, (E) North Face, 1979, (F) Northwest Buttress, 2005* (Photo by John Scurlock)

Castle Peak massif was one of the centers of ice dispersal during periods of heavy glaciation. Its wide north face still holds several sections of glacier today.

The south and east aspects of Castle Peak drain east to the Columbia River via Castle Creek and the Similkameen and Okanogan Rivers. The north and west aspects find their way south to the Skagit River via tributaries of Lightning Creek.

Castle has some notoriety, being Number 100 on the list of Washington's Top 100 peaks with 400 feet of prominence. In addition to the scramble routes, the mountain's northern aspect is loaded with alpine rock climbs—true adventure climbs where routefinding substitutes for detailed topos and route beta.

## LAND MANAGERS

Ross Lake National Recreation Area, North Cascades National Park, Marblemount Wilderness Information Center, and Pasayten Wilderness, Okanogan-Wenatchee National Forest, Methow Valley Ranger District. Northwest Forest Pass or interagency recreation pass required for parking. Free self-registered wilderness permit required for day or overnight trips. E. C. Manning Provincial Park, British Columbia, Canada; backcountry permit (fee) required.

## 97. SCRAMBLE ROUTES: GRADE I

**TIME:** 1–3 days. Both the south and southwest faces have straightforward scramble routes, depending on the chosen approach. All three approaches are popular, each with their own challenges, pros, and cons.

## APPROACHES, GRADE III+

There are a number of approaches to Castle Peak: from the west via Ross Lake or from the north via Manning Park, British Columbia.

**VIA LIGHTNING-FREEZEOUT CREEKS:** Time 3–4 days, about 32 miles round-trip from Lightning Creek Landing on Ross Lake (if not using the Ross Lake water taxi, add 30 miles round-trip via the East Bank Trail from State Route 20, about 1 mile east of the Ross Dam Trailhead). Drive the North Cascades Highway (SR 20) to 38 miles east of Marblemount, or 59 miles west of Winthrop, to mile marker 134 and the Ross Dam Trailhead; take the Ross Lake Resort

water taxi (see Resources) by prior arrangement to Lightning Creek Landing at 1604 feet. (The Lightning Creek Trail can also be reached from the north end of Ross Lake via Silver Skagit Road; see the approach for North Peak [Climb 96] on Hozomeen. Seven miles on the Skyline II Trail reaches Nightmare Camp on Lightning Creek, where the off-trail travel begins.)

From Lightning Creek Landing on Ross Lake, take the Lightning Creek Trail No. 425 east and north for 6 miles to the bridge crossing to Nightmare Camp (2160 feet).

From Nightmare Camp, the abandoned Lightning Creek Trail is difficult to follow at first, but worth looking for upon reaching the forest. It follows the east side of Lightning Creek for 1–2 miles before joining Freezeout Creek at about 2500 feet. The trail then stays on the south side of Freezeout Creek for several miles past an old cabin at about 3400 feet (expect abundant windfall—BYOS). Follow the main creek branch northeast on abandoned trail to below the west face of Castle Peak. There are nice camping areas between about 5600 and 6500 feet.

**VIA CASTLE CREEK AND MANNING PARK, BC:** Time 1–2 days. Though this is the shortest route to the south side of the peak, it includes some bushwhacking and navigation challenges. From Interstate 5 north of Bellingham, take exit 256A and follow SR 539 north about 13 miles to Lynden, then turn right onto Badger Road (SR 546) and drive east about 8 miles to SR 9. Turn left onto SR 9 north and drive 5 miles to Sumas and the border crossing into British Columbia, Canada. Continue north on Sumas Highway (BC Highway 11) for 2 miles to the Trans-Canada Highway 1 (Canadian Hwy. 1). Go east on Canadian Hwy. 1 for 48 miles to Hope. At Hope, drive east on BC Hwy. 3 for 40 miles to the exit for Monument 78/83 Trailhead on the south side of the highway at 3640 feet.

From the trailhead take the Monument 78/Castle Creek Trail about 7 miles to the border at Monument 78, where the trail becomes the Pacific Crest Trail No. 2000. Shortly after the border is a good place to leave the PCT, at about 4240 feet. Depending on the season, it is recommended to avoid the marshy areas for the lower Castle Creek valley. Farther up the valley, keeping near the stream is recommended, especially in the 5000- to 5400-foot area gaining the upper valley.

**VIA FROSTY MOUNTAIN HIGH ROUTE AND MAN-NING PARK, BC:** Time 2–3 days. This is the recommended approach for any of the north-face rock climbs, but it can also be used for accessing the southeast-ridge scramble route. From Interstate 5 north of Bellingham, take exit 256A and follow SR 539 north about 13 miles to Lynden, then turn right onto Badger Road (SR 546) and drive east about 8 miles to SR 9. Turn left onto SR 9 north and drive 5 miles to Sumas and the border crossing into British Columbia, Canada. Continue north 2 miles on BC Hwy. 11, then

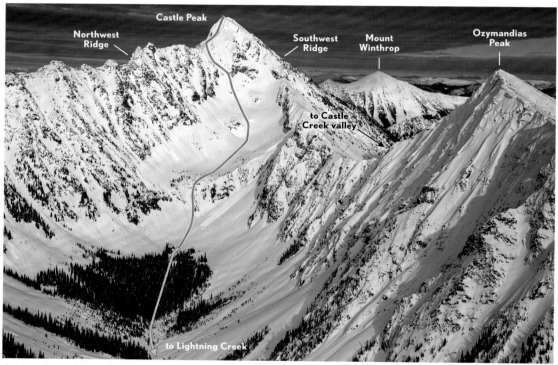

*Castle Peak from the west* (Photo by John Scurlock)

## SELECTED HISTORY

**1904**  South Route. II. USGS survey party.
**1973 SEPTEMBER**  North Face, West Ridge. II, 5.0. Fred Beckey, Philip Leatherman, Greg Markov.
**1979 AUGUST**  North Face. III, 5.8 A1. Fred Beckey, Rick Nolting, Reed Tindall.
**1986 SEPTEMBER**  North Face, Northeast Buttress. Sue Harrington, Alan Kearney.
**1993 AUGUST**  North Face, Middle Buttress. IV, 5.11. Lorne Glick, Dave Medara, Mike Pennings.
**2005 SEPTEMBER**  North Face, Northwest Buttress. IV, 5.10+. Darin Berdinka, Mike Layton.
**2008 AUGUST**  North Face, Middle Buttress variation. IV, 5.10+. Blake Herrington, Peter Hirst.
**2017 JULY**  North Face, *The Drawbridge*. IV, 5.10+ A1. Jason Schilling, Morgan Zentler.

east on Canadian Hwy. 1 for 48 miles to Hope. At Hope, drive east on BC Hwy. 3 for 38 miles to the exit for Manning Park–Lightning Lake. Drive Gibson Pass Road west 2 miles to the Lightning Lake Trailhead at about 4100 feet.

Hike the Frosty Mountain Trail for 6.6 miles south to about 7500 feet near the top of Frosty Mountain.

Leave the trail here to make a descending traverse of upper Princess Creek past a small lake at about 7000 feet, then head back up to Stronghold Peak at 7540 feet. Descend the Crow Creek–Pass Creek divide to about 6550 feet, where there is camping.

## ROUTE

The Lightning-Freezeout Creeks approach climbs from the camping areas between about 5600 and 6500 feet. The final climb is a straightforward gullies-and scree affair up the mountain's southwest face.

The Castle Creek approach climbs from the lovely upper valley starting at about 5600 feet; it's a pleasant scramble up and down the south face's central gully, which is loose but direct.

The Frosty Mountain High Route approach climbs from the Crow Creek–Pass Creek divide at 6500 feet. From the pass, traverse south to an obvious gully that is best when it's snow-filled to reach the mountain's southeast ridge at 7400 feet. Follow the southeast ridge to the top.

## DESCENT
Descend the climbing route.

# AMPHITHEATER MOUNTAIN 8358'

### PROMINENCE: 758' [87]

### MIDDLE FINGER BUTTRESS, ORIGINAL ROUTE; MIDDLE FINGER BUTTRESS, FINGER OF FATWA

Amphitheater is a sprawling mountain with two high intersecting ridges crowning the two southern amphitheaters. The north-south ridgeline abuts the 2-mile-long east-west ridge above Cathedral Pass. The southwest amphitheater presents a beautiful alpine walk to the mountain's multisummit ridgelines.

*Amphitheater Mountain from the east* (Photo by John Scurlock)

*Amphitheater Mountain from the north* (Photo by John Scurlock)

In contrast, the mountain's northern and eastern aspects are a series of rock walls, buttresses, and gullies. The attractive rock features between Cathedral Pass and Cathedral Lake have seen the bulk of the rock-climbing action to date. Middle Finger Buttress is located at the west end of Amphitheater's broad northwest face, directly above Upper Cathedral Lake. Middle Finger is the largest of several north-facing rock outcrops, all of which have solid rock for climbing. Short rock climbs, followed by visits to several of the high summits, make for a unique and relaxed outing among the vast open space of the Pasayten Wilderness.

### LAND MANAGER

Pasayten Wilderness, Okanogan-Wenatchee National Forest, Methow Valley Ranger District. Northwest Forest Pass or interagency recreation pass required for parking. Free self-issued wilderness permit required for day or overnight trips.

## 98. MIDDLE FINGER BUTTRESS, ORIGINAL ROUTE: GRADE II, 5.10

**TIME:** 3 days. This is the original rock climb on the mountain, ascending the prominent corner near the left (east) side of the buttress.

### APPROACH, GRADE III

From the North Cascades Highway (State Route 20) just west of Winthrop, drive north on West Chewuch Road, which becomes Forest Road 51, then FR 5160, for 29 miles to the road end at the Thirtymile Trailhead at 3440 feet.

There's about 3000 feet of elevation gain and 19.5 trail miles to campsites near Upper Cathedral Lake at about 7400 feet.

Hike the Chewuch Trail No. 510 north through a burned forest from fires in 2001, 2003, and 2006. At a little over 8 miles the trail crosses a small creek at about 4650 feet; shortly after, leave the Chewuch Trail and take the Tungsten Trail No. 534 north. The Tungsten Trail climbs about 1000 feet before traversing into the Tungsten Valley and passing the Tungsten Mine just before reaching the Boundary Trail No. 533 at 6800 feet, about 14 miles from the Thirtymile Trailhead. Take Trail No. 533 west, crossing Apex Pass at 7300 feet into the Cathedral Creek valley and reaching Cathedral Pass (7650 feet) at about 19 miles from Thirtymile. A final 0.5 mile reaches a large camping area a bit north of Upper Cathedral Lake (about 7400 feet). A large water container is helpful, as there is no water at the preferred campsites away from the lake. Middle Finger Buttress is a short walk from camp directly above Upper Cathedral Lake.

(An alternate approach from near the town of Keremeos, British Columbia, via

*Amphitheater Mountain's Middle Finger Buttress from the north: (A) Original Route, 1971, (B) Finger of Fatwa, 2011 (Photo by Steph Abegg)*

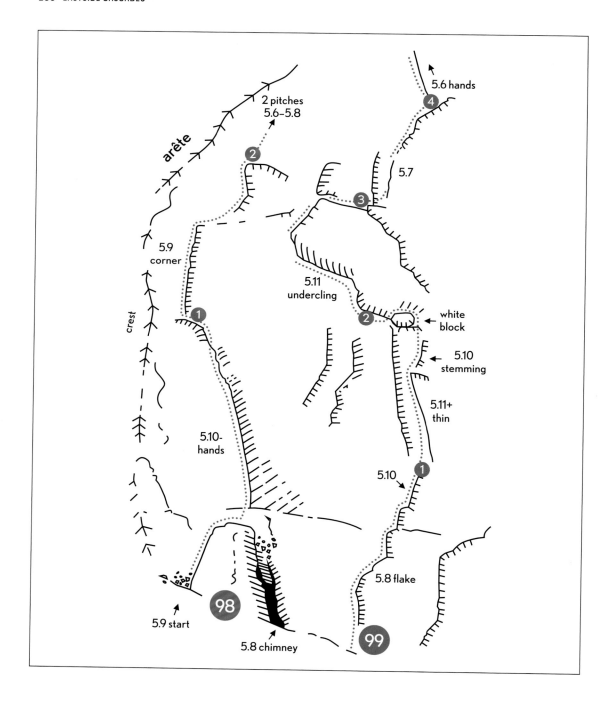

arête

2 pitches
5.6–5.8

5.6 hands

④

5.7

③

5.9
corner

crest

②

5.11
undercling

②

white
block

① 

5.10
stemming

5.11+
thin

5.10-
hands

5.10

①

5.9 start

**98**

5.8 flake

5.8 chimney

**99**

## SELECTED HISTORY

**1901 AUGUST**  Amphitheater Mountain. I. Frank Calkins, George Smith.
**1971 AUGUST**  Middle Finger Buttress. II, 5.10. Dave Anderson, Don Harder, Donn Heller.
**1973 JULY**  Middle Finger Buttress, right side. II, 5.10. Ellie Brown, Pete Doorish, Glen Wilson.
**1973 AUGUST**  North Ridge. II, 5.6. Ellie Brown, Pete Doorish.
**1980 SEPTEMBER**  *The Mosque* (east of Ka'aba Buttress). II, 5.9. Pete Doorish, Lee Nason.
**1981 SEPTEMBER**  Middle Finger Buttress, east of 1971 route. II, 5.8. Pete Doorish, Kent Stokes.
**1981 SEPTEMBER**  Ka'aba Buttress, right side. II, 5.8. Pete Doorish, Kent Stokes.
**1982 AUGUST**  *The Minaret* (west of Ka'aba Buttress). II, 5.8. Pete Doorish, Susan Halpert.
**1986 JULY**  Sunday Morning Buttress. II, 5.10. George Bell Jr., Don Monk.
**2004 JULY**  Ka'aba Buttress, *Pilgrimage to Mecca*. II, 5.9. Darin Berdinka, Owen Lunz.
**2011 AUGUST**  Middle Finger Buttress, *Finger of Fatwa*. II, 5.11. Scott Bennett, Blake Herrington.

the Wall Creek-Orthodox Mountain high route in Cathedral Provincial Park, is a shorter distance but not faster.)

### ROUTE

**PITCH 1:** Can be 1-2 pitches; climb the left-facing corner east of the chimney (5.9), or the chimney itself (5.8), to the sweet 90-foot corner hand crack (5.10-). **PITCH 2:** Move left to a nice corner (5.9) before moving back to the right toward the original corner system. **PITCHES 3-4:** Ascend mostly low 5th class near the ridge crest, with options available.

### DESCENT

There are a number of north-facing gullies east of the West Peak (8252 feet) that can be used to return to camp. Follow the summit ridgeline east to the low point in the ridge toward the North Peak (8200 feet), where the broadest of the gullies can easily be descended. The gullies are filled with snow until they melt out, lovely alpine gardens after.

(An alternate descent can also be made down the southwest amphitheater through lovely meadows and on trail back around to camp.)

## 99. MIDDLE FINGER BUTTRESS, FINGER OF FATWA: GRADE II, 5.11+

**TIME:** 3 days. This route parallels the 1971 *Original Route* and is on equally good rock.

### APPROACH
Follow the approach for the preceding climb.

### ROUTE
**PITCH 1:** Climb a crack and flake system (5.8) just right of the 1971 route, with a bit harder moves (5.10) at the top. **PITCH 2:** Begin with a steep face crack (5.11+), then stem a corner (5.10) before exposed moves left lead to a belay under roofs. **PITCH 3:** Traverse left through a first roof, followed by a second roof (5.11), and move into a chimney. **PITCHES 4-5:** Ascend toward the ridge crest with climbing to about 5.7.

### DESCENT
Follow the descent for the preceding climb.

# CATHEDRAL PEAK 8601'

## PROMINENCE: 961' [45]

### SOUTHEAST BUTTRESS

Cathedral, named in 1901 by the first ascensionists for its resemblance to a large church, is yet another classic rock peak where Fred Beckey was first on the scene. Disciples of wilderness rock climbing will be hard-pressed to find a more suitable crag for worship than Cathedral Peak. Both vertical and horizontal jointing have created endless crack systems and ledges on this mountain of granite and granodiorite.

While the Southeast Buttress is the classic long route on the peak, climbers really can't go wrong anywhere on the south face as well. Even the scramble and low-5th-class routes finish with a very exposed leap to the final summit slab. There is also The Monk, a subpeak of Cathedral with four- and five-pitch climbs on more great rock.

### LAND MANAGER

Pasayten Wilderness, Okanogan-Wenatchee National Forest, Methow Valley Ranger District. Northwest Forest Pass or interagency recreation pass required. Free self-issued wilderness permit required for day or overnight trips.

*Cathedral Peak from the northeast* (Photo by John Scurlock)

*Cathedral Peak from the southeast* (Photo by John Scurlock)

# 100. SOUTHEAST BUTTRESS:
## GRADE III, 5.10

**TIME:** 3 days. **GEAR:** pro to 4 inches is helpful. This is one of the great moderate rock climbs in the Cascades. The rock quality is excellent, and the lengthy approach helps keep the crowds at bay. Much like Prusik Peak, without the long approach both of these fine crags—Cathedral and The Monk—would be mobbed.

## APPROACH
Follow the approach for Climb 98, Middle Finger Buttress, *Original Route*. From Upper Cathedral Lake, backtrack 0.5 mile on the Boundary Trail No. 533 to just beyond Cathedral Pass, where a rising traverse reaches the base of the Southeast Buttress. The climb begins a short way up the gully between The Monk and Cathedral's Southeast Buttress.

## ROUTE
**PITCH 1:** Climb a long left-facing corner and wide crack (5.8+). **PITCH 2:** Climb the chimney—the chock stone can be climbed behind or over—before moving to the right to a good crack system (5.8). **PITCH 3:** Climb cracks (5.8). **PITCH 4:** Blocky climbing leads to a quartz dike (5.8) to a belay ledge. **PITCH 5:** Move to the left on the ledge to a layback corner and finish with a short chimney (5.8). **PITCH 6:** Climb ledges and short corners (5.7) to a belay at two trees. **PITCH 7:** More moderate climbing leads to the headwall. **PITCH 8:** Climb small cracks (5.9+) followed by hand size up the headwall. **PITCH 9:** Climb either the off-width (5.9) or nice face cracks to the right (5.10). **PITCH 10:** Climb a hand

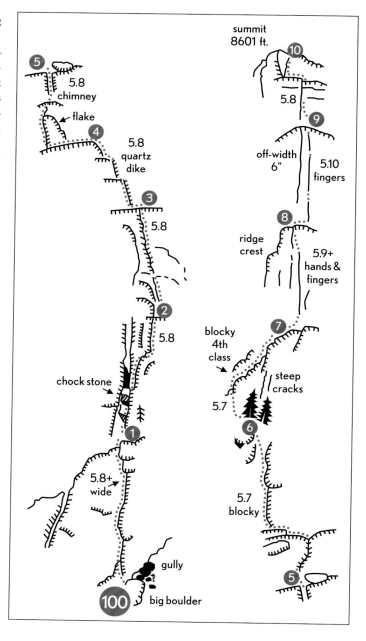

## SELECTED HISTORY

### CATHEDRAL PEAK

**1901 AUGUST** West Ridge. I, 5.0. Carl William Smith, George Otis Smith.
**1968 SEPTEMBER** South Face. III, 5.9. Fred Beckey, John Brottem, Doug Leen, Dave Wagner.
**1973 JULY** Southeast Buttress. III, 5.9. Pete Doorish, Glen Wilson.
**1973 AUGUST** Northeast Ridge. II, 5.0. Ellie Brown, Pete Doorish.
**1980 SEPTEMBER** North Rib. II, 5.6. Judy Doorish, Pete Doorish, Lee Nason.
**1987 JULY** South Face, *Sancta Civitas* (west of 1968 route). Alex Cudkowicz, Pete Doorish, Mark Landerville.
**2011 AUGUST** South Face, headwall finish, *Last Rights*. III, 5.11+. Scott Bennett, Blake Herrington.

### THE MONK (7960')

ROUTES LISTED LEFT TO RIGHT (WEST TO EAST):
**1977** West cracks, *Petronius*. II, 5.8. Pete Doorish, Don Leonard.
**1975** West cracks, *Procopius*. II, 5.7. Pete Doorish, Don Leonard.
**1982** *Thelonius* (starts in gully). II, 5.10. Pete Doorish, Susan Halper.
**1987** *Incunabula*. II, 5.11. Alex Cudkowicz, Pete Doorish.
**1991** *True Grip* (right of gully). II, 5.11. Alex Cudkowicz, Pete Doorish.
**1991** *Dies Irae*. II, 5.11. Alex Cudkowicz, Pete Doorish.
**1974** *Odine* (starts with 2-pitch chimney). II, 5.9. Pete Doorish, Bob Odom.
**1987** *Incubus*. II, 5.10+. Alex Cudkowicz, Pete Doorish, Mark Landerville.
**1987** *Round Midnight*. II, 5.11. Alex Cudkowicz, Pete Doorish.
**1973** *Le Gibet* (starts at lowest point). II, 5.9. Pete Doorish, Glen Wilson.
**1991** *Straight, No Chaser*. II, 5.11. Alex Cudkowicz, Pete Doorish.
**1973** *Scarbo*. II, 5.9. Pete Doorish, Keith Hanson.
**1991** *Succubus*. II, 5.9. Alex Cudkowicz, Pete Doorish.
**1973** *Des Moines* left (east face near descent notch). I, 5.7. Pete Doorish, Ellie Brown.
**1987** *Des Moines* right. I, 5.7. Alex Cudkowicz, Pete Doorish.
**1982** *Shelly's Leg* (from descent notch). I, 5.10. Pete Doorish, Susan Halper.

crack, followed by another hand crack that gets wide (5.8), to the summit.

## DESCENT

Down-climb the 5.0 summit block, or make the leap. Sandy scree slopes south lead quickly to the campsites near Upper Cathedral Lake.

Janet Arendall leading the first of the two headwall pitches on Cathedral Peak's Southeast Buttress (Photo by Steph Abegg)

# ACKNOWLEDGMENTS

The authors would like to start by thanking you, the purchaser of this book, for completing the loop and giving this work a purpose. If you have purchased earlier versions of this collection, we would like to thank you for your continued support and for having an open mind as well as an open wallet.

It is impossible to imagine the climbing history of Washington State without the contribution of Fred Beckey. His support for this project since the original editions so many years ago has been of inestimable value. His research and knowledge of Cascade climbing will doubtless remain unequaled.

This book would not be possible without the generous support from the following photographers. Many of the photographs would make beautiful prints, and are available directly from several of the photographers. Thank you John Scurlock at Jagged Ridge Imaging, Steph Abegg, Jaime Bohle, Mark Bunker, Bryan Burdo, Daniel Coltrane, Ed Cooper, Pete Doorish, Peter Erickson, Colin Haley, Max Hasson, Dan Hilden, Peter Hirst, Jens Holsten, Mark Houston, Doug Hutchinson, Erik Johnson, Alan Kearney, Mike Layton, Jacob Lopilato, John Roper, Brooke Sandahl, Sky Sjue, Paul Sloan, Alasdair Turner, Monty VanderBilt, Wayne Wallace, Mike Warren, Eric Wehrly, Jeffrey Wright, and Andy Wyatt.

In addition to the photographers the following people contributed their support, and knowledge. Thank you Mark Allen, Dave Bale, Fred Beckey, Darin Berdinka, Paul Butler, Geoff Childs, Carl Diedrich, Chris Dolejska, Brett Dyson, Mark Fielding, Kris Fulsaas, Mike Gauthier, Larry Goldie, Chris Greyell, Mark Hanna, Blake Herrington, Jeff Hunt, Scott Johnston, Josh Kaplan, Alan Kearney, Seth Keena-Levin, Doug Klewin, Rolf Larson, Kit Lewis, Harry Majors, Natalie Merrill, Stephen Packard, Matt Perkins,

*Jim Nelson climbing the* **Eve Dearborn Route** *on Mount Index,* **February 1989 (Photo by Mark Bebie)**

Peter Potterfield, Peter Renz, Robert Rogoz, Jim Ruch, Ira Rushwald, Stef Schiller, Gordy Skoog, Steve Smith, Mike Swayne, Monty VanderBilt, Doug Walker, Wayne Wallace, Sol Wertkin, Leland Windham, Brandon Workman, Priti Wright, and Jim Yoder.

# RESOURCES

## TRIP PLANNING

GPS tracks and KML files: uploading this kind of information to a backcountry device can be a huge navigational aid; www.peakbagger.com is one good place to start a search.

**GOOGLE EARTH:** Satellite images give a great overview of the terrain; current or recent images can be especially helpful with regard to snow conditions and location.

**TRIP REPORTS:** There are endless options— www.cascadeclimbers.com, Facebook groups, www.nwhikers.net, and www.wta.org are several.

**WEATHER FORECASTS:** These are getting more reliable all the time. NOAA at www.weather.gov is packed with current weather information and forecasts.

## TRANSPORTATION SERVICES

**HOLDEN VILLAGE:** www.holdenvillage.org for parking at Field's Point Landing and shuttle bus to the village

**LADY OF THE LAKE:** www.ladyofthelake.com for passenger ferry from Field's Point Landing up Lake Chelan to Lucerne Landing

**ROSS LAKE RESORT:** www.rosslakeresort.com for water taxi from Ross Dam to trailheads up the lake

## LAND MANAGERS

See national park and national forest websites for links to specific ranger stations or districts.

### CHILLIWACK LAKE PROVINCIAL PARK
HTTP://BCPARKS.CA/EXPLORE/PARKPGS /CHILLIWACK_LK/

Backcountry camping permit: http://bcparks.ca /registration/

Park operated by Sea to Sky Park Services, British Columbia, Canada; 604-986-9371

Chilliwack Natural Resource District, British Columbia: www2.gov.bc.ca/gov/content/industry/natural-resource -use/resource-roads/local-road-safety-information /chilliwack-natural-resource-district-district-road-safety -information

### E. C. MANNING PROVINCIAL PARK
HTTP://BCPARKS.CA/EXPLORE/PARKPGS/ECMANNING/

Backcountry camping permit: http://bcparks.ca /registration/

Park operated by BC Parks, Manning Field Office, British Columbia, Canada; 250-840-8708

### GIFFORD PINCHOT NATIONAL FOREST
WWW.FS.USDA.GOV/GIFFORDPINCHOT

Climbing permits: www.recreation.gov; 1-877-444-6777

Mount Adams Ranger District, 2455 Hwy. 141, Trout Lake, WA 98650; 509-395-3400

Mount St. Helens National Volcanic Monument, 42218 NE Yale Bridge Rd., Amboy, WA 98601; 360-449-7800

### MOUNT BAKER-SNOQUALMIE NATIONAL FOREST
WWW.FS.USDA.GOV/MBS

Darrington Ranger District, 1405 Emens Ave. N., Darrington, WA 98241; 360-436-1155

Glacier Public Service Center, 10091 Mount Baker Hwy., Glacier, WA 98244; 360-599-9572

Mount Baker Ranger District, 810 State Route 20, Sedro-Woolley, WA 98284; 360-856-5700 ext. 515

Skykomish Ranger District, 74920 NE Stevens Pass Hwy., PO Box 305, Skykomish, WA 98288; 360-677-2414

Snoqualmie Ranger District, 902 SE North Bend Way, Bldg. 1, North Bend, WA 98045; 425-888-1421

Verlot Public Service Center, 33515 Mountain Loop Hwy., Granite Falls, WA 98252; 360-691-7791

## MOUNT HOOD NATIONAL FOREST
**WWW.FS.USDA.GOV/MTHOOD**

Hood climbing permits: Wy'East Timberline Day Lodge, 503-272-3311

Hood River Ranger District, 6780 Highway 35, Parkdale, OR 97041; 541-352-6002

Zigzag Ranger District, 70220 E. HIghway 26, Zigzag, OR 97049; 503-622-3191

## MOUNT RAINIER NATIONAL PARK
**WWW.NPS.GOV/MORA/INDEX.HTM**

Headquarters, 55210 238th Ave. E., Ashford, WA 98304; 360-569-2211

Paradise Ranger Station/Wilderness Information Center, 360-569-6641

White River Wilderness Information Center, 360-569-6670

## NORTH CASCADES NATIONAL PARK
**WWW.NPS.GOV/NOCA/INDEX.HTM**

Headquarters, 810 State Route 20, Sedro-Woolley, WA 98284; 360-854-7200

Marblemount Wilderness Information Center, 7280 Ranger Station Rd., Marblemount, WA 98267; 360-854-7245

## OKANOGAN-WENATCHEE NATIONAL FOREST
**WWW.FS.USDA.GOV/OKAWEN**

Chelan Ranger District, 428 W. Woodin Ave., Chelan, WA 98816; 509-682-4900

Cle Elum Ranger District, 803 W. Second St., Cle Elum, WA 98922; 509-852-1100

Enchantment Permit Area: www.recreation.gov; 1-877-444-6777

Methow Valley Ranger District, 24 W. Chewuch Rd., Winthrop, WA 98862; 509-996-4000

Wenatchee River Ranger District, 600 Sherbourne, Leavenworth, WA 98826; 509-548-2550

## SKAGIT VALLEY PROVINCIAL PARK
**HTTP://BCPARKS.CA/EXPLORE/PARKPGS/SKAGIT/**

Backcountry camping permit: http://bcparks.ca/registration/

Park operated by Sea to Sky Park Services, British Columbia, Canada; 604-986-9371

## WALLACE FALLS STATE PARK
**WWW.PARKS.STATE.WA.US/289/WALLACE-FALLS**

14503 Wallace Lake Rd., Gold Bar, WA 98251; 360-793-0420

## WASHINGTON STATE PARKS
**HTTPS://PARKS.STATE.WA.US**

Headquarters, 1111 Israel Rd. SW, Tumwater, WA 98501; 360-902-8844

Sno-Park (nonmotorized) permits: available November 1–April 30, Winter Recreation Program, 360-902-8684; also available at all USFS offices in these Resources lists

## ADVOCACY ORGANIZATIONS

**TRAIL BLAZERS:** www.watrailblazers.org

**METHOW VALLEY CLIMBERS:** https://www.facebook.com/groups/4249916800921009/, chapter of the Washington Climbers Coalition

**WASHINGTON CLIMBERS COALITION:** https://washingtonclimbers.org

# INDEX

# ABOUT THE AUTHORS

**TOM SJOLSETH** has climbed extensively in the North Cascades for over thirty years. Learning to climb mountains with his father as a child, Tom gained an appreciation for the challenge and beauty that mountains, especially the North Cascades, provide. A resident of Washington State for over forty years, Tom moved to Arizona in 2018 to pursue his new passion, mountain biking.

**JIM NELSON** has been alpine climbing in the Cascades for fifty-plus years, and has also climbed in Yosemite, British Columbia, and Alaska. When not roaming the hills, Jim can be found at the Seattle outdoor equipment store Pro Mountain Sports.

**DAVID WHITELAW** is a well rounded mountaineer (rock and ice) with more than fifty years of experience from Yosemite to Alaska. He has helped develop many classic climbs during his years of exploring the rock walls of Washington State.

**MOUNTAINEERS BOOKS**
SKIPSTONE · BRAIDED RIVER
recreation · lifestyle · conservation

**MOUNTAINEERS BOOKS** is a leading publisher of mountaineering literature and guides—including our flagship title, *Mountaineering: The Freedom of the Hills*—adventure narratives, natural history, and general outdoor recreation. Through our two imprints, Skipstone and Braided River, we also publish titles on sustainability and conservation. We are committed to supporting the environmental and educational goals of our organization by providing expert information on human-powered adventure, sustainable practices at home and on the trail, and preservation of wilderness.

The Mountaineers, founded in 1906, is a 501(c)(3) nonprofit outdoor recreation and conservation organization whose mission is to enrich lives and communities by helping people "explore, conserve, learn about, and enjoy the lands and waters of the Pacific Northwest and beyond." One of the largest such organizations in the United States, it sponsors classes and year-round outdoor activities throughout the Pacific Northwest, including climbing, hiking, backcountry skiing, snowshoeing, camping, kayaking, sailing, and more. The Mountaineers also supports its mission through its publishing division, Mountaineers Books, and promotes environmental education and citizen engagement. For more information, visit The Mountaineers Program Center, 7700 Sand Point Way NE, Seattle, WA 98115-3996; phone 206-521-6001; www.mountaineers.org; or email info@mountaineers.org.

Our publications are made possible through the generosity of donors and through sales of 700 titles on outdoor recreation, sustainable lifestyle, and conservation. To donate, purchase books, or learn more, visit us online:

### MOUNTAINEERS BOOKS
1001 SW Klickitat Way, Suite 201 • Seattle, WA 98134
800-553-4453 • mbooks@mountaineersbooks.org • mountaineersbooks.org

*An independent nonprofit publisher since 1960*

Mountaineers Books is proud to support the Leave No Trace Center for Outdoor Ethics, whose mission is to promote and inspire responsible outdoor recreation through education, research, and partnerships. The Leave No Trace program is focused specifically on human-powered (nonmotorized) recreation. For more information, visit www.lnt.org.

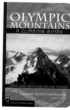
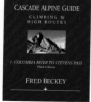